Competing in
The New Capitalism

How Individuals, Teams and Companies
Are Creating the
New Currency of Wealth

AuthorHouse™
1663 Liberty Drive, Suite 200
Bloomington, IN 47403
www.authorhouse.com
Phone: 1-800-839-8640

AuthorHouse™ UK Ltd.
500 Avebury Boulevard
Central Milton Keynes, MK9 2BE
www.authorhouse.co.uk
Phone: 08001974150

© *Lawrence M. Miller. All rights reserved.*

No part of this book may be reproduced, stored in a retrieval system, or transmitted by any means without the written permission of the author.

First published by AuthorHouse 06/29/06

ISBN: 1425931596 (sc)
ISBN: 1425931588 (dj)

LOC: 2006903297

Printed in the United States of America
Bloomington, Indiana

This book is printed on acid-free paper.

Contact LMMiller@LMMiller.com

Table of Contents

Acknowledgment
Introduction

Part One:

The Nine Disciplines of High Performance in the New Capitalism

1. Broad-Slicing the Organization
2. You Can Count on Me
3. A Pursuit With Passion
4. Thinking Together Rather than Alone
5. Dance to the Drumbeat
6. A Return to the Family Farm
7. Make Performance Matter
8. When Performance Becomes A Game
9. The Habit of Process Thinking

Part Two:

A Strategy for Creating Value

10. Organizational Strategy: A Plan for Building the Five Forms of Capital – Whole-System Design
11. Creating High Value – High Performance Teams
12. You're a Business: Build Your Net Worth
13. A Modest Proposal For A National Strategy

Index

Acknowledgement

A book such as this is the summation of many learning experiences. Much of my learning is the result of working within clients' organizations. My greatest debt is to the clients who have allowed me to exercise my ideas within their companies. Hopefully, I did them some good. They certainly did me an enormous good by providing me with those most enriching learning opportunities.

This book has been through several re-writes. Several people have been particularly helpful in providing feedback, listening to my ideas and trying to point me in a more coherent direction. I am particularly indebted to my literary agent, Margret McBride. Several of my consulting associates, particularly Al Wilgus and Will Jones, were extremely helpful in their feedback. Farsheed Ferdowsi and Shahin Sobhani were encouraging in a very important way. Others who provided helpful feedback and encouragement include Bob Dale, Harold Edwards, Kathleen Burton, Robert Tomasko, Norman Bodek and Tom Kelly.

Among the critics (and we all need critics!) who I can trust most to be forthright and pull no punches, are my two daughters. Layli Miller-Muro is the Founder and Executive Director of a non-profit organization – declared one of the ten best managed in Washington, D.C. (I would expect no less!) and Natasha Naderi, who, I am proud to say, employed some of my ideas in her work as a Training and Development Manager at Tyco Electronics, and made a real difference. My wife, Carole, has been my first editor and supporter through all of my writing and continues to provide me with immediate feedback, and is always encouraging.

Finally, Roxane Christ has been a very helpful partner in editing the manuscript and addressing my verbosity, wordiness, redundancy and tendency to say the same thing more than once, just in a slightly different way. Kind of like that!

INTRODUCTION

This book is about creating high performing organizations, teams and individuals in the new capitalism. There is now a voluntary, self-initiated, self-organized, free enterprise transformation of capitalism into something better. Capitalism is transforming, not simply because of the external force of regulation, but because of the internal exertion of virtuous self-interest.

For the past thirty years, I have worked to help companies create high performing organizations. Sometimes those efforts were linked to quality improvement, sometimes to improving the culture, and sometimes focused on improving financial performance. However, high performance results from a few common ingredients:

First, sustained high performance results from the leader's ability to define and create a culture that unites energy and effort. I have identified ***nine disciplines*** that characterize high performing organizations, teams and individuals. It is the exercise of these disciplines that creates high performance.

Second, there are ***five forms of capital*** that are linked together to form a whole-system in every organization. To achieve sustained high performance we must redefine our understanding of corporate and personal wealth. The very game of free enterprise needs redefining by acquiring a new understanding of capital. Capital is both the input and the output of every economic unit. To understand capital as simply money is to be stuck in the economy of the nineteenth century. It is time for countries and companies to embrace a new understanding of capital and build their organizations with the intent of both employing and creating all five forms of capital.

Third, maximum performance only comes when seeking the highest ideal at ***three levels*** – the individual, the team and the organization. These three levels are interdependent and success at one level leads to success at another.

There is a formula, a simple way of remembering the path to high performance. This is the culture code that when unlocked is the cause of both wealth and happiness, corporate or personal.

$$9 \times 5 \times 3 = 1$$

Before attempting to unlock this code, there are a few central ideas that will help define the playing field of competition in the new capitalism.

In the previous centuries of capitalism, money ruled. Today, a creative personality, such as Steve Jobs together with the talented minds at Pixar, may play a major role in determining the future course of a company like Disney. Yet, they exert their influence without investing one dollar in Disney stock. Their influence over Disney only exists to the degree they have established social, human and technical capital. Financial capital follows and does not lead. This is the norm in the new economy.

Many books have been written about the new economy. These tend to address the rise of technology, the knowledge economy and globalization. While these are all forces to be reckoned with, these are not my concern here. These are all external forces, the playing field on which business must compete. These issues, as important as they are, do not address the internal transformation that is now required for success. This is a book about the transformation from the inside out. The nature of capitalism, competition and management are all transforming because we have grown in our knowledge and understanding.

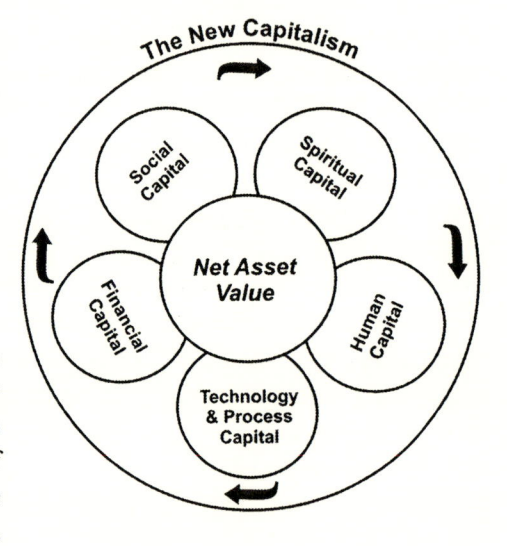

While I am an optimist, I am not blind to injustice, inequities or human failures that are often associated with capitalism. Those failures often result from the sole focus on financial capital and dismissing the power of social and spiritual capital. I believe that our civilization is advancing, moving forward on an inclining plane and moving toward a stage of maturity in which we will recognize that the good and the gold, human virtue and self-interest, must ultimately be pursued as one. If the reader wishes to find a litany of past or present evils of business, you will have to look elsewhere. My mission here is to point forward and define a path toward a more ideal future.

Capitalism is not only the private control of financial capital, it is also the private control of social capital, human capital, spiritual capital, and technology or process capital. What you own when you buy the stock of a company, is not merely the value reported on the balance sheet and income statement. If you knew that a corporation, with no current income, had just hired a team of scientists who had the capability to discover the cure for cancer, the financial statements would in no way reflect the value of that firm. You would recognize that the human capital would represent future financial capital. The same is true of Pixar and almost every other firm whose value is in human talent and creativity. Similarly, if you knew that the leaders of a company adhered to the highest ethical standards and were motivated by a worthy purpose that inspired the members of the organization to their highest possible efforts, the value of the firm would be greater than if the reverse were true. And, if you knew that the firm had instituted the most productive and effective sales, manufacturing and product development processes, you would know that the firm possessed an asset that might be deficient in another firm. True wealth, net asset value, is not measured by the financial balance sheet.

It is time that we who are engaged in the practice of free enterprise define ourselves, the nature of our system, and the future of that system. There is no viable alternative to capitalism. The only alternative is state ownership of capital and we have witnessed a one hundred year experiment which proved that whatever evils were attributable to capitalism, those of state socialism were ten times worse.

Capitalism is, however, a living thing that grows and changes form. The power of social capital to create economic value must now be taken into account. The reality that always has been, that spiritual capital, the power of purpose and adherence to shared values will determine the wealth of individuals and groups, must now be part of the equation of capitalism. Human capital, the competence and motivation of those who work in an enterprise is the real "equipment" of production in the new economy. And, process innovation and technology are among the key assets of any successful business today. Capitalism can no longer be understood by the measure of the balance sheet.

The thesis of this book is based on an assumption of change. Capitalism will evolve, not only as a result of legislation, but as a result of what works in the competitive market place. We, the business community, will transform capitalism again because we must strive to remain competitive.

One of the reasons for this transformation is our understanding of wealth at a personal level. Maturity impels one to a more profound understanding of the nature of wealth.

Doc Watson has been blind from childhood and lives in a modest home in Deep Gap, North Carolina. But, Doc Watson is one of the wealthiest men I know. He is a genius of acoustic folk guitar and spent a lifetime bringing joy to others through his music. To watch him on stage with his friends, playing together in a spontaneous conversation of brilliant licks and ancient melodies makes me want to be nowhere else on earth. Watching Doc on stage is like sitting in a good friend's living room as he plays with no stress or strain to perform like anyone else. It is not only his music, which is in harmony, but his soul. Doc sings the songs of the Appalachian Mountains, not Nashville commercial country, but the country of deep roots, deep sorrow and deep faith. When Doc lost his sight, God sprinkled the magic dust of talent on his shoulder and he has developed every measure of that talent. To know Doc Watson is to know the joy of authenticity, the demonstration of internal unity and cohesion. Then I watch Donald Trump's *The Apprentice* as the winning team receives the "reward" of a visit to Trump's gold plated penthouse mansion. The contestants stare with wide-eyed envy and dream that someday they may be this successful. They will pursue the gold and one day wake up and ask what they left behind.

Everyone wants to be a millionaire, or is it billionaire now? But will you really be happy if you have a million or a billion? There is research that answers this question and it says that you will not be any happier than someone who has very modest wealth. The pursuit of millions to achieve happiness is the pursuit of an illusion. Happiness, however, is not an illusion. It comes to those who know that they are making their best contribution, developing their unique talents and abilities, and who know that they are utilizing those talents for a worthy purpose. The ability to create unity of our material, spiritual, social and intellectual selves is like the harmonious pleasure of a well played melody.

This is not a book of academic research or theory, but of practical advice. However, there are two significant areas of research, upon which this book is based. I believe that future management thinking will be significantly altered as managers discover how to apply these new perspectives in the practical world of our organizations. The first of these is *whole-system thinking*[1] and the second is the emerging field of *positive psychology*[2]. In their essence, these are both based on simple ideas, but ideas that create a radically different approach to improving our organizations.

Most management efforts to improve performance have focused on fixing problems and analyzing the root-cause of those problems. It is a view that begins with big things and narrows the focus to smaller and more specific things. We have learned to derive satisfaction from this reductionism, finding specific causes, measuring them, and watching the data improve. This has served us well. As a result, we drive more reliable cars and every other manufactured product is delivered at both lower cost and greater reliability.

Whole-system thinking, on the other hand, looks up and out to understand the macro-system and to envision major system breakthroughs. It asks questions about the big systems and their nature. It looks at all the interrelationships of a complex system and

---

[1] A good starting point to examine the more academic or theoretical underpinnings of whole-system theory would be *Wholeness and the Implicate Order* by David Bohm.

[2] I will provide a number of references in the following chapters, but a comprehensive presentation of positive psychology applied to organizations can be found in *Positive Organizational Scholarship* by Kim S. Cameron, Jane E. Dutton and Robert E. Quinn.

seeks strategic changes in that system. Focused problem solving can never address the complexity of a whole system. It requires a complete paradigm shift from traditional problem solving. In short, if you engaged in quality improvement problem solving within a dictatorship, you might improve the efficiency of the police, administration, etc. However, you would still have a dictatorship because the transformation to democracy cannot be achieved through detailing the causes of specific problems. That transformation requires looking upward and outward to primary principles and the nature of the system. This upward and outward view is whole-system thinking.

Over the past two decades I have led many dozens of *whole-system design* projects in which my consultants and I helped our clients by rethinking the entire system of the organization. This process is described in the chapter on organization strategy.

In a somewhat similar way, positive psychology is a radical departure from traditional psychology. Traditional psychology has also been problem focused, seeking to understand mental illness and emotional disturbance. It has focused on negative deviation from the norm, just as quality management has focused on negative deviation in production processes. Positive psychology studies why people are happy and successful. It is the psychology of positive deviation rather than negative deviation.

Many of the principles discussed in the following pages, draw on the research in the field of positive psychology. While I do not reject problem solving, I also recognize that even greater good can be derived from looking at the positive exceptions in both organizations and people.

While avoiding academic language this book attempts to apply these two very significant developments in theory and research to the practical life of managers, teams and organizations. My thirty-four years of experience is entirely in the "natural setting" or the "real world" of organizations and that experience is the filter through which I must process all new theories or research.

This book is organized in two parts: the first, *The Nine Disciplines of High Performance in the New Capitalism,* defines the value creating practices of wealth creation. These serve to unify energy within winning individuals, teams and the organization. These disciplines are not necessarily new. Some are tried and true. They are simply what works to instill a culture of high performance in this age. They have been proven in hundreds of firms on every continent. Yet, their disciplined practice is rare.

The second part of this book, *A Strategy for Creating the Five Forms Wealth*, defines the five forms of capital in specific terms and outlines a process of development and change.

I never read a book from front to back in a linear process of page turning and I suspect the reader is not so obedient that he or she will do so either. Each chapter stands on its own. They can be read in any order you choose. If the reader wishes to explore the specifics of social, spiritual or other forms of capital, I suggest you skip forward to Chapter Ten through Twelve. There are four chapters in part two: one devoted to developing organizational strategy; one devoted to the development of the team as a business unit; one devoted to developing yourself as your own business unit; and lastly, a modest consideration of the implications for a national strategy.

Part One:

The Nine Disciplines of High Performance in the New Capitalism

Chapter 1

Broad-Slicing the Organization:
Creating Unity of Energy and Effort

In his book *Blink*, Malcolm Gladwell used the term *thin-slicing* to describe a focused intuitive knowledge that allows an apparent snap judgment. Thin-slicing is the act of relegating the decision-making process, to what Gladwell calls the *adaptive unconscious*, by focusing on a small set of key variables. Gladwell gives compelling examples of art experts, such as those who are able to recognize fraudulent art, even when contradicting research shows the art to be genuine. Something about it, some small clue, alerted their intuitive judgments. While this presents an interesting insight into the decision-making process, it is my observation that a very different kind of intuition is the key to creating value in an organization.

Another kind of judgment, far more essential to creating value, which I will simply call **broad-slicing** is essential to the performance of the individual, team and company. Broad-slicing is the ability to slice across an organization and see the connections, the need for solutions, which consider knowledge of the whole, knowledge that unifies the energies and effort of the members of the organization. *Broad-slicing is the presence or promotion of principles; strategic purpose; or processes that serve to create unity of energy and effort throughout an organization or culture.*

In many ways, our culture is in a period of fragmentation, dividing into ever more narrow interest groups. In our corporations, we have increasingly narrow specialization in which experts develop their own priorities, plans and even language. There is a desperate need for leadership that can unite energy and effort into one force. Such competence is essential not only for leaders, but also for all those who seek to build economic values.

Every organization should have both external and internal strategy. The external or business strategy defines the desired market position. It defines how to position products or services to serve customers in relation to the market competition. Internal strategy defines the capability of the organization that will enable achievement of the external strategy. Defining and implementing the three broad-slices of the internal strategy will inevitably generate focused effort and a sense of unified purpose toward achieving the business strategy.

The Three Levels of Broad-Slicing

The three levels of broad-slicing begin with the most macro principles and proceed to what may become highly specific and defined processes. At the highest level are cultural values and beliefs that form bonds of common purpose. At the second level are business strategies that cause all work to support shared goals. At the third level are either the detailed core work processes, a chain of activities that flow from the earliest creation of input to the final satisfied customer.

The Three Broad-Slices of Organizational Strategy

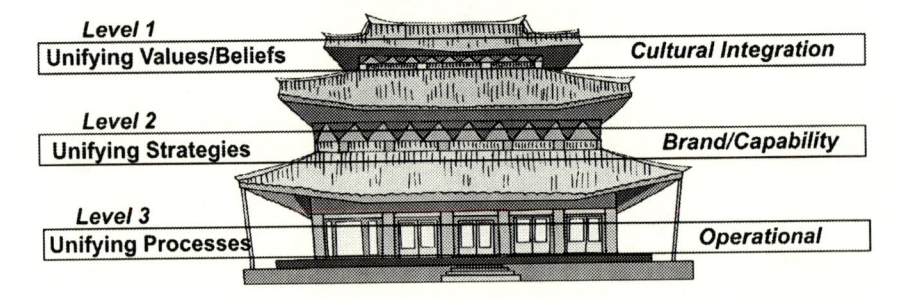

Level 1 Unifying Values/Beliefs	Cultural Integration
Level 2 Unifying Strategies	Brand/Capability
Level 3 Unifying Processes	Operational

Unifying values, cultural principles, language or religion all serve the need for cultural integration. In the political world, it is the difference between the liberation of Poland and the liberation of Yugoslavia, and possibly that of Iraq. The people of Poland were keenly aware of the broad-slices that linked them as a people – language, religion, common history and culture. In Yugoslavia, these unifying mechanisms operated in reverse and we know the result in Bosnia, Croatia and Kosovo. Today we are witnessing the struggle to create broad-slices across Iraq that may be able to hold the three primary populations together in some form of unified whole. Any country must be held together by either authoritarian force (former Iraq, Soviet Union, etc.) or by the existence or creation of broad-slices, common goals, interests, needs, philosophy or religion, that create an internal desire for affiliation. Unity of a people is ultimately a voluntary act. To be successful, the leader must elicit this voluntary response by articulating and promoting mechanisms of unity.

In companies such as Dell, Honda or General Electric there are ideas, cultural principles, which serve as unifying mechanisms in ways very similar to those in national cultures. Honda's "racing spirit" and their core competence in engine technology are broad-slices that unify the diverse business units.

Some years ago, my consultants and I worked with Chick-fil-A, in my judgment the best fast food company in the world. When you visit the Atlanta headquarters building, you may observe the cornerstone with the inscription "Dedicated to the Glory of God." The words are no mere platitude; rather their meaning permeates every function and daily life at Chick-fil-A. Their official corporate purpose is *"to glorify God by being a faithful steward of all that is entrusted to us and to have a positive influence on all who come in contact with Chick-fil-A."*

I now live in Annapolis, Maryland and when I visit the Annapolis Mall during lunchtime, there are a dozen fast food counters all handing out samples and chattering to gain your attention. Then there is the Chick-fil-A counter with four rows of three to five people deep in each row, eagerly waiting to be served. I always feel sorry for those working at the other counters.

Is there any relationship between the depth of the lines at the Annapolis Mall and the cornerstone of the headquarters building? I believe there is. Every customer knows that every Chick-fil-A store is closed on Sunday. Most know about their generous scholarship programs and other community service projects. And, of course, the food is consistently of high quality. Yet, that is not the root cause of Chick-fil-A's success. The root cause is their deeply ingrained dedication to a noble purpose – their commitment in the bonding of all employees into a set of common cultural values. This, customers can trust! Customers are attracted and loyal to a product and a brand founded on the strength of noble values.

Some years ago, Honda America Manufacturing was using one of my previous books to train their newly hired managers in the "Honda Way." When I visited Marysville, one of the striking differences in their culture was the daily team meetings held by every team and every employee, before the production line started. These meetings were to review any changes, gain the input of their associates, identify and solve immediate problems.

Some time after one of my visits to Honda, I was speaking at a quality or productivity conference. In one of the front rows, I noticed four or five men whose conference badges revealed that they were from General Motors. When I shared the example of the daily team meetings at Honda, one of them shot his arm in the air. With an air of great authority, he asked me "What is the cost benefit of those meetings if they shut the production line down for twenty minutes?"

He had me. I honestly had no idea and in front of a group of several hundreds, I told him so. He was quick to reply, "Well at GM we know the value of that line running each minute and second and you're not going to stop it unless you can demonstrate a cost benefit!"

After the conference, I returned to Marysville. Scott Whitlock was the Executive Vice President of Honda America Manufacturing and personally taught the "Honda Way" course. I told him about the above incident and I asked him if they had ever computed the cost benefit of those daily meetings. He looked at me with an expression of both disdain and distress. I was immediately embarrassed that I had asked the question. He said, "Look, we just have *faith* that if every employee and every team, every day, think and discuss how they can improve their work, it will result in better cars. I can't imagine why anyone would ask that question!"

Since this incident, more than ten years ago, General Motors market-share has shrunk and Honda's has grown. General Motors is laying-off workers while Honda is hiring. General Motors is a nightmare of brand confusion and customer doubt. Meanwhile Honda has the highest customer loyalty in the industry and everyone knows and can trust a Honda Accord or Civic. GM was insistent on cost justifying every action while Honda had faith that continuous improvement and engaging every employee in the production of high quality vehicles, would result in retaining and increasing their market-share.

The competitive advantage in both of these two cases was not some complex strategy, some technical breakthrough, or some clever marketing gimmicks. The competitive advantage was level one broad-slicing – the power of unifying cultural values. When you have the right values and you stick to them, like a train on tracks, it pays off in social, spiritual, and financial capital[3].

Broad-slices may also be a strategic direction and intention. General Electric maintains a set of values around managerial competence and accountability (a level one broad-slice) that serve to create a unifying culture. Because they have diverse business units producing aircraft engines, appliances, power generation equipment, consumer electronics and other products, it is necessary for each unit to have their own business strategy. Of course, the business strategy for selling refrigerators to Best Buys, and the strategy for selling large-scale power generating equipment to governments and major utilities, will have little in common. How then do you develop any strategic connection, and broad-slicing strategy at the second level?

General Electric has recently been promoting what they call "Ecomagination" reflecting the convergence of the need for cleaner energy, water and the development of new energy efficient technologies. This branding strategy cuts across all divisions of GE and creates a common strategic direction and purpose. Stories are a powerful tool when trying to create unified effort and the stories of innovative breakthroughs in one division can serve as a stimulus to innovation in another. Within GE, there also exists a pride, which builds loyalty in the idea that "we, GE as a company, are dedicated to the pursuit of energy efficiency."

Corporate strategy went through a period during which *portfolio management* was the preferred corporate strategy. This was the logical (or illogical) basis for conglomerates such as Textron and ITT under Harold Geneen. Geneen believed that there was no need for any link

---

[3] In the second part of this book the different types of capital will be defined specifically, and *critical success indicators* for each will be proposed at the organization, team and individual level. However, by *social capital* the author intends to include both internal trust and resulting sociability and external market capital – trust in the market place. *Spiritual capital* includes dedication to a higher purpose and strength of moral values.

between business units owned by a corporation other than that of financial competition for the allocation of capital.

These corporations were, essentially, diversified mutual funds. This approach depleted shareholder value. The absence of broad-slices resulted in division and disintegration of these companies.

The added value of a conglomerate today, a multi-business unit corporation, resides precisely in the sharing of core competencies or capabilities – some core technology or market strategy that can add value across the business units. "Ecomagination" is a good example of this. If there is no Level Two broad-slice to create value across business units, then there is little reason for those units to exist within one company.

The merger of Time-Warner and AOL was built on the premise of creating some synergy across the combined business units. However, this was only a vague intention with no serious strategy and no appreciation for the cultural differences that inhibited the creation of genuine broad-slices. The idea of an integrating strategy is not enough. The integrating strategy must be executed effectively. If Level One cultural integration is lacking, in fact working against integration, the strategy is swimming against the current and is likely to fail. It has failed at Time-Warner. Shareholders paid the price for this lack of integrating strategy.

Shared strategy may include marketing, manufacturing or technology. The same is true for broad-slicing at Level Three – the level of process.

Most readers are no doubt familiar with *lean manufacturing*, the popularization of the Toyota Production System. This is now the proven and inescapable model for production processes. The essential element of this system is the elimination of walls between departments or companies. The focus is on the horizontal flow[4] from the first step in production to the final purchase by the end-use customer. It is one seamless, interruption free process from beginning to end and one that tears down any barrier created by legal walls (companies), departments (different functions) or by personalities, which slows down the flow, add time and costs and reduce the ability to improve quality.

---

[4] See Chapter Nine for an in-depth discussion of process flow.

The father of this system is Taiichi Ohno, the production manager at Toyota whose passion was the elimination of waste – anything that did not directly add value to the product. This system has now been adopted in every industry. Dell computer is a good example of the workflow that eliminates walls and waste, and that unites the process into one rapid flow. Just as in the Toyota plant, the daily tally of Dell computers ordered by customers is a tally of parts, which flows-through directly to the suppliers who manufacture computer hard drive components or accessories. Some mysterious or complicated process does not determine the number of parts held in stock at the warehouse – the actual orders determine the inventory and the warehouse only maintains a minimal supply.

In order for this *just-in-time* system to work successfully, there must be immediate communication between those assembling a product and their suppliers. Any defect in parts or components found during assembly, must be reported to the supplier immediately, usually in less than an hour. There is no time for management to review defects and meditate on their actions. The action is reflexive and requires no deliberation, no management meetings or reports.

It is easy to see how lean production unifies those in a manufacturing process. The same is true in marketing and sales, office work, and any business process.

While complex organizations require differentiation in function, they equally require unifying horizontal processes. The competence to create effective horizontal workflow is one of the most essential competitive advantages in all modern organizations. This is Level Three *broad-slicing*.

Broad-slicing is the glue that holds companies and societies together in a unified whole. The failure to recognize or create broad-slices is one reason both companies and societies fall apart. Similarly, teams and individuals fall-apart in the absence of unifying ideas that focus their energy and effort.

We have the habit of magnifying differences and ignoring that which is common. Every public discussion seems to focus on how one group is different, better, more correct, than another. When the findings of the human genome project was announced, it was revealed that the genetic composition of individuals sampled from different races was approximately 99.99 percent the same across races. Yet, it is our learned habit to focus a great deal of attention on the differences while ignoring that, which is common. Almost every tragedy of human history is a result of an obsessive focus on differences whether political, racial, religious or cultural. Like a spreading virus, this infects our work life.

Perhaps, as we first emerged from the cave, we learned that we were more likely to be attacked by those who were different, than by those who were the same as us. And we have focused on differences ever since.

At every level of our society, we are torn between the habits of division and the bonds of unity. The downfall of every civilization and corporation is not the attack of the external barbarian, but the internal disintegration and subsequent loss of will. Internal competitors, blind to their own deeds, raise the dagger and strike their own heart, thinking they are attacking their opponent but failing to realize that they are in the boat together, rapidly circling in a descending whirlpool of debate.

It is my heartfelt belief that the greatest difficulty facing our corporations, families and society are the patterns of division and disintegration. To the degree of internal conflict, the distraction blinds one to the external threats and nullifies the potential to respond. In my opinion, the number one leadership skill required in our organizations, is the ability to promote unity of purpose and energy.

The coach of every athletic team understands the essential advantage of united effort, the multiplication of energy as one member supports and encourages the other. *"Build for your team a feeling of oneness, of dependence on one another and of strength to be derived by unity."* Vince Lombardi urged, who knew something about winning. Babe Ruth said *".The way a team plays as a whole determines its success. You may have the greatest bunch of individual stars in the world, but if they don't play together, the club won't be worth a dime.."*. Anyone who has followed sports knows the truth of these statements as very often the teams with the largest salaries and most revered players are defeated by another with great "chemistry," the magic of a unified team. And almost all work done in business and other organizations today, is ultimately the product of unified effort.

As every general knows, every military strategy is founded on the principle of united effort, coordinated attack or defense, by which the whole seeks to divide the enemy and thereby cause their defeat.

Victory goes to the united, defeat to the divided. "United we stand, divided we fall."[5] There is no great general, from Alexander to the present who has failed to understand this obvious truth. Alexander the Great went to great lengths to bring about unity within his army of diverse Macedonians, Greeks and dozens of other tribes and ethnic groups. When he conquered Persia, he incorporated the best Persian generals into his senior group of military leaders, wore Persian dress and married a thousand Greek and Macedonian men to a thousand Persian women, in a grand gesture of unity between East and West. He understood that no army could impose unity on his diverse empire unless he could instill the idea, the vision and value, of a united world. Unfortunately, his idea was a few thousand years too early.

The Bible, as well as every other Holy book of every great religion, sought to promote unity even if its followers failed to understand or act accordingly, as they usually did. *"And Jesus knew their thoughts, and said unto them, Every kingdom divided against itself is brought to desolation; and every city or house divided against itself shall not stand."* (Mathew 12:25) And the Apostle Paul said: *"If ye bite and devour one another, take heed that ye be not consumed one of another"* (Gal.5:15). The primary mission of Mohammed was to unite the warring and fractious Arab tribes under the banner of One God. The subject of spiritual unity and the connection of all living things is a predominant theme of Buddhism and Hinduism as well. *"He who experiences the unity of life sees his own Self in all beings, and all beings in his own Self, and looks on everything with an impartial eye,"* Buddha is reported to have said. And more recently, the Founder of the Bahá'í Faith, Baha'u'llah, whose central mission was the unity of religion and humankind, said, *"So powerful is the light of unity that it can illuminate the whole earth."* And the Native Americans saw in God's creation a circle of unity and believed in an eternal oneness of man, the earth and all the beings of God's universe.

If this theme is so predominant in the belief systems of every faith, how is it that our behavior falls so short? Perhaps it is the

---

[5] "United we stand, divided we fall" is the motto of the great Commonwealth of Kentucky. And it says on the state Web site: "The motto is believed to be from 'The Liberty Song,' popular during the American Revolution, and a favorite of Isaac Shelby, Kentucky's first governor."

excitement and entertainment value derived from division and the ego satisfaction of believing that "my side is right" and the others are wrong. Perhaps Dr. Seuss expressed it as well as any in his story of the Sneetches who played on the beaches:

> *"Now, the Star-Belly Sneetches*
> *Had bellies with stars.*
> *The Plain-Belly Sneetches*
> *Had non upon thars.*
>
> *"Those stars weren't so big. They really were small. You might think such a thing wouldn't matter at all. But, because they had stars, all the Star-Belly Sneetches Would brag, "We're the best kind of Sneetch on the beaches." With their snoots in the air, they would sniff and they'd snort "We'll have nothing to do with the Plain-Belly sort!"*[6]

But simple truths often demand the most tragic struggles for their realization. The history of both Christianity and Islam is the history of a united beginning and subsequent division, debate and internal conflict. Every marriage begins with vows of unity and more than half (in the West, at least) end in division. And how many corporate marriages, strategies and plans begin with a vision of the advantages of united effort and efficiency and end in disappointment following battles, mostly within?

Every form of government has struggled with the issue of creating unity within. Plato and Socrates both recognized its central role in governance. But perhaps the process of unity was never taken to be as central as when a group of Founding Fathers chose to employ the declarative "United" in the title of their state. And perhaps no state has struggled as long to bring that intention into reality. This American democracy was founded as a revolution against the vertical division of class, ruler and ruled, and it was not intended that it be replaced by the

---

[6] Dr. Seuss. The Sneetches and Other Stories. Random House, New York, 1961.

horizontal divisions of party and political dogmas. In fact, it is clear that our founders feared and warned against this very thing.

Arnold Toynbee's great work, *A Study of History*,[7] plots the rise and fall of twenty-three civilizations. Toynbee asked what could be learned from this pattern of the emergence and subsequent decline of civilization. Civilizations (and companies) when growing, expanding their borders, are integrating different people, ideas and cultures. When they cease the process of integration, they start defending their borders, building walls to keep out the energetic barbarians, and begin the process of internal disintegration. Toynbee concluded that the decline of every civilization was not at the hands of an external enemy, but rather an act of suicide, the loss of will within and the disintegration of the culture.

Whether or not you accept Toynbee's analysis of the rise and fall of civilizations, and you should read his work yourself and decide, (it is clearly one of the most brilliant works in the English language!) it is easy to see the parallels to the rise and fall of corporations and organizations.

Some years ago I wrote a book in which I chronicled the rise and fall of companies and drew the parallel to the patterns described by Toynbee.[8] Without restating the premise in its entirety, it is worth a summation here. The following diagram illustrates the essential idea.

When companies or civilizations are emerging and conquering, they are integrating different cultures and becoming increasingly differentiated within. Human resources, accounting, marketing, sales, all emerge as separate organizations, creating increasing differentiation, while at the same time integrating increasing numbers of people, territory, products, etc.

Differentiation in process and organization is a different thing than disintegration. Disintegration occurs when the differentiated units no longer perceive common interest, share common values, and employ the same language. A time comes when the different factions, political, religious or job functions no longer have empathy with each

---

[7] Toynbee, Arnold. *A Study of History*. New York. Oxford University Press
[8] Miller, Lawrence M. *Barbarians to Bureaucrats – Corporate Life Cycle Strategies*. New York, Clarkson Potter, Inc. 1989.

other and can no longer understand each other. It is a short step to civil war and actual disintegration.

Every one of twenty-three prior civilizations have gone through the life cycle curve from the birth and articulation by a Prophet to the stifling control of the Bureaucrat and the useless Aristocrat.

The job of leaders is to create the mechanisms that promote and maintain integration of the culture, rather than their disintegration. This is exactly the intention of broad-slicing, the forces of values, strategy and process that can unify a differentiated organization or culture.

Creating Personal Unity of Energy and Effort:

Personal Action Agenda	I do	I don't	I will
1. I am confident that my work-life is consistent with and a fulfillment of my personal values.			
2. I seek to align my goals with the goals of my associates.			
3. I believe in the goals of my organization and I will feel personal satisfaction as they are achieved.			
4. I feel that the organization works as one, united force.			
5. I understand how I am helping to achieve the strategy of the organization.			
6. I understand how I contribute to the process flow through the organization to meet customer needs.			
7. I feel that I am able to contribute to the elimination of waste that delays the flow of the process.			
8. My energy is focused on beating external competition and is not wasted by internal competition.			
Summary of what I will do to create unity within myself and with my team or organization:			

Creating Team Unity:

Team Action Agenda	We do	We don't	We will
1. My team is unified in its goals.			
2. My team members behave toward each other in ways that create unity of effort.			
3. Team members can be counted on to help each other with a true team spirit.			
4. All team members understand the work process that is "owned" by this team.			
5. I trust the values of other team members.			
6. There is a common spirit on our team and we do not have cliques that divide us.			
7. We consult together frequently to achieve a common understanding of what we can do to improve our performance.			
8. Our team does not compete against other internal teams, but is focused on external competition.			
9. Teams share information with other teams and seek to help all teams meet the goals of the organization.			

Summary of what we agree to do to improve the unity of energy and effort on our team:

Creating Unity of Energy and Effort in the Organization:

Organization Action Agenda	We do	We don't	We will
1. There are a clear set of values that serve to unify energy in the organization.			
2. The leaders of the organization often speak to these unifying values and reinforce their importance to all members of the organization.			
3. There is a unifying strategy that provides for shared resources and effort across organizational units.			
4. The strategy is one that all members of the organization, across divisions, feel connected to and feel that they contribute to.			
5. The strategy results in shared or common competencies that are employed across organizational boundaries.			
6. The unifying strategy results in processes that unite effort horizontally in the organization.			
7. Our organization creates competitive advantage by the excellence, speed and quality, of our processes that flow through the organization from suppliers to customers.			
Summary of what we can do to improve unity of energy and effort through the organization:			

Chapter 2

You Can Count On Me:
The Currency of Trust

"The people when rightly and fully trusted will return the trust."
Abraham Lincoln

I was conducting a workshop at the Intel Corporation headquarters in Santa Clara and, Andy Grove, Chairman and founder of the firm, one of the founders of the entire semi-conductor industry, was a participant along with about forty senior managers. At some point in the workshop, Andy Grove, not shy or soft-spoken, made a very declarative statement about something. Immediately upon completing the statement, a young man, in the back of the room, raised his hand. I suspect that this young man was two or three levels below the Chairman in the organization structure. When he rose to speak, he too was not shy. "Andy, that's wrong. And we all know it's wrong, and you keep saying it, and it keeps being wrong!"

A pregnant silence filled the room while we waited for the Chairman's response. Andy Grove slowly turned around to face the young man and said, "OK, let's discuss it. What do the rest of you think?" Then followed a twenty-minute period during which the members of staff discussed the issue with their chairman, and I lost control of my workshop.

The bold young manager knew something about his chairman and the culture of his company. He was no fool. He knew the boundaries and he trusted those boundaries.

Intel is a company built on intellectual and scientific rigor. What is valued most is the ability to think, to question, and to explore the truth of things. Andy Grove is a scientist, the opposite of an ideologue, he values people who can raise serious questions and engage in serious dialogue on important issues. This forms the social capital, which one of the strengths of Intel, and the culture begins with the norms established by the founder and Chairman.

While at the head of Intel, Andy Grove was not always the most pleasant, the most appreciative, or the most consensus oriented leader. He was, however, entirely authentic. He knew who he was, was comfortable with himself, and felt no need to conform to any standards he did not consider important. He knew his own talents and he developed them to the fullest. He was an intellectual in the best sense of that word – one who values intellectual development and inquiry and this resulted in not only his personal success, but also that of his company. And, of course he created economic value, but it was not money that he was pursuing.

The ability to trust in the honest pursuit of the truth, to trust the value of intellectual inquiry, is a *broad-slice*, which enables every other performance and which in turn, brings great technology to market. Trust is the currency that creates all five forms of capital.

Where Free Enterprise Works

Trust is the first prerequisite for the success of any group and to create trust with a group is the first and most important act of leadership. To the degree of trust, you can count on any relationship, and all business success is built on strong relationships. If you do not fully trust your relationships, you are forced to behave in-authentically, forcing yourself to share and to smile, all the while hoping that no one is taking advantage of you or your talents. As a child is free to explore new behavior in the comfort of a loving home, adults in a trusting environment are also free to explore new behavior, to be creative and to share ideas openly. This is the fertile soil from which new business emerges.

We consider ourselves a *civilized* society. But, what is it that defines a civilized society? It is not our technology, but our complex social system, most clearly seen in commerce. The ability to generate trust among a wide number of people is essential to the success of that social system we call *free enterprise*.

There is trust of people and trust of the system in which people operate. Why has a system of free enterprise had great difficulty emerging in Russia? To invest your money in some city of Russia, to open a restaurant or a manufacturing facility, you must trust the system. It must be predictable. Can I trust the legal system that provides for my right to my property? Can I trust the tax laws? Can I trust the stock market? Can I trust the banking system? Lack of trust in all of these systems is a brake on the individual entrepreneurial spirit. Similarly, within companies, trust either fuels or inhibits the very behavior that grows the business. Can I trust that my ideas will be treated with respect? Can I trust that I won't be punished for taking a risk? Can I trust that I will be fairly rewarded for my contributions? If the system is untrustworthy, the company will be robbed of individual contributions.

If you cannot trust the system in which you live, you are alienated from it. It is not yours. On the other hand, if you feel that you can trust the system, you feel some sense of ownership, you have your representatives, your candidates, and your say in the system. In both the corporate and the political worlds, it is easy to see the process by which distrust creates alienation and the breakdown of relationships, which eventually leads to the breakdown of institutions. The loss of social capital inevitably leads to the loss of financial capital.

The Decay and Revival of Trust at Tyco

When Dennis Kozlowski was still the Chairman of Tyco, the company went through forced cost reductions, each resulting in a series of employee layoffs. Down in the manufacturing plant, where real people did real work, they knew that there was no "fat." They were laying off workers with great skills, who had shown twenty-five years of loyalty to the company, and who had contributed to the success of that business unit. But, even when the manufacturing plant had orders backed up and had difficulty getting sufficient product out to customers, these layoffs continued because of the dictate from on high. No appeals to logic and reason had any effect. At the same time, workers knew that the Chairman was spending money to buy additional companies, was living lavishly in his New York Penthouse and flying around in his corporate jet. Yet, they did not know about the six thousand dollar shower curtains and the million dollars spent on a decadent birthday bash for his wife. They soon found out the whole truth however, when Kozlowski stood before the courts accused of embezzling six hundred million from the company.

It is hard for most to imagine, to have empathy, for the emotional toll this takes on employees in the operations of a company. We all gain self-respect and self-esteem by knowing that we are working for something worthy. What were these workers working for? Why should they trust any decision or decree that came down from management?

To be ruled by someone you do not trust, whether in government or business, creates the feeling of oppression and the response of rebellion. John Adams, in 1776 said, *"There is something very unnatural and odious in a government a thousand leagues off. A whole government of our own choice, managed by persons whom we love, revere, and can confide in, has charms in it for which men will fight."* At Tyco and inside the walls of dozens of other corporations, the leaders governed from "a thousand leagues off" and the employees yearned to be "managed by persons whom we love and revere and confide in."

The good news at Tyco, and a model that should be studied, is that Ed Breen, the new Chairman is restoring that trust and the employees are responding with their efforts and energy. It may seem a small thing, but Ed Breen lives in an old house and drives an old car. He closed down the New York office and sold the corporate jet. His manner is humble and modest and he listens well to those around him.

It is not surprising that appearing on the Tyco website is a letter from Breen that says in the first paragraph: "Nothing is more important to a company than its credibility -- credibility with investors, customers, government leaders and employees. Since my arrival in July 2002, my biggest challenge has been to begin the process of restoring genuine trust in the leadership of this company." And the last paragraph ends with, "Tyco's corporate culture today is built on the premise that every employee, without exception, is responsible for the conduct and success of the firm. We are working hard to make ethical business practice and personal integrity an inextricable part of this enterprise and strive to continue to identify, develop and adhere to the highest standards of corporate governance." Sure, this may sound like mushy feel-goodness. Yet, the stock has responded by tripling in price since Breen took over. Integrity, trust, and the resulting dedication of employees is good business!

Tyco is rebuilding its "social capital." Social capital is an asset of the organization and of society. It enables the creation of wealth, and its destruction will destroy wealth. One could measure the advancement of civilization by the measure of social capital. One could also measure the advancement of a business by the same measure.

Why Social Capital Equals Economic Growth

A recent book by Francis Fukuyama presents a well thought out argument that *"one of the most important lessons we can learn from an examination of economic life is that a nation's well-being, as well as its ability to compete, is conditioned by a single, pervasive cultural characteristic: the level of trust inherent in the society.*[9] Fukuyama presents a detailed argument for individual virtues, which are the bedrock of social relationships, or the tendency toward fluent association, what he calls spontaneous sociability. *"Spontaneous sociability is critical to economic life because virtually all economic activity is carried out by groups rather than individuals. Before wealth can be created, human beings have to learn to work together, and if there is to be subsequent progress, new forms of organization have to be developed."* [10] Fukuyama directly relates social capital to the prevalence of trust in a society. High trust societies are more successful at wealth creation. Those, which are low trust societies, demonstrate less ability to generate material wealth. Low trust societies, such as in the Middle East, extend trust within, but little beyond the family association. Economic relationships are often restricted to the family unit and external relationships are treated with distrust. This is a brake on economic activity. High trust societies such as the United States, Japan and Great Britain develop multiple forms

---

[9] Fukuyama, *Francis: Trust: The Social Virtues & The Creation of Prosperity*, New York, The Free Press, 1995.
[10] Ibid. p.47.

of association and ease of relationships beyond the family. These associations include the civic clubs, fraternities, political parties, trade and professional associations, as well as religious and other community organizations. This ability, spontaneous sociability, is the foundation of economic activity.

This analysis of high trust society as a foundation of wealth presents a clear warning to cultures such as the United States, in which the decline of sociability, the loss of trust, is rapid and visible. It is also a lesson for cultures in the Middle East that struggle to find the source of their own suffering and poverty. If they don't examine and reform their own low trust cultures, they will always be economically disadvantaged regardless of religion or other culture competencies. It is also a warning to executives. The exact same process takes place within the mini-society of the corporation. Leaders who create trust do so by encouraging shared learning, open discussion of problems and possible improvements, and freely share information. Just as a free and democratic society is an "open society," so too, an open society within the corporation, represents social capital and is necessarily linked to the ability to create other forms of wealth.

Just as personal relationships are voluntary, an act of attraction rather than compliance, the unity of effort that most often results in the success of organizations is discretionary. We choose to share ideas; we choose to think about problems driving in the car or while taking a shower. It is this discretionary effort, which evokes a culture of trust. The habit of discretionary effort is a form of social capital.

Social Capital within the Company

How do we experience social capital within the firm? Do I trust you with my idea? Do I trust that management will treat me fairly? Do I trust that the company or my leaders will not suddenly decide to dispense with my department, my function, and my job? Do I trust my immediate team members to value my work? The answers to these questions indicate the degree of social capital. As work is increasingly knowledge work, relying on the individual competence of the members of the organization, social capital becomes increasingly critical. Companies with low, trust-low social capital have difficulty hiring and retaining the best people. These companies are likely to stifle innovation and creativity, be slow to solve problems, and are likely to have difficulty adapting to changes in the external environment. High trust firms are more likely to possess the talent and employ that talent in rapid problem solving and rapid adaptation to external changes. Business competition is directly dependent on the ability to develop trust.

Social capital is perhaps, the least tangible of all forms of capital. Yet, in many ways, it may be the most powerful. Francis Fukuyama has defined social capital as *"a set of informal values or norms shared among members of a group that permits cooperation among them. If members of the group come to expect that others will behave reliably and honestly, then they will come to trust one another. Trust is like a lubricant that makes the running of any group or organization more efficient."*[11]. He points out that every society has some social capital, the important distinction that results in economic differences is what he calls the "radius of trust" that extends outward from the individual to the family, the community, the state and other associations. Similarly, with the corporation, there is a radius of trust that extends out from its employees to its suppliers and business partners, its customers, and to the marketplace at large. The much sought after financial returns will only follow the creation of social capital.

The Network of Community – A Mechanism of Trust

What you believe about the nature of community is also an important indicator of both success and happiness. Studies of authentic happiness have indicated that a strong social network is one of the highest causal factors. Those who live in the middle of a block of houses have a stronger social network, and report that they are happier than those who live at the end of the block.[12] How many times have

---

[11] Fukuyama, Francis. *The Great Disruption – Human Nature and the Reconstitution of Social Order*, The Free Press, New York, 1999. p. 16.

[12] Seligman, Martin E.P. *Authentic Happiness.* Free Press, New York, 2005. p. 56.

you heard people say "it's all in who you know?" Well, there is a lot of truth in that.

There was a time when the business unit was a simple, family based system. For thousands of years the work place was the home, and work revolved around the home. The original corporation was not some impersonal legal entity, with distant owners. It was the family, the family farm or family craft shop. There was trust and intimacy within the family unit, and it enabled the group to hunt or plant together. Perhaps, the inherited traits and expertise of a million years of small family units working together found their way into our genetic make-up.

In the United States in the year 1900, 60% of Americans worked on the family farm and even more in some other form of family business. Today it is less than 1.5%. With the mechanization of farming, the workers moved from the rural family structure to the organized, specialized structure of cities and factories. The CVS, Kroger's or the Wal-Mart's of today have replaced the family grocery store or pharmacy of yesterday. In the last quarter of the 1800's and the first quarter of the 1900's, every business learned the value of two things: economies of scale, or "mass production" and the application of the scientific method, or industrial engineering. These two methods, both of which increased productivity, also destroyed intimacy, the personal connection to the work and to the customer. The farm combine and tractor, and the technology of the assembly line, powered by electricity and later by computers, drove a redefinition of the social system around the work. All work systems, all companies, are social and technical systems, that are constantly seeking alignment.

In the craft shop, the worker made a complete piece of furniture and signed his name to the work, like a personalized piece of art. Workers on the family farm and craft shop did *whole* work. They made a whole piece of furniture, a whole chair, not just a leg, a seat or a back to be assembled elsewhere. They prepared the soil, planted the seed, hoed the rows and brought the harvest to market. They understood how the pieces fit together and controlled the whole process and they felt ownership for that process. Just as Native Americans believed in a unity of earth and man, the farmer felt this unity with his work. The social aspect of the craft and family farm system kept the family together. Much of their purpose as a family was their work. Once family and work were separated, neither the family nor the work unit would ever be the same.

From Mass Production to the Return of High Trust Organization

The invention of the combine and the tractor reduced the need for labor on the farm, while the factories that made the equipment suddenly needed that same labor. This transition from work on the family farm to work in the cities and factories transformed the nation and its society. The new system of production saw its ultimate expression in Henry Ford's factory. His system of mass production was based on the division of labor into specialized units, and the specialized professions of engineering and management emerged. The worker no longer designed or improved the product, he was simply

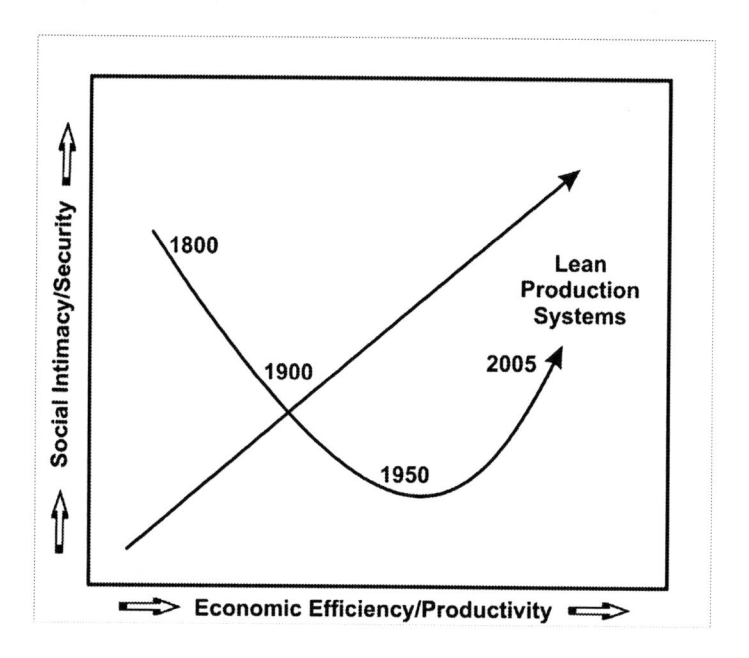

told, "do your own work," a fragment of the whole. The worker, who once worked in the united family, was now treated as a disposable item in the production process. This isolated the worker and diminished the trust placed in him and in return, it diminished his trust in the organization. Thus, the creation of a cycle of distrust and disunity materialized among the workforce.

We all seek safety and security in unified groups, a family, a tribe, a gang, or a team. We need a group to belong to, to care about and to protect us. This was removed from the factory work system. Yet, workers will do what they must. In response, they formed their own organization, they called each other "brothers" and "sisters" and they organized a union – a group whom they could trust and would represent their interests. This separation of trust from the work organization, replaced by the union, was a natural response to the system of mass production.

The mass production factory model was a temporary and passing stage, inevitably unstable because it was based on a system that contradicted human nature. By isolating the individual from his or her natural group, it instilled a form of anaclitic depression, which in infancy is known as Marasmus, and in adults has been referred to as Mussulman's Syndrome, first identified in inmates of concentration camps. In both cases, it can result in death. Infants who are left alone without cuddling and the warmth of social support may literally waste away and die a lonely death. Suddenly separated from their supporting social system, without psychological support, inmates gave way to loneliness and despair and literally perished. Prisoners of war in the Korean War gave up and died of loneliness when they were denied social support. Captain Eugene McDaniel, who was a POW in North Vietnam, reported that the probability of POWs dying in captivity increased multifold inasmuch as they were unable to receive emotional support from fellow POWs.[13]. Every POW has reported the importance of the support of fellow inmates to their survival. In North Korea, the guards worked to create distrust among the POWs to isolate them further. To the degree the guards succeeded, the POWs died. It could be argued, a bit tongue in cheek, that the typical mass production factory, as a social system, was designed to kill its workers.

---

[13] Harvey, Jerry. How Come Every Time I Get Stabbed In the Back My Fingerprints Are On The Knife? Josey-Bass Publishers, San Francisco. 1999. p. 119.

Today most factories have been redesigned into small groups – cells, work teams, in which the unity of the social system of the family farm and craft shop is at least partially restored. The redesigned factories into "lean production" units required the creation of series of interlocking teams supervised by process owners who would follow the flow from input to output throughout the organization. The effectiveness of lean production now depends on the social system of those teams. If trust fails within the team it will inevitably behave in ways that create distrust with linking teams. Our organizations cannot afford the cost of distrust.

Why Cooperation and Competition Co-Exist

We have a competitive economy and a competitive social system. We compete to be on the baseball team, we compete for grades, we compete for jobs, and we ultimately compete for business. We value those who are highly competitive and who strive to win. Yet, even the winner's success depends not only on the ability to compete, but also on the ability to cooperate.

Most sports are team sports. Baseball, football and basketball are all highly cooperative, as well as competitive endeavors. Cooperation, trusting relationships, trust based contracts, are built into every sport. When we go to the basketball game, we focus on the competition between the two teams. It is likely that we do not notice the cooperative behavior, even though it is critical both within the team as well as between the teams. Within each team, each player is trained in a role that is supportive of other players. The point guard's primary function is to pass the ball to someone else who will score, and to set up plays to create opportunities for his teammates. We measure "assists" for each player in each game. Each player has a role, not only to make an individual contribution, but also to behave in a way that does more than simply add to his own statistics. If a player focuses mainly on his own numbers, he is likely to become an unpopular player and other members of the team will react in a way that will lessen his own opportunities to score. Therefore, cooperation is in the player's own self-interest.

Yet, while we see the cooperative behavior within the team, we may miss that the entire performance requires extreme cooperation between the teams. They agree on the rules and those rules define the cooperation. They agree to give up the ball and hand it to the other team immediately after they score, presumably to give the other team an equal chance. They agree on the boundaries and agree to abide by the judgments of the referee. They even agree to switch sides at half time, just in case one end of the court has an advantage. Cooperation is so common in sports that we barely notice it. After every significant victory of a football team, the star quarterback is interviewed and without fail, with the first thing out of his mouth, he credits his offensive line without whom he couldn't have done it! While he is no doubt sincere, he is also acting out of self-interest. He knows that he would be buried out there if it were not for the dedicated support of his linemen.

Of course, some sports are individual sports – tennis, golf, swimming, auto racing. However, even in those sports there is a team of supporting actors around the golf or tennis pro. The success of these athletes, much like in the team sports, depends on his or her ability to create cooperation and trust.

Economic Complexity Requires "Nonzero" Logic

Robert Wright, in is excellent book *Nonzero – The Logic of Human Destiny*[14], argues that human history and human evolution have a direction. That direction, simply put, is from simple to complex organization, requiring ever-wider circles of trust and cooperation. The challenge of unity grows as we move from the simple organization of the family to the complexities of modern organization. He also argues that genetic selection is hard-wiring a tendency toward what he calls "non-zero-sum" behavior. It may be hard for us to see the forest from the trees when we are bombarded each night with the miseries and distrust in the Middle East or the Balkans. Just as we may focus on the competition in sports and fail to see the cooperation, we may fail to see the ever-expanding forms of cooperation required for us to survive, and even compete, as a human species.

---

[14] Wright, Robert. *Nonzero – the Logic of Human Destiny*, New York, Vintage Books, 2000.

Let's demonstrate "non-zero-sum" behavior by observing our basketball players. Imagine that there was a fixed amount, a zero-sum of credit – applause, appreciation or respect afforded to a basketball team. Let's call that amount of credit 100 units. If the star center performs so well that his amount of credit goes up from 20 units to 30 units, the ten-unit gain must come from the other players. In this "zero-sum" competition, the other players are diminished proportionally to his success. In other words, this transaction is a win-lose transaction because it is zero-sum – the sum of credit remains the same. It is not hard to imagine the type of behavior this transaction would create within the team. They would compete to the detriment of each other and reduce the probability of the team's victory.

The fact is that credit, or respect, is highly elastic. In other words, if the team performs extremely well, they win the NBA championship; consequently, the amount of credit expands greatly. If they lose, the amount of credit shrinks. Therefore, the real game is a win-win game in which the amount of credit is what Wright calls "non-zero-sum", or highly elastic. Because of the realities of this basketball economy – the earning and payoff in appreciation, applause, etc. – the sport generates highly cooperative behavior among the players on a team. The goal of the players is to increase the amount of total credit available to all team members because they know that their amount of credit will then increase. Our ability to see that the economy of the sport is non-zero-sum leads us to develop cooperative relationships. Non-zero-sum games lead to unity, zero-sum games, lead to disunity. The biggest sport of all is the sport of business, which is also a non-zero-sum game. Wealth is elastic.

Businesses compete with each other while, at the same time, they cooperate. Within every industry, there is cooperation among competitors. Oil companies, car companies, software or computer companies engage in a variety of legal forms of cooperation. Every industry, every profession, has an "association." There are associations within the oil industry, semi-conductor industry, publishing industry; there is even the American Truck Stop Owners Association to which I once spoke. What is the purpose of these associations? First, they come together to martial their forces before Congress and the bureaucracies of Washington. They understand that they have little power divided, but considerable thrust when united. They come together to share learning and best practices. They even come together to engage in almost ritualistic trust building exercises (golf!) that will allow them to call upon each other if needed. Within each industry, competition and cooperation co-exist because the members recognize that it is a "non-zero-sum" game.

With complexity, the challenge of unity becomes more difficult and requires more sophisticated means of trust-building. Wrights says, *"As history progresses, human beings find themselves playing non-zero-sum games with more and more other human beings. Interdependence expands, and social complexity grows in scope and depth."*[15]. The earliest and most primitive social organization[16] (Wright uses the Shoshone Native American tribe as an example) relied almost exclusively on the family structure. The Shoshones were well known for their lack of a cohesive tribal structure. They lived in small family units, foraging for roots and other simple forms of food, which required little organization beyond the family. However, even the Shoshones periodically required assistance from the other family units to hunt rabbits. On these occasions, they fabricated a net that necessitated a larger group to come together to herd the rabbits into the net so others could club them to death. Single families could not do this. They then shared the poor rabbits among them. This was their most complex, even though temporary, form of social organization. While generally distrusted by other Native American tribes, the Shoshone families who worked together engaged in ritualistic trust building behavior in order to enable this simple non-zero-sum hunting.

All companies today are members of a supply chain. Virtually no company does it all. Even the local farmer, who may do everything within the borders of his farm, is dependent on the agricultural agent, the seed and fertilizer manufacturers, the distributors and grocery market. We are all members of a chain of customer-supplier relationships and our success depends on our ability to create social capital built from the currency of trust.

The Seven Keys to Building Trust

---

[15] Ibid. p. 19.
[16] By the term "primitive" I am not intending a value judgment, but a judgment about the social and technological complexity of their society.

What then are the concrete things we must do to build trust in the culture of an organization? The following seven actions are at least a good start:

1. Transparency:

Secrets create distrust. What are you hiding? Why are you hiding it? We have all heard these questions, which are a natural reaction to secretiveness. Twenty years ago, supervisors considered it their job alone to know how the work of one group connects to the work of another and each worker was told to "just do your own work!" The world has changed greatly. It is now a requirement of ISO Certification (International Standards Organization) that each work process be documented and transparent. Knowledge of the work process across groups enables problem solving and creativity that would be impossible if one were only "doing one's own work." Quality depends on process and performance transparency.

Transparency in measurement and finance builds trust. *The Great Game of Business* [17] and other books on *Open Book Management* [18] advocate open accounting, sharing financial information with every team, even providing every work team with a weekly or monthly accounting statement, so that every team can play the "great game of business." Transparency, or open-book management, takes the practice of employee empowerment or teams to a new and more profound level.

On a larger scale, the business scandals of the last few years that rocked the stock market, most particularly the Enron fiasco, have illustrated the disastrous consequences of failed transparency. Even the board of directors did not understand the accounting at Enron. The Chairman claims he didn't. Of course, it is the job of the Chairman and CEO to understand the accounting. Nevertheless, the books were so

---

[17] Stack, Jack. *The Great Game of Business*, New York, Doubleday, 1992.
[18] Schuster, John P; Carpenter Jill and Kane, Patricia M. *The Power of Open Book Management: Releasing the True Potential of People's Minds*, Hearts & Hands. New York. John C. Wiley & Sons, Inc.

constructed as to make the accounting opaque rather than transparent. One lesson is; if you can't understand it, don't trust it, don't invest in it!

It is common for executives to present financial results and financial goals to their employees. While this is good, it is far short of a genuine transparency in financial reporting. Break down the balance sheet and the profit and loss statement for employees. Give them credit for the ability to understand these financial statements. They are all available (for public companies) on the Internet anyway. Break them down by division and business unit. Explain which assets increased or decreased and why that is desirable or not. Many employees (heck, many managers) don't understand that corporate assets are not like storing stuff in your basement or closet, which we always seem intent on filling up! Reducing assets is good, because it increases return-on-assets. Explain how a business unit succeeded in increasing ROA by selling off some of its unneeded equipment, or sharing with another division. Explain the income statement and the reasons for the increase or decrease in different streams of income. Make them owners, through open information. This will create bonds of unity and energize them to contribute to financial results.

The behavior of managers must be consistent and understandable in the light of the financial information. For example, one company executive reported to his employees that they were doing very well toward meeting their quarterly revenue and cost targets. Then during the last two weeks of the month, he pushed everyone to cut expenditures and work overtime to get product out, all with no explanation. How did this message jive with the prior message? The problem with transparency is that it is a check on your own behavior. Suddenly, with everyone understanding the numbers, they expect you to behave in a way consistent with those numbers. Once employees have the numbers they start thinking, they start reasoning, they start asking questions. You must share your reasoning with them so they understand why pursuing different strategies and actions may be necessary.

2. Shared Communication:

We trust those who communicate openly and honestly and we trust those who listen well to our communication. Good communication skills are the foundation of all good relationships and successful careers are built on relationships.

Good communications in business cannot be occasional or serendipitous. There must be regularity and it must be planned. Quarterly meetings with suppliers and customers; monthly meetings between work teams; weekly team meetings to share performance data and problem solving improvements – these are just examples of the type of regularity in communication that must be established as routine practice in the organization if trust is to be built.

Well-managed companies today are thinking carefully about their communication strategy within the company because they recognize the link between communication, trust and performance. As corporate communication consultant Jim Shaffer said, *"You can't not communicate. It's going to happen whether you think it should or not. It's like the wind when you're sailing. You have the choice of ignoring it or managing it. Sailboats tend to sail better when you don't ignore the wind. Businesses tend to run better when you don't ignore communication."* [19].

The manager today is well served by thinking through a planned series of messages, somewhat like a politician decides on the three to five key issues and positions, that he believes will appeal to voters. However, in the case of managers, they are not trying to appeal; they are trying to influence behavior. Is a certain type of customer interaction most important? Is improving productivity a key goal? Is increasing creativity and input form employees, or safety the key goal? Is an effort to recreate the corporate culture an important priority? The manager must develop a strategy for reinforcing the same message repeatedly. Consistency and repetition drive home the message. Yet, it is equally important that managers are conveying positive messages, uplifting and energizing views of the future of the organization. This is the positive vision around which people will unify.

3. **Deep Listening:**

---

[19] Shaffer, Jim. *The Leadership Solution.* New York: McGraw-Hill, 2000. p. 50.

To each of us, we are the most important person in the world. If you value what I say, if you listen to me as if you are intently interested in learning from me, it shows extremely good judgment on your part. Obviously, you are someone who is not only clever, but someone whose judgment I can trust. We trust those who listen sincerely to us. Listening is an act of regard, of valuing the other person. And if we value each other, we can trust that we will do each other no harm.

Chapter Four of this book will focus on the quality of communications and its importance to performance. Let us just be reminded here that the performance of all social groups, families, teams or businesses, is dependent on the quality of communication, and in a knowledge-based economy, it is dialogue that creates value – not debate.

4. Reliability:

Do what you say and say what you do. No more common sense prescription for trustworthiness was ever given. We trust those who show up when they say they will show up; who do what they say they will do; and we cannot afford the expense of having our own time and efforts wasted by those who don't.

There is a cost to poor reliability in human relationships, just as there is in the quality of products and services. To go back to our "non-zero-sum" basketball team: if a player is not reliable in executing plays, it not only reduces his performance, it reduces the performance of others on the team. A player who unreliably executes plays in practice is quickly noticed by other players, who then cannot rely on him. They quickly learn to compensate by avoiding plays that involve that player. Moreover, the competing team will react equally to the opponent player's unreliability and adjust their game accordingly. Now, with one hand (one player, actually) tied behind their back, their chance of success is diminished. Poor personal reliability within a team or organization is just as costly as poor reliability in a product. I have seen the exact same occurrence on management teams as members of the team come to distrust the reliability of one player and find ways to compensate, diminishing the success of the whole team.

5. Responsiveness

Have you ever sat and talked with someone who was motionless? No head nodding. No smile. No verbal acknowledgment. A true stone face! You don't know whether they understand, appreciate, agree or disagree. How can you trust someone who is not responsive to you? You can't. A natural reaction is not to trust those who fail to respond to us.

I had a policy, a standard of operation, in my consulting firm, that when a potential client called inquiring into the capability or availability of my firm, we would respond both in writing and over the telephone in less than twenty-four hours. I am certain that the likelihood of a successful sales relationship is directly proportional to the speed at which the client receives a response. We trust that someone who responds quickly is motivated, cares, and will get the job done for us, versus someone who delays or defers his response.

6. Demonstrate Win-Win Relationships:

I want to work with someone who will help me win. I am more than happy to return the favor. Win-win relationships are based on an abundance mentality, a mentality that there is more than enough goodies to go around and we can help each other without diminishing our own success – again, a non-zero-sum relationship.

While we may think and feel that we are in a win-win relationship, it is important to verbalize this belief clearly and openly. In every relationship, it is worth engaging in the conversation of "what we each get out of this," so there is transparency of understanding. I need this from the relationship, and I understand that you need that. We trust those who are sincerely motivated to help us win.

7. Alignment of Rewards:

A statement of values can not compete with the reward system. A consulting firm (not my own) had a wonderful statement of values encouraging all the right things. The reward system was simple: you earned bonuses based on personal billing and personal sales of contracts. The firm had different sectors or specialties of consulting. It was not unusual for an individual in one specialty to bring in members of different specialties who could aid the client. However, there was a frequent problem. Assuming that there was a zero-sum of money the client would spend, individuals from one specialty would advise the clients that they really didn't need the first consultant, who had invited them in initially. By this means, they hoped to maximize their personal billing at the expense of the others. What this did to trust within the firm is obvious. Many of the most capable and creative consultants left because of their distaste for this cut-throat culture.

The zero-sum fallacy is obvious. What was less obvious was that the firm had a compensation system that directly encouraged behavior contrary to their stated values and to the best interest of their clients. Aligning reward systems to encourage trustworthy behavior is not a simple matter, but one that must be pursued if the firm is to build its social capital. The first chapter in the second part of this book presents a process for designing the system of the organization based on the values required to create the new currencies of competition.

Managing and leading in a manner that builds trust creates unified effort toward common goals. The success of organizations, whether in business, military or service organizations, is the result of the degree to which unified effort and energy, is created by authentic leaders. This *broad-slice* cannot be separated from any other part of the culture. Every form of capital, true wealth, is dependent on the currency of trust.

Creating Personal Trust:

	Personal Action Agenda	I do	I don't	I will
1.	I behave in ways my associates regard as trustworthy.			
2.	I tend to display trust toward my associates.			
3.	I am very open and don't keep secrets at work.			
4.	I enjoy participating in discussions about how we can improve and I share my ideas freely.			
5.	I don't just accept the obvious, but enjoy hearing different opinions and considering the importance and meaning of issues.			
6.	I do what I say and say what I do.			
7.	If I am needed by any of my associates, they can count on me responding to them quickly.			
8.	I enjoy sharing credit with others and end to give credit to others.			
Summary of what I will do to improve trust in my personal relationships:				

Creating Team Trust:

Team Action Agenda	We do	We don't	We will
1. My team behaves in ways that are trustworthy toward our customers and suppliers.			
2. My team members behave toward each other in ways that engender trust within the team.			
3. Team members are open in sharing information with each other.			
4. We do not keep secrets within the team.			
5. The team has active and open discussions about how it can improve its work.			
6. My team can be trusted to fulfill our obligations and commitments.			
7. My team responds quickly when improvements are needed.			
8. We listen carefully to our customers and engage them in dialogue.			
9. My team gives credit to other teams when we have a shared victory.			
Summary of what we agree to do to improve trust in our teams relationships:			

Creating Organizational Trust:

Organization Action Agenda	We do	We don't	We will
1. My organization is respected for its trustworthiness.			
2. We have a culture of honesty and integrity in this organization.			
3. The organization promotes win-win relationships within the organization.			
4. We share information openly, transparently, with members of this organization.			
5. The leaders of our organization are open in their desire to seek improvement.			
6. Fulfilling obligations to our customers and other stakeholders is required in this organization.			
7. This organization can be trusted to respond quickly to our customers and to seek rapid improvement.			
8. We listen carefully to our customers and we engage them in dialogue.			
9. This organization has reward systems, formal and informal, that promote sharing and giving credit to others.			
Summary of what we agree to do to improve organizational discipline:			

Chapter 3

A Pursuit with Passion
The Currency of Purpose

"True happiness...is not attained through self-gratification, but through fidelity to a worthy purpose." Helen Keller

Purpose is the most pure energy source emerging from the deepest well of our soul. It is the answer to every important question about our being. Why are we here? Where are we going? What difference will it make if we get there? It is the motivation of motivations; it is the reason to seek reason; it is not merely what people will work for, it is what people will die for. The pursuit of purpose was in the beginning and in the Word. Without it you are nothing, mere dust, because you are going nowhere and don't know why.

How Leaders Create Energy

The capacity to lead is directly related to the pursuit of worthy purpose. Purpose may be the most powerful *broad-slice* to link people and processes in common effort. Authentic leaders know and display purpose in their lives. Why? Because it is the degree, to which we pursue an ennobling purpose that we attract others. Leaders must attract others if they expect to have followers. Purpose attracts and therefore serves as a unifying force. There is unity of effort and energy to the degree of shared purpose. Our level of satisfaction and our level of energy are directly related to not only our understanding of our own purpose, but whether the organization, the team, the family to which we contribute, share that same purpose.

Individuals have a personal need to find their purpose, to create their own energy source, and they may find it in their faith, family or career. Teams are structured around a common purpose and manage their work to be of service to their customers, those who care about their work. Purpose may be found in genuine caring for others, customers and fellow team members. The purpose of larger organizations should be found in its statement of mission and strategy. Why does the company exist? What will it contribute to the world at large, to its customers, shareholders, employees? Most often, the answer to these questions rolls off the tongue as parroted repetition of published papers posted on the wall. However, it can be a deeply felt and sincere reason to go to work in the morning, to seek improvement and dedicate discretionary energy, the distinction between common and superior performance.

While individuals should each take responsibility for finding their own purpose, it is the function of leaders to provide a reason, a shared and ennobling purpose that will cause energy to be focused on the goals of the organization.

Finding the Noble or Eating the Apple

Purpose is found at many levels – common and profound. Earning money to feed and educate your children is a sensible purpose. Sacrificing for a church or charity, enlisting in public service and even politics, may be motivated by a genuine desire to contribute to the betterment of fellow citizens. Of course, not every purpose is noble and inspiring. The cocaine dealer, the politician appealing to fears and hatreds, the business person seeking personal gain without regard to the interests of others, are all fulfilling a perverse purpose. But, there are natural laws. We are all tempted to pick the apple off the tree rather than defer gratification. Even though we have knowledge of our best long-term interests, we would rather just grab the ice cream than resist our temptation and do what we know to be in our long-term self-interest.

Something within our nature, perhaps it is a seed planted by God within us, determines that we all seek and will sacrifice for that which is noble. Every leader understands, perhaps intuitively, that followers will sacrifice for a noble purpose, and the leader defines the mission of the organization in terms of a worthy purpose. We will sacrifice, even our lives, for a cause, we perceive to be noble and worthy. Why? Because we understand the mystery of sacrifice and when we sacrifice our money, time, or energy to that which we hold to be noble, there is no sacrifice, but only an investment – one with a guaranteed return – and that return is in that which is most precious to us, our own nobility and worth. The mystery of sacrifice is that we become like that unto which we sacrifice ourselves. When we sacrifice our self to that which is noble, we become more noble.

Just ask yourself how you felt the last time you sacrificed your time, money or energy to something you believed to be noble (your faith, family, country or community). How did you feel? You felt better about yourself. You felt more worthy. You felt more worthy because you became like that unto which you sacrificed. Conversely, the person who sits home all day glued to the boob tube, sacrificing himself to the trivial, becomes himself, more trivial. And how does he feel about himself? He feels depressed and less worthy. And he, or she is witnessing the same truth that he is becoming like that unto he sacrifices himself.

In Jack London's novel *Martin Eden* there is a wonderful line – *"God's own mad lover should die for the kiss, but not for thirty thousand dollars a year."* God's own mad lover, the seeker after that which is noble, will die for the kiss, to be near, to touch, that which is most noble; but, not for the material and transitory thing. This is the mystery of sacrifice. This is the mystery by which human energy is created.

Leaders lead by communicating a sense of purpose. Followers respond with pleasure because they know that by sacrificing their energies they will be ennobled in return. This is the contract between the leader and the led and when it is fulfilled they become a unified whole.

Happiness is Found in Finding Your Purpose

The case can be made that happiness is found in fulfilling one's purpose. Martin E.P. Seligman has studied mental health, what he calls *positive psychology,* as opposed to the more usual topic of psychologists, mental illness. Seligman presents the common sense hypothesis that more people are likely to achieve a healthy psychological condition by pursuing health and happiness, rather than continually seeking a solution to their problems. He has conducted an exhaustive study of happiness and arrived at a description of the conditions leading to what he calls *authentic happiness.*[20] Authentic happiness is distinct from temporary pleasure and is much more then the sum of continuous pleasurable events. In other words, if money, candy, sex or other pleasure inducing events were all that was required for happiness, than the person who could acquire the most of these pleasures would be happiest. The data says otherwise. The extremely rich are no happier than those who are just moderately well off. Easy access to sex or candy or any other instant pleasure does not cause one to be "authentically happy" – happy with oneself and one's life.

Seligman says, *"The belief that we can rely on shortcuts to happiness, joy, rapture, comfort and ecstasy, rather than be entitled to these feelings by the exercise of personal strengths and virtues, leads to legions of people, who in the middle of great wealth, are starving spiritually. Positive emotion alienated from the exercise of character leads to emptiness, to in-authenticity, to depression, and, as we age, to the gnawing realization that we are fidgeting until we die."* On the other hand, his research found that *"The positive feelings that arise from the exercise of our strengths and virtues, rather than from the shortcuts, is authentic."*[21] *"Authentic happiness comes from identifying and cultivating your most fundamental strengths and using them every day in work, love, play and parenting."*[22]

This says volumes about our personal performance, and that of our teams and organizations. We know that we are ennobled, feel better about ourselves, when we are pursuing a worthy purpose. And, we know from Seligman's research that authentic happiness results

---

[20] Seligman, Martin E.P. *Authentic Happiness.* New York: Free Press, 2002.
[21] Ibid. P. 8
[22] Ibid. P xiii

from *"identifying and cultivating our strengths and using them every day in our work."* Therefore, knowing our strengths and using them for some purpose we believe to be worthy leads us to happiness and self worth. This then results in greater energy and motivation, learning and developing greater capacity, and higher levels of performance.

The task then, is to identify those strengths within our self or our group; develop and strengthen those through exercise; and dedicate them to a worthy purpose.

Finding Purpose in Business

We must learn to create and utilize purpose, not only in our own lives, but also in the management of our teams, our businesses and even our nation. Businesses can have a noble purpose if we recognize the five forms of capital or wealth – social, spiritual, human, technical and financial. The purpose of business is the creation of wealth not only for shareholders, but also for the society at large.

The only way to eliminate poverty is to create wealth, as the only way to combat the dark is to turn on the light. We who are able to produce wealth can eliminate poverty and disease and may free humanity from the chains of mindless toil so that we can pursue and utilize our higher capacities of mind and soul. Peter Drucker made a similar observation a number of years ago: *"The achievement of business management enables us today to promise perhaps prematurely (and certainly rashly) the abolition of the grinding poverty that has been mankind's lot through the ages... In a world that is politically increasingly fragmented and obsessed by nationalism, business management is one of the very few institutions capable of transcending national boundaries."*

Many people believe that their higher purpose, their spiritual life, and their work life are necessarily different and disconnected. Because of this belief, they behave in entirely different ways at home, on Sunday and at work. They are not united in their own character. They are living dual lives and there is a personal toll, a loss of energy that results from this fragmentation. They can bring these lives into harmony if they realize that their work, whether making steel, farming potatoes, producing cars, or processing information, each in its own way contributes to a collective purpose. We, who have the opportunity to choose, must meditate and develop a clear sense of purpose, both personal and corporate.

Purpose is found in knowing and serving customers. Some years ago, I was working with a foundry in Monongahela, Pennsylvania, deep in the heart of the adversarial culture of steelworkers and coal mines. A foundry is a rough and tough environment where the buildings aren't heated, where they pour molten iron to form castings and where union and management are often at war. Listening as best I could to the experience of workers, I discovered that even though some had worked there for thirty years, they had never met a customer face-to-face. They knew that their castings were put on a truck and shipped to another company, but that company had no human face.

Some times the simplest things have the strongest effect. We found that one of the customers was no more than fifty miles away. We gathered some of the experienced union members and drove to the customer's plant on a day when their product was going to be delivered. There, they watched the workers of that plant unload and inspect their castings. These other workers, it turned out, were members of the same steelworkers union. They were brothers, brothers they had never met. And these brothers explained to them the problems they had with their castings, in language more direct and more forceful than their managers would have dared. Suddenly the purpose of their work, rather than meeting the requirements of managers they did not trust, became doing work that met the needs of their brothers. Their entire purpose had changed.

These workers had been denied a sense of purpose, not by any fault of their own, but by the system in which they worked.

Civilizations and Companies Decline with the Decline in Purpose

Organizations and civilizations are defined by their culture. Over time, cultures go through a cycle from their birth to their death, and this cycle is much like the cycle of individual life. A few years back, I wrote a book describing the rise and fall of corporate cultures[23] and their parallel with the rise and fall of civilizations as described by Arnold Toynbee in his great works.[24] There are periods of high energy and there are periods of comfort, ease, and decline.

One of the most interesting things I found in Toynbee's great data base of human history is his description of what leaders do and what results in the progress of civilization. Toynbee said that cultures advance by recognizing and responding to challenge. The "condition of ease" does not lead to progress, but the crisis, the reason to exert one's muscles and one's creativity. Toynbee said that leaders are those who recognize the challenge and issue forth a creative response. These leaders are not necessarily the formal leaders, but rather those who are creative, who respond to the challenge. This creative response, when successful, does not result in a "condition of ease" but rather in a higher-level challenge, requiring a higher level and creative response. Now the old response will not work. If the leaders rely on yesterday's successful response, to meet today's new challenges, it results in a failure. This failure of creativity is the signal event in the decline of a culture. Leaders, rather than discovering a creative response, mechanically pull the same lever, harder and faster, all the while knowing it is without effect. The mechanical response, rather than the creative response, is the clear signal of the approaching end. Sell!

The job of the leader is to recognize and respond to challenge. Leaders instill purpose, unity, and create energy through this challenge-response mechanism.

The Deception of a Condition of Ease

The concept of a "condition of ease" is worthy of reflection and has implications for our own purpose. One of the great tricks of life is that we seek that which will kill us. We seek a condition of ease. We all want millions of dollars well invested, no more work, no more

---

[23] Miller, Lawrence M. *Barbarians to Bureaucrats: Corporate Life Cycle Strategies*. New York: Clarkson N. Potter, Inc. 1988.
[24] Toynbee, Arnold. *A Study of History*. New York: Oxford University Press, 1962.

schedules or demands by unreasonable managers or customers, and we want the complete and absolute freedom to do what we want and when we want. My father died at the age of 95 recently. He worked until just months before his end. I think he worked out of fear, fear that if he stopped, if he had no reason to get out of bed and get to work, he would not get out of bed. And, several months after he ended his work, he didn't get out of bed.

While longevity in life is the result of many factors including genetics, diet and exercise; it is also the result of mental activity. People who live longer tend to be those who are still curious, reading, exploring, responding to challenges. I was always impressed by the energy and drive displayed by Dr. Edwards Deming, one of the founders of the quality movement. In his late 90's he was driven, constantly giving speeches, consulting and trying to reform business to focus on the needs of its customers and clarify their thinking with statistical methods. Agree with him or not, he was driven by an animating purpose and he was full of life until the end.

Our culture has conditioned us to seek ease. Every advertisement of the vacationer laying on the lounge chair on the beach, beer in hand, beautiful bodies in abundance and free from care, seduces us to seek leisure. We want the most comfortable car, the most comfortable house, the safest neighborhood, the safest retirement fund, and every labor saving device that responds with a click of a remote control. Why do so many things come with a remote control? So they do not disturb our ease and comfort. But does this lead to either happiness, the deep satisfaction of knowing that we are growing and developing? No, they are only those immediate pleasures that we confuse with authentic happiness.

If leisure led to happiness, everyone in the wealthiest neighborhoods would be happy and everyone living in a remote village in Tibet would be miserable. Suicide, drug abuse, divorce and general misery are far higher in the wealthy neighborhood. Financial wealth does not result in higher levels of happiness. For example, there was no difference between the happiness level of 22 lottery winners and comparison samples of average people or paraplegics. There are many studies demonstrating that once a minimal level of wealth is achieved, additional wealth has no effect on happiness.[25] Ease does not produce happiness. Employing our talents toward a worthy purpose does. A condition of ease leads to reduced energy, while dedication to a passionate purpose creates energy.

Managing Our Personal System with Intention

Systems thinking is a way of looking at an organization, or any organism, in terms of its interaction with its environment. A farm is a system, the performance of which is impacted by the inputs into the farm (rain, sun, seeds, tractors, etc.); then the processes (planting, fertilizing, harvesting); and, finally, the response to the output by the customer. All systems have these same three critical steps of input, a process, and outputs. A healthy system is adaptive or learning, adjusting to the quality and quantity of inputs and responding to the feedback from those who receive the output. Systems which do not learn, die. This is easily seen in companies that fail to employ the latest technology (input) or fail to gather intelligence on social trends and market preferences; or, fail to listen to their customer's reaction to their product (output); or, fail to improve how they do things (process).

Individually, we are also a system. We respond to our environment whether parents, peers or customers. But, if we only respond to the immediate pull and push of the environment, we are victims, slaves to whatever is presented to us.

As a human being, we have a freedom other organisms' lack. We can exert our will. We have the capacity of *intention*, willful direction based on an understanding of our purpose. We can choose and control our environment and therefore, we have the opportunity to exert our will. This power of *intention*, purpose turned into action, allows us to exert control on our environment.

Without a clear purpose, we are not clear in our intentions regarding our own behavior and development. Without purpose, why should we read, exercise or study? Purpose is necessary for our own development and this progress ultimately leads to our happiness.

---

[25] Seligman, Martin E.P. *Authentic Happiness*.

Meaninglessness is Funny, But Deadly!

Most of us have enjoyed watching the Seinfeld show. What is most interesting about this sitcom is that Jerry and his band of buddies never appear to do anything meaningful or important. They never seem to learn any lessons, contribute anything to society, or even ask significant questions.

I remember the show in which George Costanza comes very close to marriage. Recognizing that he is approaching a lasting and significant commitment in his life, George is in a near panic to find a way out. His fiancé, licking envelopes for their wedding invitation, dies of poisoning from the glue. At her funeral, someone suggests that George have some moments alone at the grave so he can talk to her in private. George is puzzled. He can't think of anything to say. So, he stands over her grave and tells her about last night's baseball game with great enthusiasm and how the Yankees beat the Orioles. Of course, it is funny. But, it is funny precisely because it illustrates how completely shallow his life is. He is a person who can think of no important or meaningful thing to say.

Why do we laugh at this? Is it because we are relieved that here we see people who seem to be happy and carefree, but who are more lost and lacking direction than even we are! They live in a state of purposeless bliss, a complete and total illusion!

Seinfeld and company never engage in serious reflection for more then twenty seconds. It would ruin the show. When we reflect we tend to reflect, not on the trivial, but on the important. As we reflect on the important, we inevitably meditate on our own importance, our own lives. Seinfeld will not prompt this kind of reflection. Martin Eden, or virtually any other serious book, will. This reflection helps us achieve a sense of purpose.

Earlier I referred to the quote from Martin Eden, a wonderful novel by Jack London ("God's own mad lover…"). The book is about a young uneducated seaman near the beginning of the last century. He is rough and crude and through a series of misfortunes falls in love with a young woman who is from a prominent upper class family. He decides that the way to win her love is to be an author and he starts writing. Needless to say, he doesn't have a great agent! He finds it almost impossible to get his work published. He works day and night, almost starving in his apartment with no heat or comforts. Neither the girl nor her family has any sympathy or interest in his plight. Suddenly, he gets an article published. It is a hit and the publisher wants another. He has accumulated a pile of unpublished and rejected work in the corner of his freezing apartment. He takes another story off the pile and sends it to them. Again, it is a hit. His royalties go up, his popularity grows, and suddenly the girl and her family invite him over for dinner and want him to meet their friends. Success! The girl is now in love with him, admiring his brilliance and determination.

But, Martin Eden knows a secret. From the time of his first publication, he does nothing but take articles off his pile of previously rejected and unpublished work. He never writes again. He is now popular, but he is not producing, not writing. While the outside world now appreciates him and thinks he is great, he knows better. He knows that he was great when he was starving, cold and writing all through the night. Now he considers the girl's love meaningless and even despises her for her bad judgment. I won't tell you the end of the story, read it yourself!

What is the significance of this story? Martin Eden discovered something. He thought he loved and wanted the girl. He thought he wanted fame and fortune. But, when he acquired these, he recognized that what was of greater value was the actual work he had been doing when no one gave him any attention. Now the attention was meaningless because he knew that he was now unproductive and undeserving. What he discovered was that his true purpose, the act of being creative itself.

The other significance of this story is that this insight gave this author purpose, helped clarify my own values, interests, and helped me understand the truth of success and failure. But, it only came because of the input and reflection on that input.

This process of managing the inputs into your own personal system is yours, and yours alone, to manage. What is the input to your personal system that gives you insight and understanding?

Finding Purpose in the Team

Just as an individual is motivated by her purpose, so too is a team or any other social group. If we are leaders of these groups, we own the task of helping develop a shared purpose. Every coach understands this. Every general or military platoon sergeant understands this as well. It is no different in the office or factory.

How does the system affect the purpose of a team? Do we manage the inputs within a team of people at work? How do we find time to reflect, to think deeply about those inputs, and then to engage in dialogue, a reflective exchange among the team, to find meaning and clarify purpose? If this is not done, the team is likely, like the television viewer, to become obsessed with the trivial and transitory, failing to think about the important things, failing to understand their true purpose and be energized by that purpose. Teams have routine work that occupies most of their time and to which they must often respond immediately. Time must be set aside for strategic considerations – the big questions. Why do we make this? Who cares about it? What is really important to our customers?

These are not trivial questions. They are like Martin Eden's questions about why he was writing and why others did or did not value him. The ability to answer these questions leads to the creation of energy; the daily issues of immediate improvement do not.

The Hierarchy of Purpose

There is what I will call a hierarchy of purpose from the eternal to the instant, from the spiritual to the material. You can visualize this as a pyramid. At the top of the pyramid is our largest understanding of our existence. Most of us gain understanding of our purpose from our religion or our parents. The concept of purpose is a spiritual concept. It is not merely intellectual and it is certainly not material. Most religions tell us that our purpose is to become like God, to acquire the spiritual attributes of God and his Divine Teachers. We go to our place of worship to gain greater understanding of our purpose in this life.

The concept of purpose creates a link between spiritual capital and financial, social and other forms of capital. In the second part of this book, I will provide more specific definitions and indicators of each form of capital. However, spiritual capital can be viewed to include both one's connection to a higher source of purpose, for most God; and to a strong commitment to moral values. A team or larger organization can possess spiritual capital to the degree the members

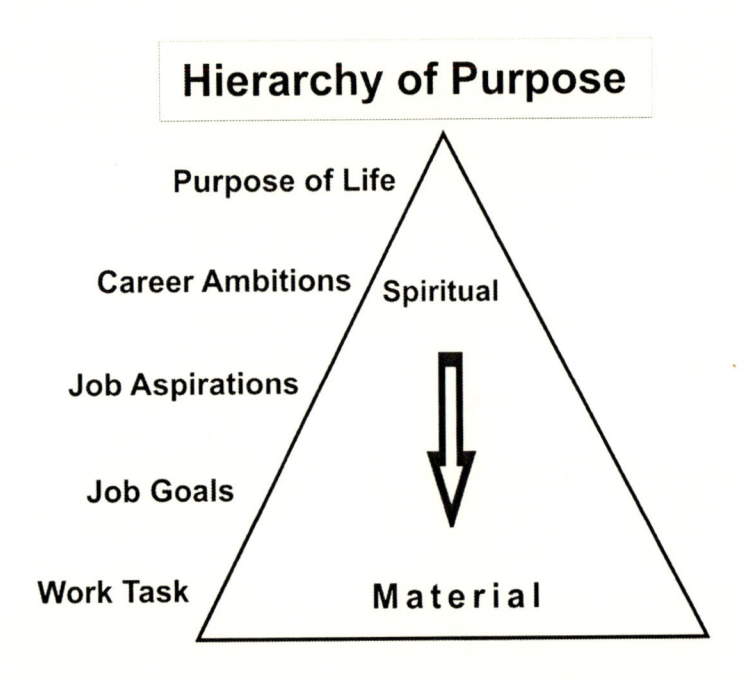

Hierarchy of Purpose

- Purpose of Life
- Career Ambitions — Spiritual
- Job Aspirations
- Job Goals
- Work Task — Material

share both an ennobling purpose and moral or ethical values.

Many people have great difficulty relating spiritual purpose to their daily work-life. Yet, merely struggling with the question of how my work fulfills my spiritual purpose is in itself, a step forward. Spiritual progress always comes from the internal struggle to resolve questions. If one has no questions, one has no spiritual progress. By asking this question we are seeking connection, we are seeking meaning; we are seeking unity between our spiritual and material lives; we are seeking an integrated life.

If this were a simple question, everyone would have a fulfilling job and a fulfilling life. However, more often than not, people are doing work that is not related to their purpose, or they have not figured out what their purpose in life is, and therefore can never derive meaning from their work. They may derive material benefit, but not a lasting satisfaction. It is a lifelong quest to seek meaning and spiritual connection in one's daily life.

Answering these purpose questions is also the job of senior executives, even the board of directors in a corporation. They are the ones who must define the over-arching purpose and values of the business and the answers have a huge impact on the motivation of all in the organization. Unfortunately, even boards of directors and senior executives are distracted by the trivial and avoiding reflection. They too, should attempt to create a hierarchy of purpose throughout their company, with a clear mission statement, which is ennobling of efforts and which connects all work toward this worthy purpose.

Creating Personal Purpose:

Personal Action Agenda	I do	I don't	I will
1. If asked, I can describe my life's mission in a simple and direct sentence.			
2. In the past six months, I have discussed my life's mission with someone close to me.			
3. I read and study books and magazines that help me understand and clarify my purpose in life.			
4. I can describe specific goals in my personal life that are to fulfill my purpose.			
5. I regularly take account of myself to check that I am pursuing my purpose.			
6. I am not distracted by the trivial entertainment and television and am able to focus on purposeful activities.			
7. I take time to dialogue with other people who share my purpose, or have a similar purpose, to deepen my own understanding.			
8. I deliberately control my environment to keep me on a purposeful path.			
9. I am genuinely happy with my life.			
Summary of what I will do to improve my pursuit of personal purpose:			

Creating Team Purpose:

Team Action Agenda	We do	We don't	We will
1. My team knows that we add important value to our customers.			
2. We know that we are responsible for an important part of the process that serves our customers.			
3. We believe that the product or service we help to create is a worthy product or service, contributing to a larger good.			
4. My team discusses our purpose with some regularity.			
5. My team has an agreed understanding among the members as to our purpose.			
6. In addition to the daily work of continuous improvement, we take time to think about the strategic decisions, the "why?" questions.			
7. Our team engages in dialogue with our customers and others who help us gain a sense of purpose.			
8. We engage in development activities that help us understand our purpose.			
9. Knowing our purpose gives us a satisfaction, a sense of "joy" about our work.			

Summary of what we agree to do to improve our team's self-discipline:

Creating Organizational Purpose:

Organization Action Agenda	We do	We don't	We will
1. Our organization contributes something noble and worthy for our society.			
2. Our leaders communicate the worthy purpose of this organization.			
3. We have a strategy that fulfills that purpose.			
4. Associates and I discuss and understand this purpose.			
5. I am able to describe the purpose of this organization to outsiders in a way that makes me proud to work here.			
6. I know that I am involved, and making a contribution to fulfilling that purpose.			
7. Our customers feel that the work we do is important to them.			
8. This organization contributes to the growth and development of employees or associates.			
9. I feel energized to come to work here.			
Summary of what we agree to do to improve organizational discipline:			

Chapter 4

Thinking Together Rather Than Alone
The Currency of Dialogue

"A dialogue is more than two monologues.."
Max M. Kampelman

We have a crisis of conversation. It is going down hill rapidly and if it continues we may all be left watching ourselves on Crossfire, further depleting the gene pool from stress related deaths. Our ability to make effective decisions depends on our ability to listen, to gain understanding, to explore ideas and to consider alternatives while getting beyond preconceptions – in other words, to engage in genuine dialogue in a spirit of humility and common interest. Wisdom is not achieved through the combat of debate, but through the exploration of dialogue. Dialogue is a conversation of shared discovery.

In every conversation, there is a mysterious process by which we are forming attractions and bonds of unity, or we are distancing ourselves, creating separation from the other person. It is not simply a matter of what we say, and it certainly is not a matter of being right or wrong. It is in the spirit of the discourse; the spirit of winning a contest by displaying superior wit; or, the spirit of shared discovery and appreciation. The first creates alienation while the second unites the parties. One is an exercise in thinking and acting alone; while the second is an exercise in thinking together. Those who are always thinking and acting alone are likely to be less happy than those who tend to think and discover with others.

At the time of this writing, my son is in Baghdad working for the organization charged with planning the elections and helping to develop the capacity of the Iraqi Election Commission. After one of the several elections, I asked my son, "So, is all of this going to work?" He replied very simply. "It will if they can learn to talk to one another." His response was short, yet very meaningful. Democracy is not built on the formal process of elections and laws alone. Democracy is built on a culture in which people can talk to each other in a trusting and trustworthy manner; in which leaders are willing to compromise and take into account the views of different groups. It is a very precious form of capital, social capital.

When to Invest in Deep Conversation

We find it difficult to engage in the effort, or take the time to think deeply together. We are all in a rush. We rush by our children's important events. We rush by our friend's crisis without stopping to engage them in serious thought. While at work, we are always in a rush – measuring our performance by how quickly we make decisions, rather than by how well we think them through.

Of course, you may say, "but the reality is that I am under pressure. I do have to make decisions quickly and don't have time to think deeply with others, to dialogue, about every little decision." True enough. I would not suggest that you engage in deep dialogue for "little decisions," only big ones. But, are there times when an investment in gaining collective wisdom is worth the costs? Of course there are.

When we are investing millions in training and development and quality improvement, the biggest quality problem in modern corporations is virtually ignored. That is the quality of decision-making by senior management groups. Repeatedly, in corporate and government history, there are cases of major decisions that completely overlook simple facts, leading to extremely costly mistakes. Executives of one petroleum company with whom I was consulting admitted that they had invested approximately one billion dollars drilling for oil in a land-locked African country. When they finally found oil, someone asked the obvious question, "How are we going to get it out of the country?" Incredibly, there was no possible way to transport the oil to market. One billion dollars had been wasted because no one had asked an extremely obvious question. Everyone had assumed that someone had the answer. These were smart people. How does that happen?

It happens because they had a very habitual pattern of conversation leading up to decisions. Someone studied the matter, made a presentation with a few overheads showing facts and figures, there were questions and answers, and they then made a decision. Someone was always an advocate for a decision and the decision would be a personal victory or defeat for that person. Egos were on the line before the meeting began. Challenges to a proposition were challenges to the person, and within the group, there were well-formed alliances. Challenges might fracture an alliance and cost one support in a following case. Everyone judged comments or questions based on whether they were from perceived advocates or opponents. Decisions took on the quality of sport, with teams lined up and a sure winner and loser. They did not think deeply together, they did not seek to learn and explore together without prejudice. They didn't ask the "what-if?" questions that might have reveal weaknesses in a proposal. It doesn't take much imagination to see how the same failure of decision-making occurs in the political realm.

The Roots of Dialogue

Much of the literature on dialogue stems from the work of David Bohm.[26], a physicist who thought deeply about the "wholeness" of our systems. He promoted a form of group dialogue that would lead to self-awareness and insight, but would not necessarily lead to decisions or the use of other problem solving tools. In his view, a dialogue should continue without any time constrain or any "goal" of making a decision. I have spoken with a number of practitioners of dialogue groups and, in general, they have conceded that his original form of dialogue is not practical in the business world. Bohm was not a manager and did not have to integrate his ideas with the day-to-day world of getting results that every manager faces. Yet, there is great

---

[26] Bohm, David. On Dialogue. Rutledge. London and New York. 1996.

value in the process he developed and the potential to integrate dialogue with management decision-making in a selective way.

The value that dialogue can contribute to management decision making is two fold: first it can help us come up with more creative and higher quality decisions based on unbiased listening and reflection on the views of others. Second, the process of dialogue creates unity within the group and shared commitment to a decision. Many decisions fail, not because they were wrong, but because they did not have the shared understanding and commitment of those who were responsible for implementing the decision.

The Stages of Group Decision-Making: The Four Containers

Group decision-making is not one thing. There are steps in the process, different stages that a conversation goes through to arrive at a decision. In each of these stages, different modes of thought and techniques are appropriate. One can think of these as different "containers" that one enters for a period of time. If the members of the group know in which container they belong, it can help everyone to be on the same page.

In the work of groups, there is a stage of *structure and organization.* This stage begins before the meeting when you determine the purpose of the group or meeting, the membership, the different roles and responsibilities within the team. This stage also includes understanding the team's relationship to other groups or individuals. This container also includes deciding on the agenda and the time to be allocated to each topic. It is very common that groups have problems because of poor structure. They may not have the right people in the room; they may lack the authority to make the necessary decisions; they may not be structured properly within the group with assigned roles and responsibilities.

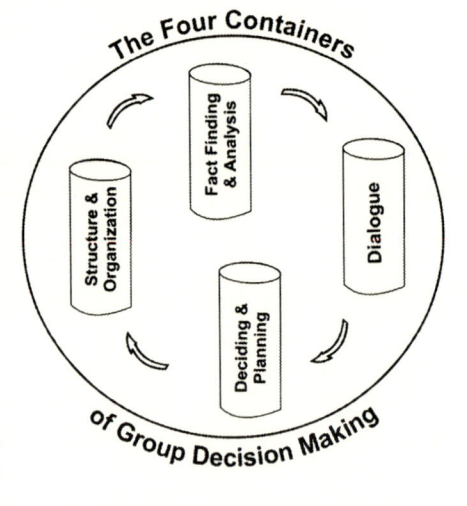

The second container is that of *fact-finding and analysis*. This container may last as little as five minutes or may extend over more than one meeting as the members seek information or data relevant to their decision. Within this container, techniques such as cause-and-effect diagrams, histograms, Pareto charts, affinity diagrams and other techniques may be used to seek knowledge of a problem and analysis of causes.

The third container is that of *dialogue*. Dialogue is the process of seeking meaning and understanding. It is thinking below the surface. Dialogue occurs when a group seeks to "think together" in a process of discovery. This process requires patience, silence, finding your voice, and the search for what is important. This stage is almost a meditation, a period of reflection on the subject in order to see things in a different way by getting beyond assumptions that block alternative perspectives.

Finally, there is the container of *deciding and planning action*. It is useful to separate decision-making from the previous steps. Often members of teams jump right to "here is what we should do" when they have not gathered any facts, even considered where the facts might be, or who might have them, and have certainly not considered their meaning or importance. Decision-making requires a different mental process than either fact-finding or dialogue. Neither fact-finding nor dialogue involves judgment of any kind, but rather learning and exploration. Decision-making does require identifying alternatives and making judgments as to the best course of action. When you know that you have gathered the facts and considered their meaning, you feel prepared to make sound judgments. This container also includes developing an action plan that specifies by *whom*, *what* and *when* things will be done.

Since this book is not intended as a training manual for teams or decision-making groups, I will not spend additional time here on the first and last two stages of group decision-making. I will focus on dialogue because of its importance in achieve unity among group members. This is in no way intended to lessen the importance of the other three stages.

From Debate to Dialogue

One understanding of conversation in a group is to think about the group as a number of different people, each member of the group sharing his or her ideas and the group deciding which idea is the best. With this understanding, each individual is thinking alone, forming his or her own ideas and opinions and then attempting to convince the others of the value of those ideas.

Another understanding of group conversation is to consider that the group is thinking as one collective mind. With this understanding, the individual members are not so focused on their own ideas; they are focused on learning and exploring an issue and its meaning. They are no longer focusing solely on convincing others to accept their ideas. They are no longer trying to *win*. When thinking together the members are interested in encouraging and supporting the ideas of others because those ideas become their own. The objective is to create "collective wisdom," to find the best answer for the group, with no concern for whose idea it is.

It may be useful to define our terms.

Conversation will be used to describe all interaction among a group of people in their effort to reach understanding or a decision regardless of the quality or nature of that interaction.

Debate is a conversation in which the parties assume opposing positions at the outset and view the goal of the conversation to be the victory of their position over that of their opponent.

Discussion is a conversation in which the goal is to reach a decision that both parties can accept and which may represent a compromise or combination of positions previously held by the parties.

Dialogue is a conversation that explores the meaning and nature of an issue in an effort to create insight and understanding on a deeper level. Dialogue seeks to gain the insight of all parties and create collective wisdom, unity, or a new way of looking at an issue.

It may be helpful to visualize how we communicate with others. The following triangle illustrates the different mental frameworks from which we engage in conversation. In most conversations people are thinking about their own ideas and how to persuade the other person to accept their ideas. Unfortunately, the other person is doing the same. This defeats the opportunity for shared understanding and may result in conflict. When we are in our own corner, thinking alone,

Competing in the New Capitalism 79

we are in a win-lose posture, searching for victory for our position at the cost of defeat for the other person.

Any night on America's talk shows, you witness the culture of debate, not dialogue. "Crossfire, from the left comes the liberal, from the right comes the conservative, and may the best person win!" It is interesting to examine the conversation and ask whether the two combatants ever acknowledge that the position of the other could be valid or worth considering. Most often, the two protagonists are listening carefully with an eye to disagreement. This guarantees that neither can learn from the other. The very act of learning, of accepting

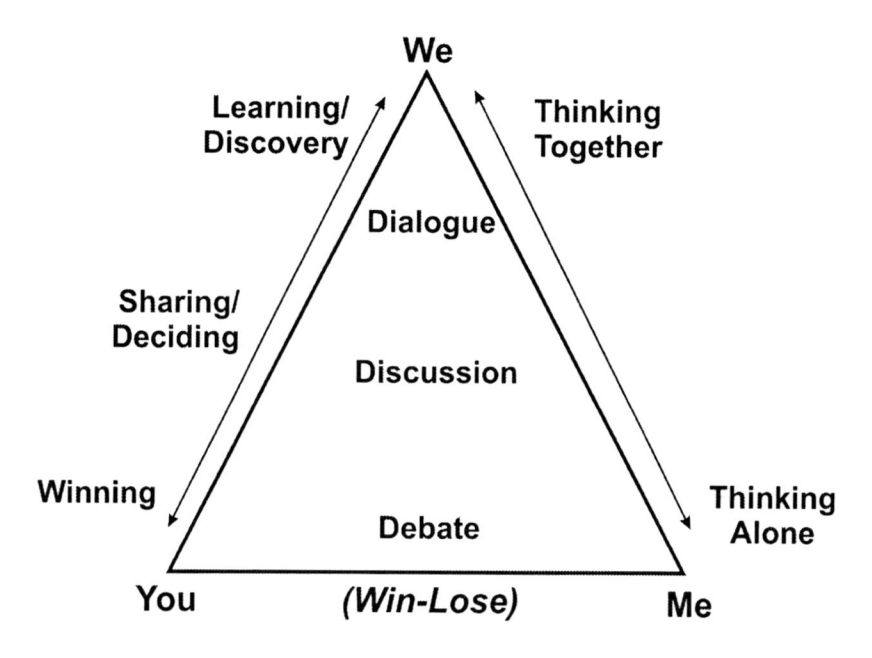

```
                       We
        Learning/     /\      Thinking
        Discovery    /  \     Together
                    /    \
                   / Dialogue \
        Sharing/  /          \
        Deciding /            \
                / Discussion   \
               /                \
      Winning /                  \ Thinking
             /     Debate         \ Alone
            /_____\
         You      (Win-Lose)       Me
```

or appreciating the ideas of the other, would be regarded as an act of weakness or defeat.

The Corruption of Debate

When we are trying to win a debate, to have our ideas victorious over the ideas of another, we listen to the other with an ear to exclude and label ideas in a way that makes them unacceptable. During the time of the second Iraq war in 2003, a member of the country music group, The Dixie Chicks, spoke out against the war. A conservative talk show host commenting on this said to a guest, "Well you have to understand that these Hollywood types really hate America and all that it stands for." This interpretation of a very young woman's position against the war is exactly the kind response that destroys the democratic process, which relies on dialogue to form understanding and consensus, rather than the victory of one group at the expense of humiliating another. The young country music star was not a "Hollywood type," but was from Texas, the home of the President, and could never have had the thought of hating her country. However, by labeling her in this extreme way, by creating black and white distinction between good and evil, it eliminates any possibility of understanding what her view actually was or why she held it. It also creates the environment in which anyone attempting to understand this person's views is likely to be attacked for being soft, or comforting those who "hate America" and surely no good American would want to be in that position.

From the other side of the political tug of war, Bill Maher, who has made a career of mixing comedy with politics, repeatedly lashes out at Southerners as "Bible thumbing, redneck bigots," who in his own words, "might as well go off and form their own country." Having lived in the Atlanta area for thirty years, deep in the South and the center of the civil rights movement, the home of excellent black colleges, Dr. Martin Luther King Jr., and as healthy a pattern of racial harmony and cooperation, as any metropolitan area in the country; I find this characterization not only absurd but highly offensive. If it was intended to be funny, alone it might be excused. But he offered this view absolute sincerity. It is just as destructive to the national dialogue as the assault on The Dixie Chicks.

This type of discourse hardens the corners of the triangle and is the exact opposite of dialogue. Debate creates discomfort with opposing views and attempts to lower the stature of anyone who holds those opposing views. Dialogue creates a zone of comfort for others to contribute without fear of being assaulted, or insulted. In debate, generalizations are used to label a point of view in a manner that discounts its consideration. In dialogue, questions are used to uncover the true meaning of another person's contributions. In debate, you look for the error in the position of another. In dialogue, you look for what may be learned from the ideas of another. Debate suffocates intellectual inquiry; dialogue fuels intellectual inquiry. Debate creates or hardens distance or alienation between the parties, dialogue creates connections, appreciation and unity.

When to Practice Dialogue, Discussion or Debate

You are driving in your car and your child shouts, "Mom, there's a McDonald's. Can we get a Happy Meal?" Should Mom now enter into a deep and meaningful dialogue about why the child really wants a Happy Meal, or the true understanding of a Happy Meal? I think not. Mom will probably, and correctly reply, "No, it is almost dinner time and we will be home soon." End of discussion and hopefully with no debate.

Our lives are filled with simple decisions, and our concern is often for efficiency and not depth of meaning. In team meetings at work, much of the time may be spent reviewing numbers, brainstorming a cause or solution to a specific technical problem; or, deciding who will fill-in for someone who will be absent next week. These decisions do not require in-depth dialogue.

Dialogue should be employed for questions of significance. Why are we organized the way we are? Are we genuinely meeting the current and future needs of our clients? Are we assisting each other in the development of our personal capabilities? Are we doing the best we can to make this an enjoyable and fulfilling place to work? Why do we do this work at all? These are important questions and they are not matters of just choosing "A" or "B". Rather, they are issues with several levels of meaning and possible action. These are the types of issues around which we should engage in genuine dialogue.

Dialogue is more appropriate when there is a great degree of shared purpose. The degree to which we lack common purpose is the degree to which we are likely to remain at the bottom of the pyramid, focused on our self, our individual needs. If we are focused only on our personal needs our conversation will tend toward debate and we will remain motivated to win all we can.

As we achieve common purpose, the nature of our motivation and conversation will change. We move from simply trying to win to teaching, sharing, understanding, learning, and serving as we move up the pyramid to a condition of genuine dialogue. Imagine a congress in which every representative had no self-interest, no concern about his or her election, no concern about winning any personal or party victory. Rather, every member would focus on only one purpose, the collective, shared good of the country. In a true attitude of service, they would seek deep understanding and meaning, striving to make decisions that would be in the best interests of the country. No one's name would be on any bill. Or, all their names would be on every bill. The entire spirit would be transformed, the quality of decisions would accelerate, and the country would benefit.

Dialogue can be a frame of reference. Once the team understands the potential of dialogue, a team member may recognize that we are engaged in a debate when we should be engaged in a dialogue. It is helpful to simply ask "shouldn't we have a dialogue on this issue for a while?" This will trigger a different thought pattern in all the members of the team.

Failures at every level of the organization, from the CEO to the first level, are often the result of the failure to recognize when genuine dialogue is needed.

The High Price of the Failure of Dialogue

One of the more amazing realities of recent corporate history is the much-discussed collapse of the Enron Corporation. This failure can be described in many ways – a failure of corporate ethics, poor strategic judgment, or outright stealing. But, how did this happen? The Board of Directors of Enron was highly regarded as a model of Board structure and composition. Only two insiders served on the Enron Board. No corporation could have had a more financially competent and experienced board. The list included a former Stanford University Dean of the School of Accounting, a former CEO of an insurance company, the former CEO of an international bank, a hedge fund manager, a prominent Asian financier, and an economist who is the former head of the U.S. government's Commodity Futures Trading Commission. These were all extremely smart and competent individuals and all financially sophisticated. Yet the members of this board have all claimed to have been confused by Enron's financial transactions and claimed not to have understood the financial statements.[27] They were all thinking alone.

How could this group of experienced and respected individuals have provided oversight of a corporation whose books were so complicated that no analyst could figure out where the money was coming from or where it was going? Thousands of deals were being made that amounted to little more than a shell game of moving money around to give the appearance of profits where there were none. Why didn't they inquire? None of them understood the financial statements, so why didn't they discuss this? Why weren't they troubled enough by this lack of transparency to insist on accounting statements and explanations that they could understand?

Jeffrey A. Sonnenfeld, writing in the Harvard Business Review[28] on the Enron case said, *"We need to consider not only how we structure the work of a board but also how we manage the social system a board actually is. We'll be fighting the wrong war if we simply tighten procedural rules for boards and ignore their more pressing need – to be strong, high-functioning work groups whose members trust and challenge one another and engage directly with senior managers on critical issues facing corporations."*

Was the Board of Directors, or the senior management team, engaged in dialogue? Were they thinking deeply and understanding the meaning of the facts presented to them? Of course, they were not. Rather there was a classic case of "group-think" in which even the most analytic and sophisticated managers did not question the surface facts presented to them, did not dig deep to understand how and why the numbers did, or did not, make sense. Perhaps it was the simple fact that each person around the table had so much respect for the other that they were saying to themselves "Well, if it makes sense to him, it must make sense." Perhaps this was a case in which a "court jester" was needed, someone to ask the absurd questions, someone who could display complete lack of respect and ask "why," "how could that be,"

---

[27] "What Makes Great Boards Great", Sonnenfeld, Jeffrey A., Harvard Business Review, September, 2002, p.108.

[28] J. A. Sonnenfeld, Harvard Business Review, September, 2002, p.106.

or ask other members of the Board to explain where the money was coming from.

Systems thinking became the topic of much conversation during recent years. Peter Senge's book *The Fifth Discipline*[29] is about the creation of the "learning organization" and at the center of that discipline, is systems-thinking. The most costly system problem in our corporations is the system of conversation. The system to which most managers and executives have become accustomed does not dig deeply, does not seek genuine meaning or significance in information, and often fails to uncover important facts or opinions. When you realize that in the knowledge economy, processing information and making decisions is the core function of almost every organization, the cost of this failure is huge.

How Can We Develop the Competence of Dialogue?

How do we develop the ability to engage in dialogue? What skills do we need to develop? The following are the skills that will help us engage in dialogue. Simply stating them is a start, but not sufficient. Managers and teams need skill development, training, that develops these as habits.

1. Practice Deep Listening:

When you walk into a debate, your mind is set on convincing the judges or audience of the superiority of your point of view. You plan your "arguments" and voice those arguments in the most convincing manner possible. Your tone of voice conveys confidence if not certainty in the correctness of your argument. The purpose of a debate is not for the parties to engage in learning. Rather it is to convince the audience that one participant has a superior position and has most skillfully argued that position.

When the motive of a conversation is to search for meaning and to learn there can be no thought of winning or losing. There is no

---

[29] Senge, Peter. *The Fifth Discipline: The Art and Practice of the Learning Organization*. New York: Doubleday-Currency, 1990.

external audience to convince in a dialogue. You are the audience, the team is the audience, and the purpose is to gain knowledge and meaning and this does not result from authoritatively arguing pre-packaged positions. It derives from listening and reflecting.

There are many levels of listening. Of course, there is the simple act of being quiet and tuning in to the voices of others. Yet, there is also the capacity to listen to what is really going on, to listen to the story behind the words and faces. Each pained expression tells a story. Each deep sigh tells a story. Each expression of impatience tells a story. At times, it is worth inquiring as to the nature of that story. Sometimes it is valuable simply to seek insight by imagining the story that each person has to tell.

Some time ago, I fancied that I would become a "real" writer. I read a wonderful book, "On Writing" by Ernest Hemingway, a compilation of his letters to his editor, Charles Scribner. In addition to bemoaning his own trials and tribulations as a writer, he spoke of the awareness required of a writer. He said that a writer is always writing, always forming characters and imagining possibilities. When sitting in an airport awaiting his plane, the writer is studying the face of the old woman across from him and imagining the life she has led, imaging who she is going to visit, and what it must mean to her to visit this person. The writer can develop an entire story by just staring at this person and imagining the meaning of her wrinkles, the cause of the worried look on her face, or the reason why her shoes don't seem to fit quite right.

According to Hemingway, you become a writer, not because you know grammar or sentence structure, but rather because of the capacity of observation and imagination. Consider the young person walking through the airport with earphones plugged in, listening to his Ipod. Is he observing anything? Is he imagining the story on anyone's face? And, isn't his life that much poorer for the inability to imagine the story told by the rushed walk of the young woman toward her plane; or the story told by the old man on the park bench? In our cities people walk around plugged in to their Ipods or other devices, bumping into each other, staring ahead as if they can't see, hear or recognize anyone. What are they listening to that is of such great value that it is worth missing out on the sounds and stories of real life?

Dialogue requires the listening of the writer, the ability to hear the voice of the other person, to listen to their story, to take pleasure in the details that give meaning to each story.

As you listen to another, go beyond what they are saying to imagine their story. How does their story affect the members of their family? How do they feel in this situation? What do they imagine about their own future? Where does their story go from here?

2. Practice Inquiring versus Acquiescing:

Groups that are formed around some ideology or political point of view are likely to be extremely accepting of the views of its members, particularly when those views are expressed by the person in power or framed in the legitimacy of their ideology. Most Washington "think-tanks" are comprised of individuals selected for their ideological consistency, whether on the left or right. So you have a group of like minded people sitting around all day talking to each other and then devising policies, writing books and articles. Obviously, they reinforce each other's views and they become more convinced of how right they are because the group around them agrees. They shouldn't be called "think-tanks," they should be called "acquiescing-tanks." A "tank" that was actually designed to promote thinking would assure the greatest possible diversity of opinion and a culture of sincere inquiry.

In a group of political conservatives, someone might say, "Well, as we conservatives all know, the more we can reduce taxes the better." In a group of political liberals, someone might say, "You know we have to reign in the power of corporations." And in both groups everyone nods approvingly, demonstrating their acquiescence. Such statements create an assumption that then stifles creative thought. What if one said – "How can we increase the power of corporations to provide better health benefits to their people?" Is this coming from a liberal or conservative view or is it just an open door to think in a different and possibly creative way. Dialogue requires questions that escape from the assumptions of ideological views. Otherwise, rather than inquire into the meaning of things, the members of the group will simply acquiesce to the "politically correct" point of view.

This acquiescence avoids the intellectual inquiry, the asking of questions that are the fundamental tool of learning. Members of the

Enron board acquiesced and failed to inquire. But even the CEO, Ken Lay, who claims not to have known what was going on, acquiesced to his subordinates. In the WorldCom case, Bernie Evers also claims the "I-was-too-stupid-to-know" defense, claiming he didn't understand the finances. These CEO's are either dishonest or they engaged in extreme, and self-serving acquiescence.

Questioning is the foundation of science. Without questioning, there would be no science or human progress. Inquiring minds, questioning minds, seek meaning, significance and underlying truths. The ability to ask questions, to ask the simple question "why?" is the first skill of acquiring wisdom. No one is more important in a group than the one who recognizes when to ask "why?" It is all too common for groups to be heading in a direction, while no one can explain *why* the group is heading in this direction. Jerry Harvey, in *The Abilene Paradox*,[30] tells a wonderful story about a family sitting on the porch one evening, in the sweltering heat of west Texas, and Pa asks what's for dinner? Ma then mentions a restaurant down the road in Abilene. Somehow, they end up in the car, with no air conditioning, the dust blowing through the windows in 90-degree heat and everyone is miserable, when Ma asks Pa, "Why the hell are you dragging us to Abilene anyway?" To which Pa says, "I ain't draggin' you anywhere, you wanted to go to Abilene." "Did not" replies Ma. It turns out that no one in the car wanted to go on this trip. And the question comes, how did they end up on the road to Abilene when no one wanted to go in the first place?

As Jerry Harvey, a college professor, tells it, he was sitting in his office one day when an attractive young woman student came into his office and sat down. She looked rather depressed.

Dr. Harvey, concerned professor that he is, asked, "What's wrong? You look rather depressed."

She replied, "Well, you'd be depressed too if next weekend you were marrying someone you didn't love."

To which Dr. Harvey naturally responded, "Well, why are you marrying someone you don't love?"

---

[30] Harvey, Jerry. *The Abilene Paradox*. Jossey-Bass, New York, 1988.

She explained, "Well it was a moment of passion, and I couldn't say no, it would have broken his heart. And, he told his parents, and they called mine, and the wedding got planned, and I can't say no now. I just couldn't do that to him."

The next day Dr. Harvey was sitting in his office and a young man came in and sat down, looking rather depressed.

The ever-empathetic Dr. Harvey asked, "What's wrong? You look rather depressed."

He replied, "Well, you'd be depressed too if next weekend you were marrying someone you didn't love."

To which Dr. Harvey naturally responded, "Well, why are you marrying someone you don't love?"

The young man explained, "Well it was a moment of passion, and I couldn't say no, I would have broken her heart. And, she told her parents, and they called mine, and the wedding got planned, and I can't say no now. I just couldn't do that to her."

Witness a young couple "on the road to Abilene."

Well, how do people get on the road to Abilene, on a course that they do not support in the first place? This is how a billion dollars were spent drilling for oil in a country with no ports and no way to ship the oil to market. This is how the entire board of the Enron Corporation ended up in Abilene. Even country Presidents, the congress, the press, and the entire population can find themselves stranded in Abilene - some country… not anyone in particular, of course.

3. Practice Suspending Judgment:

A judgment is something that comes "down" at the end of a "trial." If a judge or jury entered a trial with a judgment already in their mind, we would suggest that they be disqualified. We ask judges and juries to suspend judgments, to hear all sides, to reflect and to consider alternative explanations.

When we make decisions in groups we are often hindered by our tendency to judge quickly. There is an unstated value in our culture, which rewards quick decision-making. This is a remnant of the military culture of command. On the battlefield, the officer was required to make judgments quickly in order to win a victory or save the lives of his men. Dialogue or consensus decision-making would not have survived the demands of the battlefield where victories were often won by fast and decisive action and strict obedience by the troops. The military did not want soldiers to ponder the "meaning" of their actions. They could do that for the rest of their lives, but not while the bullets were flying.

Perhaps because the military was, for most human history, a male domain, it is entirely possible that men came to associate the ability to make decisions quickly with "manliness." While delaying, pondering, considering alternatives in a reflective manner, may have become more associated with women. How ever it evolved, it is certain that men in particular, find the ability to make decisions quickly an attractive characteristic and associate delay with weakness. We are therefore, quick to judge.

One of the best qualities of a leader is humility. Contrary to the television image of the charismatic leader, most corporate executives who achieve sustained superior performance are not the demanding cheerleader. Rather, they are patient, and behave with humility. Jim Collins, in *Good To Great*[31] documents leaders who possess this quality of humility. He describes what he calls Level 5 Leadership: *"We were surprised, shocked really, to discover the type of leadership required for turning a good company into a great one. Compared to high-profile leaders with big personalities who make head-lines and become celebrities, the good-to-great leaders seem to have come from Mars. Self-effacing, quiet, reserved, even shy – these leaders are a paradoxical blend of personal humility and professional will. They are more like Lincoln and Socrates than Patton or Caesar."*[32]

Humility is being open to the ideas of others. Humility is the ability to learn and change course when the evidence points in a different direction. Humility is the capacity to suspend judgment and listen to the voices of others.

Humility and suspended judgment are most important when it comes to how we present our ideas to the group. It is important to

---

[31] Collins, Jim. *Good to Great*. Harper Business, New York: 2001

[32] Ibid. pp. 12-13.

listen to yourself as you present an idea. Is it presented as a gift to the group for their consideration? Or, is it presented as your judgment that you are now asking others to approve? Is it presented as an argument that should be "right"? If it is the latter, you have attached your ego, your self-worth, to your ideas. Naturally then, you will defend your idea. If, on the other hand, you present your idea as a gift to the group with the intention of letting go, allowing the group to take ownership and do with it as it wishes, you would observe its transformation, its merger into the stream of thought and wisdom of the group. Rather than the joy of seeing "your" idea adopted as the best idea, it is possible to gain joy from seeing your idea contribute to the shared ideas that become the *group's* final decision or point of view.

4. Avoid Dismissive Categorizing

We seek order in conversation as we seek order in life. To order our surrounding we place things in categories: good or evil; friendly or hostile; left or right; with me or against me. There are a hundred ways that we can categorize people, comments, or entire conversations. How we categorize contributions to conversation will have an impact on our ability to enter into a meaningful dialogue.

When we hear a comment we do not like, one that differs from our understanding or point of view, we may have a tendency to place the comment in a category, or place the entire person in a category.

Imagine that you are meeting with a team and you are discussing how the team can improve its own that learning and development. A young woman who has been employed for only a couple of months speaks up and says, with some hesitancy and emotion in her voice, "I thought people would be more friendly when I first came to work here. I thought it would be more fun, and people would help each other more." The manager of this group, somewhat uncomfortable with this expression of personal feelings and emotion may think to himself, "Well, she just said that because she is young and inexperienced."

By placing the young woman and her comment in the category of "young and inexperienced," it alleviates his need to deal with her comment in a meaningful way. By categorizing this comment and the person, the issue is likely to receive little serious consideration. Having taken the risk of speaking up, the young woman will now feel exposed and if her expression is ignored or dismissed, she is much less likely to offer her true feelings in the future.

How else could the manager have responded? Without judging the comment as true or false, he could have expressed appreciation and looked for the value or truth in her comment. For example, he could have said, "I know that it is important when you first come to work, to feel that people want to help you succeed. It is always a bit scary starting a new job. And, I think you are making the point that we learn well, when we help each other, whether we are new or old on the job. Is that right?"

By acknowledging the truth or value in the young woman's comment, he has created a unifying bond, the opposite of alienation. This appreciative comment will make her more comfortable and more likely to contribute in the future; and, by checking it out, by asking whether he has understood correctly, she will be able to acknowledge or correct his understanding.

Every night on television, we are bombarded with examples of dismissive categorization. "Well, that's because you're a racist!" Well, that dismisses anything you may have to say! No need to seek any further understanding. Or, "You liberals (or, right wing extremists) always say that and that's why this country is in trouble!" It seems that most of the evening talk shows are a shallow monologue by opposing parties, never acknowledging any validity in the views of the other and continually categorizing the opponent to dismiss their views. This is the opposite of dialogue. (Just because two people are delivering monologues, does not make it a dialogue.) It only serves to reinforce the views of those who "know how those people think."

5. Look at the Whole System

Rather than looking only at the immediate issues, consider the system around those issues. Insight is often gained by making connections between parts of a whole. Our country, our community and our company, may be described as a "whole-system." The ecology is a whole-system comprised of numerous interconnected and interdependent parts. One cannot understand the growth of a tree without understanding the larger ecology of the forest, changes in climate, or animal species that depend on the tree for survival. The study of ecology is the study of interconnected parts, or sub-systems of a larger whole system. The economy is a whole system comprised of sub-systems such as the banking system, the transportation system, the taxation system, etc. To study the economy one must study the interconnection of the various sub-systems.

To think about the topic under discussion, as a component of a larger system, furthers the dialogue. If a team is discussing a quality problem, a part they receive from a supplier that has excessive variation from specifications, it may be useful to consider how that problem is related to a larger system. For example, how was the supplier selected? What specifications were given to the supplier, and did the design of the part lead to ease of manufacturing? How often does the supplier receive feedback, how immediate is that feedback and in what form is it given? Do we know to whom that feedback is communicated within the supplier's organization?

Rather than simply focus on the problem of the part itself, the solution is more likely to come from an examination of the whole system around that part.

Just as we have a tendency to categorize and dismiss comments by individuals, we have a tendency to fragment a problem and deal with only isolated components of the problem. We do this because it is easier. It is easier to say that the supplier "doesn't care" about us, and we should find a new supplier. When we do this, we don't need to go to the trouble of understanding the feedback system, the supplier selection and communication process, etc. Unfortunately, however, when companies fail to analyze the system and simply dismiss a supplier and find a new one, the problem often reoccurs because the system that was the root cause of the problem hasn't changed.

6. Seek Diverse Input

Groups of corporate decision makers who are all engineers, or all finance managers, or who all come from the same industry or corporate culture, are similarly likely to become a closed system. One of the advantages of the push for diverse Boards and diverse management teams is simply because minorities or women, not conditioned to the same corporate culture and assumptions, are more likely to ask the questions that force the group to think about the meaning of what they are doing.

Members of a group may stay in the "you-versus-me" corner of the triangle because of their perceptions of others. It is normal to value the contributions of those who have the same background, training or experience as yourself. If you are trained as an engineer, and the primary work of the organization is engineering, it is normal for you to value the ideas of other engineers. Senior management teams will typically have several operating managers who rose from the area of core competence of the organization, such as engineering. But there will also be a finance manager, a human resource manager, possibly an attorney or others with supportive expertise. The value placed on these areas of expertise, independent of the actual merit of a contribution by a team member, often prejudices the nature of conversation.

Some years ago, I had the good fortune to be a member of local decision-making body of a religious organization in Raleigh, North Carolina. The nine members of this spiritual assembly could not have been more diverse. Two young women were doctoral students in clinical psychology. Another was a professor of physics at the same university. Another had completed his doctoral work at Harvard and was currently with the Environmental Protection Agency. And then there were James and Marie Brodie. James and Marie were both in their sixties and were African Americans, born and lived all their life in the South. James washed dishes at a restaurant and Marie served as a maid. While other members of the group excelled in their apparent intellect, James and Marie excelled in their constant display of the spiritual virtues of humility, compassion, and service to others.

I was elected chairperson of this group. The responsibility of the chairperson was not one of authority, but rather one of facilitator – giving each member the opportunity to contribute to the conversation. A video tape of the conversation among this group would be a good case study in different styles of communication. The young candidates for their clinical psychology degrees had no trouble expressing how they felt on any issue and were quick to do so. The professor, while a bit more reflective, addressed the group with authority. The Harvard graduate was quick on the draw, and always presented his views with both wit and precision.

I remember on a number of occasions Marie Brodie would have her head down and her eyes closed while the conversation was taking place. The well educated were quick to offer both analysis and solutions to every problem. The group would appear to be ready to reach a conclusion and move on to the next topic while Marie had yet to say a word. As the chairperson, I would then ask Marie if she had any thoughts or feelings on the matter. I remember Marie lifting up her head and opening her eyes, or even with her eyes still closed, saying slowly in her soft voice, "I feel that we haven't considered how this other person will react to this. Maybe we should consider...." And, it turned out that Marie had been listening carefully, but considering the issue from an entirely different point of view, a view that when heard by the rest of the group, often completely turned the conversation in a different direction, to a solution that would never have been discovered were it not for Marie's soft voice.

When I told this story, I often felt compelled to say, "God bless Marie Brodie," and meant that in the most sincere way. Early on, she gave me a gift, the opportunity to learn a lesson about how individuals from very different backgrounds, and apparently very humble circumstances, can contribute wisdom and insight that would otherwise be absent. But I also learned that this wisdom can easily be by-passed or ignored, if one has an ear for only one type of voice. The voice of the Ph.D. candidates is one voice. The voice of Marie Brodie is another one entirely, almost an entirely different language. One must make the effort to tune in, to invite the contribution, to respect the wisdom that may emanate from a completely different voice.

7. Seek Your Authentic Voice

To some degree, we all seek to speak in a voice that will produce approval from our audience. It is normal to seek the approval of our peers. However, to discover meaning through dialogue, we must seek the most honest, authentic and genuine self. Do we even know our own voice? Do we know what are our personal thoughts, or feelings are? Do we have the courage to voice those thoughts, simply because they are our honest thoughts or feelings, our true voice? This is not an easy question.

I have known people who almost always seem to be speaking with a reactive voice, a voice that is a reaction to their audience and a voice in which they expect to elicit a positive reaction. However, it never quite works. The audience somehow senses a lack of authenticity and does not react as desired. The question becomes, does this person know her own voice? Does she have the internal courage to listen to her own thoughts and feelings and then give voice to those thoughts and feelings?

The inability to speak with an honest, authentic voice, may be the result of fear that one's own voice is not adequate, that one's own ideas are not clever enough or profound enough. However, the paradox is that what is most appreciated by others is not cleverness or profundity, but simple honesty.

I have recently served on the Governing Board of a small private university in Switzerland. The academic council comprised of the resident faculty supervised the academic program. I attended the meetings of this council as the representative of the administration. To increase participation and unity between students, faculty and administration, a representative of the student council was added as a member of the group. The truth was that the academicians had some fears about a student sitting in and listening to their internal debates that often concerned problems that would have impact on the students. They also knew that their meetings were often much more like debates then dialogues.

A popular professor decided to leave the university and the academic council was conducting a meeting to decide how to explain his departure to the students. The conversation by the faculty expressed a number of rational reasons why he was leaving, and rational explanations as to why his departure would not prevent students from fulfilling their course requirements. They seemed to have taken care of the matter when I invited the Student Council representative, Vivian, to share her feelings. I knew that this professor was one of her favorites, and until this point, she had remained silent. Vivian was sitting somewhat slumped down in her chair when I asked for her views. She sat up and then, with her head tilted to one side, struggling to maintain her composure, said with considerable emotion, "I don't know…I just feel that the faculty I came here to learn from is abandoning me! I don't know how to explain this." And with this expression, her hands were now covering her face as if to prevent others from seeing her eyes, from which she feared she could not control the welling tears.

The group was silent for several seconds as they digested this new voice and the intense emotion they had not considered at all in their quest for rational explanations. The student had the courage to speak in her own voice, in the voice of honest emotion, without which there could be no honest dialogue. To understand how to communicate to the students genuinely, the group had to recognize that the student's reaction was on an emotional level, and these emotions demanded recognition by the faculty. Perhaps it would have been easy for the student to remain silent since all of the conversation had been on the level of facts and schedules and qualifications and she had little to contribute to that. But, from the perspective of the student, the customer in this case, the matter was an entirely different one and voicing an entirely different perspective required detached courage, a willingness to speak in her honest voice without knowing how it would be received.

The ability first to listen to your own voice, to search for your own authentic thoughts and feelings, and then to express them honestly, is often by-passed in our rush to get through an agenda. William Isaacs, in his book on dialogue wrote *"Finding and speaking one's voice requires first a willingness to be still. Daring to be quiet can seem like an enormous risk in a world that values articulate speech. But to speak our voice we may have to learn to refrain from speaking, and listen. Not every word that comes to us needs to be spoken. In fact, learning to choose consciously what we do and do not say can establish a great level of control and stability in our lives."* [33]

Developing the ability to engage in true dialogue is not a simple skill or technique. It is a different level of relationship and communication, which some people never achieve. It is the difference between the casual conversation you may have with an acquaintance, and the intimate sharing of the most private feelings with one who you love and trust deeply.

Dialogue is a critical currency that contributes to social capital. Like money, dialogue is something that is exchanged between two parties and the fluency of the exchange will determine the depth of social capital.

---

[33] Isaacs, William. *Dialogue and the Art of Thinking Together*. New York. Doubleday, 1999. p. 163.

My Personal Contribution to Dialogue:

Personal Action Agenda	I do	I don't	I will
1. I recognize those times when I should engage in dialogue.			
2. I can tell the difference between other forms of conversation (discussion or debate) and the search for meaning and understanding (dialogue).			
3. I help my team consider when we should engage in dialogue.			
4. I feel comfortable "thinking together" with a group of people.			
5. I feel that I inquire into the story or meaning behind points of view that are expressed in dialogue.			
6. I am able to suspend judgment and explore a topic for learning before reaching a judgment.			
7. I don't dismiss the views of others by thinking about the "category" to which a person may belong.			
8. I am able to think about the relationship between a topic or point of view and the larger system.			
9. I feel that I am able to speak in my own honest voice because I have taken time to consider my own thoughts and feelings deeply.			
Summary of what I will do to improve my ability to engage in dialogue:			

Helping the Team to Engage in Dialogue:

Team Action Agenda	We do	We don't	We will
1. My team discusses and recognizes when it is appropriate to engage in dialogue, rather than fact-finding or deciding.			
2. My team recognizes the value of engaging in dialogue.			
3. Our team's facilitator will invite the group to engage in dialogue when appropriate.			
4. I would describe our team as capable of "thinking together" versus "thinking alone."			
5. Team members do inquire into the meaning or the story behind the contributions of team members.			
6. We don't dismiss comments by categorizing the kind of comment or who said them.			
7. We discuss the relationship between a topic and the larger system or process in the organization.			
8. We have diverse input in our conversations and we value the diversity of views.			
9. My team members are comfortable speaking in their authentic voice without fear.			
Summary of what we agree to do to improve dialogue in our group:			

Encouraging Dialogue in the Organization:

Organization Action Agenda	We do	We don't	We will
1. The leaders of this organization encourage a process of reflective dialogue on issues affecting the organization.			
2. We have large group dialogues or conferences in which there is time for open exploration of important issues.			
3. The organization provides training to facilitators to lead dialogue sessions.			
4. The culture of this organization encourages diversity of input and ideas.			
5. Leaders of this organization consider how problems or issues are related to not only one solution, but to system problems that need improvement.			
Summary of what we can do to improve dialogue throughout the organization:			

Chapter 5

Dance to the Drumbeat
The Currency of Discipline

"Discipline is the soul of an army. It makes small numbers formidable; procures success to the weak, and esteem to all." George Washington

One night a long time ago (I am tempted to say when I was a very small child) I was watching the Johnny Carson show. His guest was the prolific playwright Neil Simon, winner of numerous Tony Awards and successful by any measure.

Johnny asked him, "Where do you get the inspiration to write a play?"

Neil Simon looked at him puzzled. "I've never had the inspiration to write a play."

Somewhat shocked, Johnny said, "But that's impossible, you've written so many plays, you must have had inspiration to write them!"

Simon shook his head, "Nope, never had the inspiration."

"Well, then," Johnny asked, "How do you know when to sit down and start writing?"

Again, Neil Simon looked at Johnny puzzled. "Well, that's easy. Eight o'clock in the morning. That's my job. That's what I do!"

"But, what if you don't have anything in your head to write?" Johnny asked with some frustration.

"It doesn't matter. I write anyway. Then I look at what I wrote. Sometimes I like it and I keep going. Sometimes I don't and I throw it away. That's my job."

For someone attempting to write his first book, this was the best advice I ever heard. It was perfect. Forget inspiration! Sit your butt down in the chair and write! The drum beats at eight in the morning! Neil Simon was successful because he had conquered himself. He had developed self-discipline.

If You Dance to Your Own Drumbeat, You Dance Alone!

All cultures, all organizations, dance to the beat of their own drums. The beat of the drum creates unity of action and spirit. It must be in the human genetic code, a natural and universal need to bring order and energy to people. Every culture has a calendar that proclaims a regular drumbeat – days, weeks, months and years. The religion found in every culture, has its drumbeat of daily and weekly worship, annual periods of sacrifice and self-reflection.

All work, going back to ancient times, progresses with the rhythm of the drum. All work songs, sea shanties to which sailors hauled in the lines; the drums of the galley slaves; the field songs and hollers of African-American slaves and prison camps that are the most fundamental roots of blues, and later rock 'n' roll, all reflect the primal need in our soul to dance to the rhythm of the drum.

Without drumbeats we would all be "doing our own thing," on our own time, and to our own pace. This may be fine in your leisure, but it is not fine at work. Work is a dance and without the drumbeat we would be stepping on each others toes.

Even the chaotic dance of voodoo in the villages of Caribbean islands is a story of the need for discipline and unity of action. The dance starts with one drummer beating his drum and the dancers dance to that one rhythm. Then a second drum starts and beats to a different rhythm and the dancers move one part of their body to one drum and another part of their body to the second (its not easy, try it!). Then a third drum starts to yet another rhythm and the dancing becomes more chaotic. Soon the dancing appears to be a mad, drunken, confusion of waving hands and feet. Then from outside the village a large and overpowering drum begins to beat. The drummer carries the drum into the village maintaining the beat. Gradually all the drums and dancers come into synchronization with the big drum and the dancers are once again dancing together. Some say this is a religious prophecy of the coming of the Promised One of ancient African religions. But, it well illustrates the primal unity at the earliest of time.

When Companies Are Possessed by Voodoo

Many companies appear possessed by the voodoo dance. Any organization without clear drumbeats will miss the discipline of the dance and risk the madness of voodoo. And perhaps the greatest personal madness comes from the inability to recognize a rhythm and join in the dance of others, to be alone wondering within your own tune. Even the solo artist must maintain his own beat.

I was once in a meeting with a senior executive of a client to discuss the executive's communication of the company values. In some frustration, and after several efforts to communicate the company's values, he asked, "How often do we have to communicate this?" I responded without thinking very deeply (and certainly not with any great concern about the value of my consulting contract), "How often do you go to church?"

The client looked at me startled that I would ask such a personal question. In truth, I had startled myself. "Usually, each week," he replied.

"How often have you been doing that?" By this time, he had accepted my impudence. "A long time," he replied.

"Well, don't you think you should have gotten it by now?" I may as well dig the hole all the way down to the bottom, I thought. "Seriously, (I stopped the game) why does God want us to go to church, or other place of worship, each week? I think it's because he knows us and he knows how crummy we are about 'getting it'. It is our nature to have to hear the rhythm, the regular drumbeat of our Faith, if we are to keep dancing to the music. If this is true in our general life, it must also be true at work."

Daily life in the organization often destroys the rhythm. Managers respond to events as if they were crisis when they are actually part of the normal course of events, and they shift resources and activities, disrupting the flow. This often does more to hurt long-term performance, even when the immediate crisis is successfully solved. High performance can be described as "flow" that state of natural, focused, performance that is achieve by great athletes and teams when every move just seems natural and effortless. Musicians achieve a state of flow, where the fingers are moving with no apparent connection to their conscious mind, and they seem completely lost in their music, blocking out all external distractions. When we are in this state of "flow"[34] there is an almost spiritual satisfaction, a feeling of having achieved a perfect state of balance between one's capabilities and the task at hand. It is the state in which teams perform best. And this state is achieved, with a regularity of rhythm, a 2/4 time, and not in sporadic bursts.

Corporations instill order and discipline with monthly reporting, quarterly and annual reports. Teams instill discipline with weekly or daily meetings to review scorecards, daily or weekly feedback on performance, or regular feedback from customers.

Discipline is Consistent, Reliable Performance, Not Punishment

The word discipline is sometimes confused with punishment ("I disciplined my child after he..."). There is a positive discipline movement and practice, based on the idea of creating disciplined behavior in children through the use of positive reinforcement, rather than the use of punishment.[35] Similarly, in organizations, discipline can be instilled without resorting to punitive means. The military is highly skilled at instilling discipline without the use of punishment. All of the rituals and habits of the military center around creating disciplined behavior.

When I was a young man, a very long time ago, and right out of high school, I joined the Army. For me, who had graduated 83rd out of a class of 84, it was definitely the best thing. In addition to seeing a good bit of Europe and a small and troubled corner of Asia, I learned one or two critical lessons. I will never forget standing in the rain at five-thirty in the morning outside the basic training barracks at Ft. Dix, New Jersey, and the five foot six Puerto Rican drill sergeant, bless his heart, standing nose-to-nose (and I mean literally!) and yelling at the top of his lungs, "Son, are you tired and wet and miserable? Well, no

---

[34] Csikszentmihali, Mihaly. *Flow: The Psychology of Optimal Experience.* Harper & Row, New York. 1990.
[35] Nelson, Jane. Positive Discipline. New York, Random House, 1981.

one cares how tired you are, how wet you are, or how you feel. You are going to stand here and then you are going to run. Then you are going to stand here some more, and then you are going to run. And, then you are going to do it again, every day! And, you are going to do it because I gave you the order to! Do you understand that, recruit?" And the only possible answer without the self infliction of greater humiliation, was to yell back "Yes, Sergeant!"

Why this scene is a thing of beauty, an act of performance art, an act of liberation, I can probably not adequately convey to those who have not experienced this first hand. But to realize that you can, and you will, do things that you would never have thought you could or would, and that all of your compatriots around you will do it with you, and that you are doing it not because you awoke to the realization that this would be fun or desirable, but because this little man is screaming at you and because it is your job, your duty, and your absolute requirement to obey. And you will obey. This is the magic that the Army runs on. This is the real fuel that makes the Army a disciplined, winning machine. And it frees you from the slavery of dependence on your emotions, waiting to feel like you want to do something, free to do it just because it must be done. God bless that drill sergeant! I owe him a lot.

Am I proposing that you arouse your employees at five in the morning for drills? Of course not! But, I am proposing that every individual, team and organization requires a fair measure of discipline to succeed and this need not contradict involvement, empowerment, and the most positive forms of motivation. Anyone who follows sports knows that discipline is at the heart of every good athletic team or individual athlete. The same is true at work. Examine the practices of world class manufacturing plants or sales organization, engineers or programmers, and you will find a culture of discipline.

Successful Change Requires the Discipline of the Drumbeat

Successful change efforts require disciplined implementation. One of the great virtues of Six Sigma and lean manufacturing is that they demand a disciplined implementation. They are not voluntary or sporadic. For much of my career I have been implementing *team management*. Team management is based on creating *managing* teams that assume ownership of the routine work process from top to bottom in the organization. These teams cascade down the organization to include every first level employee. Every team, regardless of rank or function, defines customers, suppliers, processes, develops a scorecard, and seeks improvement in process and performance. When implemented properly, team management always improved performance, not because it is a brilliant technique, but simply because of the discipline it brought to pursuing improvement. It created a culture of total involvement in continuous improvement.

One of the most important steps in the success of this process is during the initial meeting with senior executives, during the sales presentation. I told them that a key to success was their leadership team. It was critical that they not only verbally supported the effort, but that they provide a model, provide leadership by participate in the same training as every other team. It was important that they do the things teams do – define their customers, interview their customers, develop a team scorecard, etc. And the critical moment came when I told them that I recommended they NOT hire us unless they were willing to provide this active leadership. "Will you provide this leadership?" The question always met with a positive response. I told them that if they proceeded they were entering into a contract, and this commitment was their contract and I would hold them to their word. More than once, I had to meet with senior management teams and remind them of their commitment.

Change management is most successful when "we are all going through it together." There is something powerful about all marching to the same drum, all experiencing the same difficulties, the same learning. It gives others the motivation and courage to move forward. When leaders can talk about their own experience and their learning, it is a powerful model and motivation for others. This then forms the basis for disciplined practices.

While I have always been a proponent of positive motivation and employed punishment as a last resort (whether at work or at home), there is a time when discipline can only be instilled with a strong hand.

When Discipline Must Be Imposed… and Is Appreciated

Some years ago, my consultants and I were implementing a number of improvement efforts within a firm in the heavy construction industry. I was coaching the senior management team to develop as a team, and practice effective group decision-making and other team processes as a model for the rest of the organization. The culture of this organization reflected the culture of the industry, very "macho," and the senior leaders were "tough guys" who had fought their way up the ranks of the organization. The problem was that they were still married to their habit of fighting. The three leaders of the three major operating divisions had a real problem with each other. They had been in conflict for a long time and would sit in the team meetings and politely discuss issues, then reach an agreement, and then they would go out and not implement a single decision they made. Worse yet, they would backbite to their subordinates, telling them why decisions of the team were bad and insulting their fellow team members. This poisoned the atmosphere in the organization and made teamwork across divisions at lower levels a very futile effort.

I was very direct and confrontational in dealing with this problem. I gave them feedback as a group and in personal sessions. When I did this, they confessed their guilt, agreed that it was damaging to their own image and the work of the organization, and pledged to do better. And then, they immediately did it again! It was stunning, their ability to contradict themselves. I again confronted them in their next team meeting. Again, like children caught stealing candy, they confessed and admitted that it was a terrible thing. I then asked them what would make a difference, what did they need to change their behavior?

After a short moment of reflection, one of the senior executives spoke up – "We need John," nodding toward the President, "to kick our butts when we screw up!" I am sure it was one of the more honest moments in their team meetings.

I turned to John. "Will you kick their butts if they do this again?" Poor John had never been asked to kick the butts of his senior vice presidents and wasn't sure exactly what this called for. However, sensing a true leadership moment, he replied – "Yes, I'd be happy to." And with that there was almost a sigh of satisfaction around the room, as if to say "Thank goodness, it's about time!"

I can't swear that they never did it again, but I am told that it definitely improved. I have seen many other cases where senior managers simply needed to experience that their performance, adhering to a commitment in this case, would result in consequences. If the leader isn't, on some occasion, willing to administer the paddle, in some fashion, he or she will have great difficulty maintaining discipline and respect. The irony illustrated by this case is that it is exactly what the group wants. They want to know what the rules are, they want everyone to play by the same rules, and they want to know that it will matter!

The Requirement to Adhere to Contracts

Discipline is the habit of adhering to contracts. As children we make contracts with our parents (if I do this – then you will do that). The disciplined child learns to adhere to contracts. The inability, or the failure to learn adherence to contracts is a common characteristic of delinquent children, and of children who perform poorly in school. This same attribute carries over at work. If an environment, a set of social habits, becomes favorable to breaking contracts, adherence is lost. With the failure of individuals to adhere to contracts, trust is lost, and with the loss of trust the ability to work in teams, to share learning, to cooperate in problem solving, are all diminished.

Some may feel that this idea of discipline and drumbeats contradicts the need for creativity and spontaneity. So much of the work in our organizations requires creative thought. The freedom to engage in out-of-the-box thinking should not be stifled in any way. But, consider Neil Simon. Was he creative? Of course, but the drumbeat of regular performance stimulated, even forced his creativity. Musicians do not abandon rhythm to find creativity. Regular practice, regular performance, regular drumbeats within the music are all the canvas on which they paint their creative sounds. There is a difference in rigidly requiring a particular performance and the regularity or rhythm of performance. If a painter were asked to paint the same picture over and over again, that would soon become mind numbing; the same with a musician or writer. Discipline and rhythm provide the pattern for individual and team performance, and enable large groups to dance together.

Achieving Self-Discipline:

Personal Action Agenda	I do	I don't	I will
1. Self-discipline begins with knowledge of direction, *where* am I going and *why* do I want to go there? I have a clear long-term goal for my personal achievement.			
2. What am I trying to achieve this *year* that will lead me in that direction? I have an intermediate goal.			
3. I have a clear goal or objective for this *month* or *week* that contributes to my long-term goal.			
4. I take *specific actions* each day to contribute to achieving my goals.			
5. I have planned a prompt, a cue, a signal, a drumbeat to alert me to engage in this behavior.			
6. I measure and record my performance of this action on a regular basis to take account of myself each day.			
7. I have planned some reinforcement, some reward, for successfully achieving some amount or portion of this performance or goal.			
8. I share this and gain support from others (spouse, team members, friends)			
9. I think about the natural negative consequences of my failure to perform these actions.			
Summary of what I will do to improve my self-discipline:			

Achieving Team Self-Discipline:

Team Action Agenda	We do	We don't	We will
1. Discipline within a team begins with knowledge of direction, where are we going and why do we want to go there? We have a clear long-term goal for our team's achievement.			
2. What are we trying to achieve this year, or this month that will lead us in that direction? We have an intermediate goal.			
3. We have a clear goal or objective for this month or week.			
4. We take specific actions, behavior, each day to contribute to achieving our goals.			
5. We have planned a prompts, a cue, a signal, a drumbeat to alert us to engage in this behavior.			
6. We measure and record our performance of this action on a regular basis to take account of ourselves each day.			
7. We reward ourselves for successfully achieving some amount or portion of this performance or goal.			
8. We share this and gain support from others (manager, other teams, customers, suppliers).			
9. We have discussed and recognized the natural consequences of our failure to engage in these actions.			
Summary of what we agree to do to improve our team's self-discipline:			

Achieving Organizational Discipline:

Organization Action Agenda	We do	We don't	We will
1. We have clearly defined our desired market position.			
2. We have clearly communicated the strategy and vision to our employees. They get it.			
3. What are we trying to achieve this year that will lead us in that direction? We have an intermediate goal.			
4. We regularly (quarterly or monthly) communicate our actions and progress toward our strategy.			
5. We have planned prompts, a drumbeat that reminds members of the organization to behave in ways that lead to achieving our goals.			
6. We have a regular goal setting and review process that creates both involvement and accountability.			
7. We measure and record organization performance toward these goals on a periodic basis and we publicize our progress or lack of progress.			
8. We have a system of planned rewards for members of the organization for successfully achieving performance toward our goals.			
9. The senior management team of the organization reviews progress toward our goals and the process of managing that progress regularly (at least quarterly).			
10. We have discussed and recognized the natural consequences of our failure to engage in these actions.			
Summary of what we agree to do to improve organizational discipline:			

Chapter 6

A Return to the Family Farm
The Currency of Teamwork

"I am a member of a team, and I rely on the team, I defer to it and sacrifice for it, because the team, not the individual, is the ultimate champion." Mia Hamm

The social capital of a nation is founded on the strength of its families. The social capital of an organization is founded on the strength of its work groups or teams.

Teamwork has become so popular and well accepted as an important part of our corporate culture, it has taken on a faddish silliness, which drifts off the path from the teamwork that creates economic value. Too often team-building exercises fail to translate into any real and significant change in behavior in the work place. Teamwork that is important is that which is focused on winning the business game – serving customers, achieving breakthrough innovations, managing core work processes, and keeping score on the financial and quality scorecard. The teamwork that matters is that of the work team, at every level of the organization, from top-to-bottom, where the important decisions are made. Chapter 13 details a step-by-step approach to implementing *team management*.

Teamwork has become synonymous with any effort to cause employees to feel good about each other, to talk nicely to each other, and generally to behave themselves. They may have great relationships, which are nice, but they may actually do no work in teams. *Team management* is work getting done in a team environment, teams of managers or employees making decisions as a group, and most important, teams assuming responsibility for business performance.

Many of us enjoy working alone. Some work is best done alone. Writing a book and scientific study are good examples when solitary work is preferred. But, this work quickly is turned over to a team, or requires a team, to see it to its desired end. Even though we may do solitary work, we inevitably become a partner in a team of professionals who realize the potential of our own work.

The family system was the first work group, and families are the foundation building block of every society, every civilization, in every corner of the globe. We don't do many useful things by ourselves. If you are not effective at working in groups, you are crippled. Unfortunately, many people are crippled to some extent! And perhaps they are crippled because the building blocks are crumbling.

Creating teamwork, or high involvement/high-performance work systems, is something about which I am entirely biased. Yes, biased! I am biased because I have seen how lives have been changed by transforming the work system.

I well remember when my firm was working with Clark-Schwebel Textile Manufacturing in Georgia and South Carolina and we were establishing a system of team management at every level of the organization. In one of the plants there was a young woman named Hazel, she had the lowest job in the plant, floor-sweep. She worked alone, given little attention or notice, yet was happy to have her job so she could support her children. The team system established teams for all work areas, so every employee was on some team. Hazel was on the maintenance team. The team had a scorecard with their own business measures; they consulted together weekly about their performance; they tried to come up with ideas to improve their performance and their contribution to the overall plant performance. Hazel was full of ideas. As the team was trained in problem-solving techniques, she came to lead brainstorming sessions. She was elected, by the team, to be their team leader. She was so enthusiastic and so effective that when it came time to train an internal consultant to assume the role of training and coaching other teams, Hazel became that internal consultant.

If you walked into the plant and met Hazel before the experience, she was one person – shy, unsure, yet pleasant. If you returned after a year in the team system, Hazel was a different human being – confident, outspoken, and sure of her self. And, it wasn't only Hazel. Ricky Wolfe the Vice President of Manufacturing who had hired us, after visiting one of the plants told me "These aren't the same people who were there six months ago." I said, "Yeah, they're the same people." He said, "No, they're not." He then told me why he had hired us (I thought I knew). "I hired you because of my mother. My mother and father worked in a textile mill in the small town in South Carolina where we grew up. Every day my mother would come home with lint in her hair. She was a 'lint-head' (a somewhat derogatory word used to describe textile workers). And she talked about how the supervisors talked to her. And, I knew how much it hurt her. I don't ever want anyone to go home and tell their children the things my mother told me. That is why I hired you." He then quietly added, "I wish my mother could visit our plants today."

Having run my own business for many years, and consulted with a hundred corporations, I am pretty business focused. However, I don't ever want to lose sight of how the work systems we create influence the lives of the human beings who work in those systems, and their children. This is why I feel very strongly about creating team based organizations, in which every employee has the dignity to be heard, to participate in solving real problems and improve real performance. This responsibility results in dignity. It is transformative of the human personality.

It has become a team-based world. The leaders of the G8 countries get together once a year to discuss global economic policy. The leaders of every country rely on something like a Cabinet, with sub-teams for national defense, health and education issues, or finance and economics. Within a country, there are hundreds of groups – the Conference Board, the coalition for this and that and every cause you can imagine. Within industries, there are associations and working groups proposing standards and policies. Companies are constantly partnering through a supply chain to share capital and risks; and, within any corporation today, not only is there a Board of Directors and an executive management team, but everyone is on a team for something. Teams are our way of life. The payoff for improving team effectiveness is huge!

What prevents us from functioning well in groups?

If I told you there was a society whose survival depended on a certain skill, a certain type of behavior and attitudes, yet from an early age, it systematically taught its children that this very behavior was bad and doing the opposite was good; what would you think of such a society? Dumb! Not only dumb, but one in which Darwin's law would soon catch up and it would be extinct. If early hunters on the Serengeti Plain taught their children how not to throw a spear, and that spear throwing was a bad thing, they would have become very good at gathering berries or burying their young. Of course, they didn't do this. They survived. Yet, I am not so sure about our society. There is a fair chance that our genes will soon obey Darwin's Law if we don't figure out how to work better in groups.

The family farm was a work and social system based on high intimacy, high trust, and high ownership of the work. Psychological and social needs were well met by this system. That is why it lasted for hundreds of thousands of years. But the invention of combine, the tractor drastically improved efficiency and now required less labor. Labor moved to the cities to work in the factories and now everything changed.

The mass production model of Henry Ford's factory increased productivity but destroyed intimacy. Units produced relative to hours of work went up dramatically due to the innovations of mass production. We gained economic efficiency and productivity, but with that system, we sacrificed social intimacy and psychological security.

Because so many families lived in the city, near their factories, children didn't learn in small group settings as they did in the rural areas. They were hustled into large factory like schools, production was specialized and they learned history, social studies and math, and were taught by production specialists. They were required to sit at small square desks and God forbid if they looked at someone else's paper! After "let's be quiet!" the phrase uttered most often by teachers became "Johnny, do your own work!" This same model was prevalent in the factory. Every worker was told to do his own work and not to worry about the work of anyone else.

Doing *your own* work was good! Looking at your neighbor's paper was bad! I never understood that because I knew there was nothing useful on my paper and I thought I might learn something by looking at the paper of my neighbor! The student who could work alone for hours on end was a "good student." The student who needed to communicate with others frequently, who was highly social, particularly in a way that entertained others, was a "troublemaker" and was often sent to the Principal's Office, an intended punishment, which was probably more reinforcing than sitting listening to the boring teacher drone on endlessly. I am willing to bet that most entrepreneurs were troublemakers and most good students became librarians.

Jerry Harvey, a professor of organizational behavior whose writing I admire greatly, wrote a wonderful piece on *Encouraging Future Managers to Cheat*.[36] Recognizing the organization "unlearning" that is perpetuated by most schools and universities, and how this cripples students to engage in useful behavior at work, Dr. Harvey has developed his own cheating policy. Of course, most schools have an honor code or cheating policy. It no doubt says something like "I swear that the work I hand in is entirely my own and I have neither given nor received help from any other person." Harvey says he has a moral responsibility to encourage cheating (as defined above) and has his own policy, which is somewhat different. It says the following:

"You may take your examination alone, with another person, or with as many people as you like. I frown on cheating. In fact, I go blind with rage if I catch anyone cheating. I define cheating as the failure to assist others on the examination if they request it. You may refer to notes and reference materials during the exam. You may bring friends, relatives or associates to help you. You may also bring equipment... You may not cheat. If possible, have fun. If not, be competently miserable."

---

[36] Harvey, Jerry. *The Abilene Paradox*, New York, Jossey-Base. 1988. pp 123-137.

You may regard Jerry Harvey as insane. I am sure others have. However, you might ask, "Is he insane or is what we normally do insane?" I think a good case can be made for the latter.

Most of us over forty have been taught to "do your own work" and not to cheat. We have been promoted for our own work and want to make sure we get credit for our own work. No team is going to be promoted or earn a raise! Individuals earn raises. The very system we live in, encourages behavior that is self-serving and often contrary to effective teamwork. Overcoming this is an act of heroism. Heroism is not doing what the system calls for. Heroism is acting sanely in the face of an insane system, disregarding the fact that others will consider you insane.

There is hope, however. Schools are changing. Just as they adopted Henry Ford's factory model, schools are beginning to engage in more group study, group projects, and group papers. Even team grades are being given in some schools. But, it will be years before the schools modify their systems to the reality of how work gets done in the modern world.

The principles in this book are mutually reinforcing. Strong trust and purpose, and an understanding of dialogue, enables teamwork. Effective scorekeeping and an understanding of the flow or processes are also essential to teamwork. In a sense, all of these come together in the work of groups, at every level of the organization. As I sincerely believe that a society is no stronger than its families; similarly, no corporation will long be stronger than the effectiveness of work groups.

In the second part of this book, you will find a chapter that lays out an action-plan for developing and improving teams in the organization. The following are what I believe to be the essential principles of teamwork in organizations.

Clarify the Purpose of Teams:

There are, fundamentally, three types of teams and they have completely different functions. Many constraints occur because teams are expected to do things they are not structured to do. Teams can be either, *problem-solving teams*, *managing teams* or, *networking teams* and they each perform different functions.

The majority of teams in corporations have been formed as a result of a quality improvement process. They are formed to solve a problem; are most often comprised of volunteers or members selected for their knowledge in an area related to the problem; and are trained to study the problem and propose a solution. Most frequently, these teams will dissolve after a management group accepts their solution, although they will sometimes follow through with implementing and evaluating the solution to the problem.

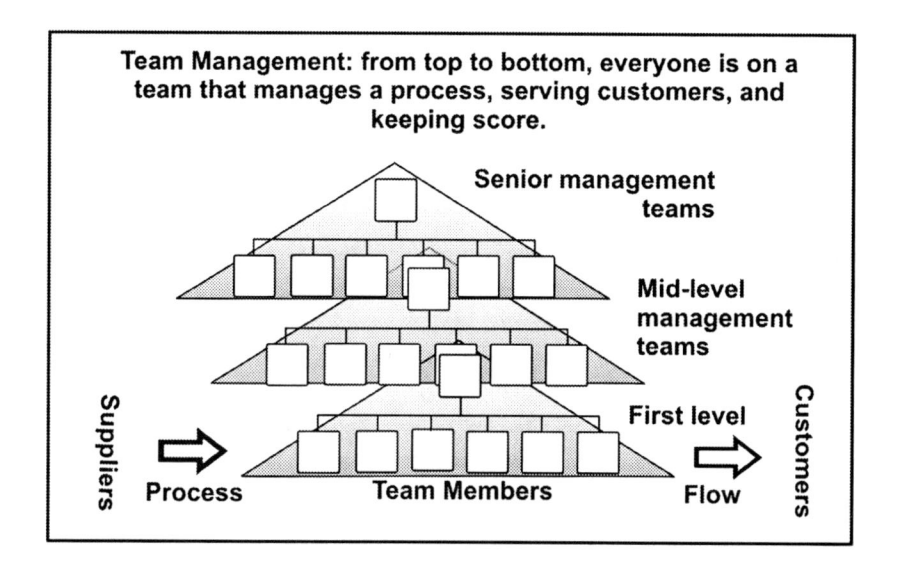

Team Management: from top to bottom, everyone is on a team that manages a process, serving customers, and keeping score.

- Senior management teams
- Mid-level management teams
- First level
- Suppliers → Process
- Team Members
- Flow → Customers

This is all good and well accepted. The quality of the problem solving by teams is entirely dependent on the skills of the members, the effectiveness of their facilitation, and the support and encouragement they receive from management. The Six-Sigma and Total Quality Management programs, as well as the Quality Circle and Employee Involvement programs that came before, have all gone a long way to improving the quality of group problem-solving. Ironically, because of our quality management programs, most of this improvement has come at the lower levels of the organization, and bypassed the top.

Problem-solving teams only have responsibility for proposing a solution, not responsibility for the on-going performance that resulted in the need for a problem-solving group. They also generally cannot be held responsible for results since they lack the power and authority to implement significant changes. They can only be accountable for "proposing" a solution, not for actually implementing and getting results if they lack the authority to make those decisions. Only managers can be accountable for results if they hold the decision-making authority.

Managing teams, or what my associates and I have called *team management* for many years, is based on a completely different premise than problem-solving teams. Team management assumes that a team is responsible for the on-going, day-to-day, management of a process and has the authority to make decisions regarding that process. These are not temporary teams, which go away after a problem is solved. The Board of Directors, the CEO's team, and other senior management teams are permanent and they have the authority to make decisions. They are responsible and accountable for performance. Work teams or professional teams are organized around the flow of the work. From the creative conception of a product or service to the delivery to the customer, teams can take responsibility for doing and improving the work. Organizing teams around work processes is the most "natural" kind of team and organization. In this manner, all processes have "process owners," teams responsible and accountable for the performance of that process. This organization of teams around the work is at the heart of "lean-manufacturing."

Team management is an organization formed into team from top to bottom, with full responsibility for all of the work processes in that organization. It redefines the culture of the organization to make group responsibility (such as on the family farm and craft shop) the norm in the organization.

Problem-solving teams and managing teams are not incompatible. They co-exist, and the best-managed organizations have both; the managing teams responsible for day-to-day performance and problem-solving groups formed to solve the systemic problems that cut across work-team responsibilities.

In order to implement team management successfully, several things are required, possibly including the redesign of the organization structure and systems. Most of our current structures and systems came about in a world in which accountability resided in individuals and those individuals were structured in vertical silos, not structured in teams that followed the horizontal flow of the work. Chapter Eleven addresses the issue of aligning systems and structure to this change.

Networking teams are again, something very different. Networking teams have neither the responsibility to solve a problem, nor the responsibility to manage performance. They exist for the purpose of learning, sharing and support, particularly among those with common professional skills. Within the large corporation, there may be dozens or hundreds of individuals with particular skills, who are isolated from others with those same skills. These may be engineers of a specialty, finance managers, human resource development managers, graphic artists, or lawyers. Each of these individuals is in the process of learning and often learns lessons that would benefit his or her peers in other parts of the organization. They are also able to share tools and solutions across the organization. These networks may exist only in virtual space, sharing information on a web site or through some in-house software like Lotus Notes.

Networks are most often self-organizing and outside the formal structures of the organization. It is very easy to form a discussion group on Yahoo, for example. Many companies or associations sponsor discussion forums on-line and these serve as network teams that share information, where members can ask questions and get help from their colleagues. A good example of an open network system is that of the Six Sigma quality professional's forum (http://www.isixsigma.com/).

Again, these networking teams can and should co-exist with problem-solving and managing teams. Each of these teams performs entirely different functions and their membership, schedule of meetings, and agenda should all reflect their unique function.

Do it Top to Bottom:

There is magic in everyone doing it together. Every army has understood this as everyone wore the uniform, did exercise, ate together, and marched to the same drummer. Why, it is human nature to go with, rather than against the norms of a culture.

One of the absolute rules of change management is this: the likelihood of successful and lasting change is directly related to the degree to which that change is practiced at the top, expected below, and reinforced from the top down. It is unrealistic to expect change to succeed in a narrow slice of an organization. It is expecting people to be deviant from the larger group. It rarely happens.

Some years ago, I initiated a team process at Delmarva Power and Light in Wilmington, Delaware. During my first visit, I met with Nev Curtis, then the Chairman of the company. As we talked about how to increase the probability of success I said, "If you want this to succeed you need to be the model, you need to do it yourself, and do it first. He replied, "Absolutely, my team needs to be Team #1." And they were. They participated in exactly the same training and went through the same steps as everyone else. Delmarva Power and Light became a model of quality management and their team process was the heart of their effort.

That effort was guaranteed success by the leader's willingness to create a spirit of unity of effort through his personal behavior. Many of our organizations, particularly our large corporations, have created a disunity of class, a great divide between top and bottom, rich and poor. A study of the progress of cultures will reveal that an excess of class distinctions results in an increasing discontent, a reduction in entrepreneurial motivation and a growing likelihood of rebellions.[37] The culture within companies is similar.

The importance of *modeling* cannot be overstated. We tend to imitate the behavior of our superiors, our mother and father, teachers, and managers. If those above are doing it, it must have value, it must be a standard.

Be Business Focused

Stephen Covey said, *"Begin with the end in mind."* That is good common sense. If you want to achieve improvements in business performance, start with a focus on business performance. Too many teams do good things, but do not impact business performance. Teams should focus first on business results and then ask, "What are the

---

[37] Toynbee, Arnold. *A Study of History*. London, Oxford University Press.

processes that impact those results and how can we improve those processes?"

Florida Power & Light and the Wallace Company both won the United States National Quality Award and immediately encountered severe business failure. Motorola, the founding home of the Six Sigma quality management process, was in business decline during most of the time they were gaining recognition for their quality programs. The processes, as good as they were, were not connected to, or focused on business performance.

Analysis of many change failures leads back to the same point – begin with the end in mind. Many failures are the result of a lack of focus. What results do you really want to achieve? If you want to achieve improvement in business performance, design it into the change process, from the beginning. The very idea of moving toward a *business team* approach is that every team and every employee is clearly focused on measurable business results which they can impact.

A clear business scorecard helps to focus efforts in a way that will produce reinforcing results. It is particularly effective if that scorecard can be integrated from top to bottom in the organization. To the degree that teams are focused on similar measures, they will have a unity of purpose.

A few years ago, I consulted with a major oil company that we were helping to implement a team management process. Every team had a scorecard focused on their performance. Overlaid onto this was a *business model*, the idea that shareholder value is the result of two key variables – revenue growth and/or return on operating assets. You can think of this as the "Investor's Matrix" and it can be understood by all employees. Employees can understand that it is their job to grow the business and increase the return on assets. With this understanding, they can be motivated to find ways to contribute to growth and asset utilization. This is the very thing for which the board of director held the CEO accountable. This idea became the key driver of the business model, with every team in the organization developing a matrix, with these two key variables, and seeking to move their dot on the matrix northeast.

When the CEO visited the West Texas oil fields, the wellhead teams displayed their charts reflecting revenue growth and return-on-assets and were able to discuss what they were doing to "move the dot." This created a unity of purpose, language and motivation in the organization. Everyone became business focused.

What defines a group of people as a business or managing team?

You are a business-focused team if...

...You have on-going responsibility for a work process that results in business revenue and/or expends operating costs.

...you know your customers and communicate with those customers concerning their requirements and satisfaction.

...you measure your financial performance, measures of current cash flow or income, expense and assets.

...you measure your operating process performance in terms of quality and productivity.

...you have the capability and responsibility to evaluate your performance, solve problems and make decisions to improve your operations.

Clarify Who Makes What Decision and How:

Members of a group want to understand how decisions are made and who makes them. Many of the conflicts that arise around teams involve a failure to create this clarity. If team members think they are going to make a decision, and a manager makes the decision alone, they will be upset even if they don't disagree with the decision. Disunity results from differing expectations and feeling betrayed that an agreement (real or imagined) isn't being followed. In my company we had a once a month team meeting when all of the consultants and administrative staff would meet for the day, share learning, discuss the companies finances, marketing, etc. More than once, I would put an issue before the group and ask for input. Someone would ask me, "Larry, are you asking us for input so you can make the decision, or are you asking us to reach a consensus and make the decision?" Good question. Sometimes I wasn't sure and needed to clarify that in my own mind. Several times, I asked them whether they thought I should make the decision or let the group reach a decision. On most of those occasions, they preferred that I made the decision after listening to their input. They didn't want to spend the time to reach a consensus.

Here is a quick primer on assigning decision responsibility: Three types of decisions: Command, consultative and consensus. Think - *who knows, who cares, who acts, when must it be made?* The answer to these questions determines how decisions should be made.

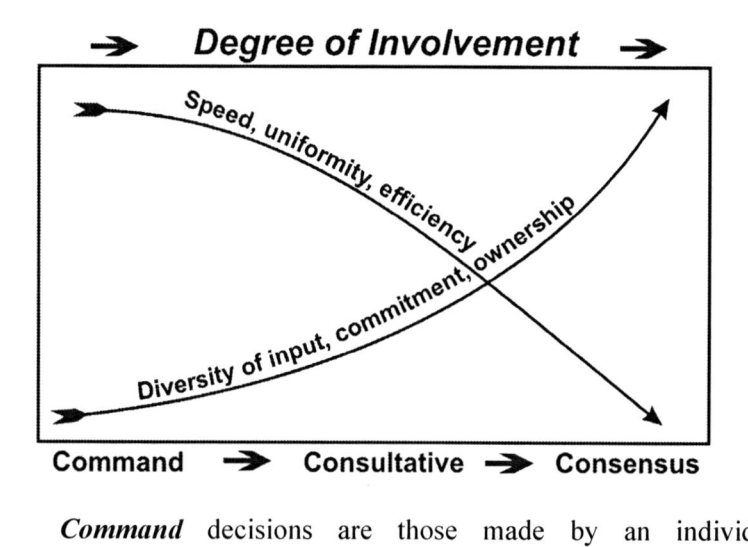

Degree of Involvement

Speed, uniformity, efficiency

Diversity of input, commitment, ownership

Command → Consultative → Consensus

Command decisions are those made by an individual. Individual command authority is not dead and not merely a left over dinosaur of the military organization. Of course, command worked well on the battlefield on which quick decisions were required and obedience won battles. Even today, if the building is burning down, if the machine is spitting smoke and oil, if the customer calls and is furious that he got the wrong package delivered – is the right answer to call a meeting? Definitely not! These are decisions where time, speed, is more important than reaching consensus. These decisions are best left to individuals who are on-the-spot and have expert knowledge.

Speed and expert knowledge are two reasons for command to be the preferred decision style. In the operating room, with the patient cut open and the cardiologist holding a heart in his hand that has just stopped beating – do you want him to call a meeting? Of course, you want him to use his expert knowledge and make a decision, fast! The greater the degree of knowledge an individual has, the more likely a command decision is appropriate. The greater speed required, the more likely command is appropriate.

Consultative decisions involve selective involvement by those who know, care, or must act. If the customer calls and was shipped the wrong order, you may say, "I am very sorry about that. Let me look into it and call you back within an hour. We will definitely solve your problem." The customer will likely say "fine." The customer does not want to be told it will be taken up at the weekly meeting. And, it is likely that you personally do not have sufficient information to know what to do to solve the problem. You will then walk down the hall, gather the two or three people who have knowledge, who may have some investment in this decision (they care), and who may have to take action to solve the problem. You can do this quickly. You are consulting, while still maintaining control of the decision, involving those who know, care or will act.

Consensus decisions are true team decisions where you turn over the decision to the group and you give up control to the group. When do you do this? First, when the conditions of speed and individual expertise are not the most important factors. Consensus decisions involve a cost – the cost of time, energy of the group, and the risk that you may not like the decision. When do you employ consensus decision-making? For those decisions that are strategic – involve long-term goals, and how we do things, our on going processes. All members of the group have an investment in the goals of the group and the "how" and "why" we do our work. Involvement in these types of decisions gains commitment, gains the wisdom of the group, and provides for shared learning.

If you can ask yourself, or ask the team, which of the decisions we make should be command, consultative or consensus, and provide them with these simple explanations, you can create a great deal of clarity and have the group focus on those things that are most value adding for the group. The time and energy of teams is often wasted with trivial and inappropriate decisions. Use common sense.

No One is Self-Managing!

I am guilty. Along with a legion of other consultants, we promoted the idea of *self-managing* teams. Self-management was good – authoritarian management was bad! How nice and simple.

We perpetuated a myth that I have since come to view as less than helpful. No one is self-managing, not even an individual solo professional. He or she is managed by their customers, by market forces, by the bank, and if married, no doubt by their spouse and

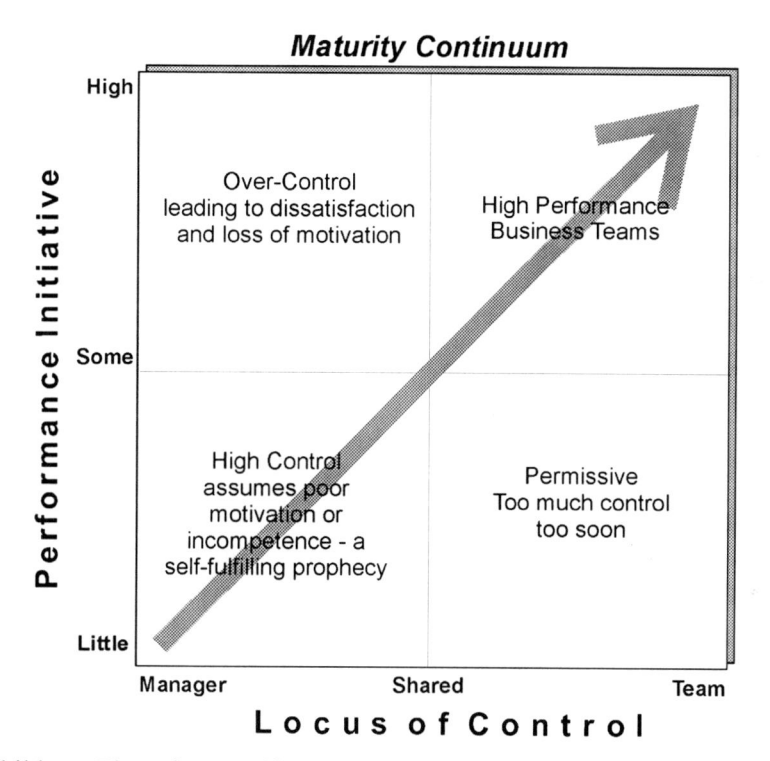

Maturity Continuum

	Manager	Shared	Team
High (Performance Initiative)	Over-Control leading to dissatisfaction and loss of motivation		High Performance Business Teams
Some			
	High Control assumes poor motivation or incompetence - a self-fulfilling prophecy		Permissive Too much control too soon
Little			

Locus of Control

children. There is no self-management. The President of the company has to report to the Board and Chairman. I can assure you, having spent a lot of time with corporate CEOs none of them feels self-managed. On the contrary, they feel managed from the top, bottom and sideways.

Of course, the more autonomous a team can be, the more it is able to make responsible decisions and act on its own - the better it feels about itself, the faster it can act, the more it will learn, and the lower the cost of management. This was, and is still, all true. This is simply a definition of maturity. Treating individuals and teams as adults, causes them to act with responsibility. Maturity is good.

The same is true with individuals. The faster they can grow up, make their own decisions and take responsibility for their own performance, the better. However, all who have been parents well understand the learning, maturing process. It doesn't happen over night for either individuals or teams. Individuals need training, coaching and feedback. So do teams.

There is a significant danger that if teams are given too much independence too quickly, it may arrest their development. If teams feel that they are "free" to do as they wish, without having developed a responsible understanding of performance, what I will call *performance initiative*, they may suffer the ills of the permissive parent and become "spoiled children." The opposite problem occurs if the manager fails to let loose of the reins of control when the team is ready to take initiative to manage performance. This over-control leads to dissatisfaction and loss of motivation.

Clarify Roles and Responsibilities:

There is nothing worse than the tyranny of a group in which the members do not know whose job is whose, and who does what for whom, and when. Many conflicts and divisions occur simply because roles and responsibilities are unclear. In chaos, personal power takes over.

If you recall the four containers of group decision-making described in the previous chapter, the first is the container of structure. This includes defining the purpose of the group; its relationship to other teams or groups; relationships within the team; roles and responsibilities; the agenda; and the pattern or requirement for external communications. These formalities, while they may appear simple matters, are often those, which inhibit the flow of work or result in damaged relationships within the team, or with others in the organization.

Within the team, there may be several different roles. There must be someone to facilitate meetings. This may be a permanent position, or it may be one that is rotated among members of the team. In either case, this person should receive training in group facilitation skills. This person has the responsibility to prove the environment and opportunity for all voices to be heard and this is not always so simple. The *facilitator* may be the formal manager of the team. On the other hand, there may be a manager, yet he or she may decide to ask others on the team to serve in the role of team facilitator. Facilitating and the authority to make decisions do not necessarily go together.

Someone needs to record decisions, action plans, who will do what by when, at each meeting. This can be done by a *scribe* who writes down actions and decisions on their laptop or on paper, but it is even more desirable that an action plan (who, what, & when) be posted on a flip chart for the entire group to see. There is something uniting about a group, together, looking at the flip chart and seeing the action step written down, their name being placed next to an action item, and with a date for completion. This has far more effect, than the agreements typed privately into a laptop. Someone other than the person who is facilitating the meeting should do this.

Another role that may be separate or included in either of the first two is that of *timekeeper*. It is very helpful to begin each meeting by reviewing the agenda, and agreeing on how long will be spent on each item. The timekeeper can do his or her job by having a separate flip chart, on which they write "30" at the beginning of a discussion on an agenda item, if thirty minutes has been allocated for that topic. Then, with five or ten minutes to go, they rise and walk over to the flip chart, cross out the "30" and write "5". They don't need to say anything to interrupt the discussion. Four minutes later, they walk over to the flip chart, cross out "5" and write "1". A minute later, they cross out the "1". This silent reminder of the time remaining has a strong effect on the group. If they need more time the facilitator can then ask "Do we need more time on this, or can we make a decision?"

There are other possible internal roles, but these are the three essential ones.

Every team must also be clear to whom it reports. Every team reports to someone or some other team. Who are their customers? Who are their suppliers? What are their other external relationships? Clarifying these relationships is an important part of establishing a healthy structure.

Families are the foundation stone of every society and teams or small work groups are the foundation of every organization. For the organization to perform well it must be built on the foundation of high performing teams. This is continual challenge, not a passing fad.

My Personal Contribution to Teamwork

Personal Action Agenda	I do this	I don't	I will
1. I participate on at least one team at work.			
2. I feel a clear purpose and responsibility to manage a process or serve a customer.			
3. I know our measures of performance to customers.			
4. I have been trained and feel competent in problem solving skills.			
5. I also serve on a problem solving group that seeks to improve quality or solve problems that cut across teams.			
6. I know which decisions I can make alone.			
7. I contribute to consensus decisions.			
8. I feel that my team listens and respects my ideas.			
9. I listen well to my team members ideas and respect their contribution to the work of the team.			
Summary of what I will do to contribute to teamwork:			

Making Our Team Effective:

Team Action Agenda	We do this	We don't	We will
1. We are organized in teams to take responsibility for our work.			
2. Our team feels a clear purpose to manage a process or serve a customer.			
3. We measure our performance to customers and solve performance problems.			
4. We manage business performance by reviewing financial results that we impact or control.			
5. We also have problem solving groups that solve problems that cut across teams.			
6. It is clear who makes what decisions on our team.			
7. We know which decisions are true consensus decisions.			
8. Our manager serves as a helpful coach to our team.			
9. Our team genuinely feels accountable for the performance of our team and initiates efforts to improve without any external pressure.			
Summary of what we agree to do to improve our teamwork:			

Making Teams Effective in the Organization:

Organization Action Agenda	We do this	We don't	We will
1. Our senior management team is a model of teamwork.			
2. Management is organized into teams at each level.			
3. Management teams set a model with their own behavior and reinforce teamwork below them.			
4. Teams are organized around the flow of the work, from input to output.			
5. The manager's job has been defined to include providing support and coaching teams.			
6. Our system of performance review rewards good team performance.			
7. Teams are not something outside the management system; they are the management system.			
8. We provide financial information to teams so they can manage business performance.			
9. Our organization provides effective training in the skills of teamwork and problem solving.			
10. Our organization supports networks of individuals who share professional experience and knowledge across the organization.			
Summary of what we agree to do to improve team effectiveness throughout the organization:			

Chapter 7

Make Performance Matter
The Currency of Appreciation

"The roots of all goodness lie in the soil of appreciation for goodness."
The Dalai Lama

It is tempting to say that there are two kinds of people: those who go through life focused on problems; and, those who go through life recognizing progress and opportunities. I am sure it is not that simple. We all have a little of those characters within us. Yet, it is perfectly clear which of these two qualities acts as an attractive force, unifying others; and, which serves as a source of irritation, conflict and is depressing to others.

It is also clear from the research in positive psychology and optimism[38] that the positive outlook on life will lead to personal happiness, a longer life, more money, and a variety of benefits.[39] It is also possible to be positive, yet not foolishly naïve and blind to problems. You can be appreciative of the good, while also recognizing and solving problems.

Much of the history of productivity and quality improvement is a history of fixing problems. Consultants are hired to fix the cost over-

---

[38] Seligman, Martin E.P. *Learned Optimism*. New York. Alfred A. Knopf. 1991.
[39] Seligman, Martin E.P. *Authentic Happiness*. New York. Free Press. 2002. pp 30-44.

runs, to reduce the number of quality defects, or to solve the problems of poor morale. Consultants and changing processes have generally focused on fixing problems. Is it possible to improve an organization's culture and business performance, by focusing on the good aspects of that culture? Doesn't the rule "if it ain't broke, don't fix it!" apply? Or, is it possible to improve things by focusing on what is already positive and reinforce those positive qualities?

The answer to this lies in some very fundamental ideas as to how people learn. The power of appreciation is always unifying, always draws people together, and can be employed to improve both individual and organizational performance. In this chapter, I will first present some experiences and principles regarding the application of appreciation to individual learning; and second, a few ideas regarding appreciation and organizational learning.

Appreciation and Individual Learning

Early in my career, I learned a valuable lesson in the power of the positive. My first serious job after college was that of a counselor in the North Carolina Correctional System. In all my enthusiastic idealism, I took a job as the one counselor for three hundred and fifty young inmates at Polk Youth Center in Raleigh, North Carolina. If you think you have an impossible job, try being the one counselor for three hundred and fifty young inmates, ages ranging from sixteen to twenty-one. If you want to focus on problems, this is your place.

What I learned in prison was a few very fundamental rules of human behavior: how people learn, and how the organization's systems can either promote or inhibit good performance. Learning occurs in all organizations, all the time. The question is "who is doing the teaching and what are they learning?" Unfortunately, the answer in most prisons is that the inmates are doing the teaching and what they are learning is how to be even more anti-social. You are paying for it. Of course, this is not the intention of prison administrators, but intentions often don't matter. What *you* do, however, does matter.

If you wanted to teach someone to behave in ways that lead to success in the real world, you would teach basic skills, such as interviewing for a job, filling out applications, communicating with your supervisor or, how to handle conflicts at work. You would also strengthen those skills with some type of reward/recognition system since we all know that habits are developed as behavior is reinforced. People learn to do what leads to rewards. Unfortunately, there was no such system in my prison, and there still isn't in most prisons. Prisons are almost entirely focused on punishing the bad in people and have little time or resources to devote to any positive learning.

From the Grocery Store to Prison

The most successful way for a parent to do away with bad behavior on the part of a young child is consistently to demonstrate appreciation for the opposite positive behavior. In other words, if a child screams and fusses in the grocery store, the parent may choose to *punish* the child for bad behavior; or employ a positive approach by *praising* the child when it *does not* scream or behave badly. Strengthening the child's good behavior through appreciation will cause good behavior to replace bad behavior. Unfortunately, many parents are too often focused on the negative. In so doing, they not only create miserable children, but they make their own lives miserable. Many managers are slaves to the same self-defeating cycle.

In 1971, I started an experimental program in a second prison. It was the first free economy behind prison walls. This prison had one hundred and fifty young inmates. They worked in a license manufacturing plant and a printing shop, printing government forms. They worked a normal workweek and they had industrial supervisors who came in to manage the operation and their work. There was, however, no reward system: no pay, no benefits, no vacation, and no promotions. Nothing good happened if you did a good job. If, on the other hand, you really messed up you could get fired. If you got fired, you were sent back to the living area where there was little to do except sit and watch TV, read, or play cards.

Let's see – work hard in a hot and smelly environment, or sit and watch TV and play cards with my buddies who also got kicked out? Which is more rewarding, and which is more punishing? What are the lessons of this system? The answers are – all the wrong ones!

When followed by rewards, behavior is reinforced, it strengthens. In the above case, getting fired is getting reinforced! It's a learning organization! The fact is that there was no reinforcement for any desirable behavior in this prison. There wasn't even an opportunity to practice most of the skills that would allow you to succeed in the "real world." On the other hand, the inmates were excellent at showing appreciation for the kind of behavior they thought was desirable within their sub-culture. And, none of that behavior was behavior we wanted to see outside of prison.

I created an economy, with no real money, but a point system by which inmates doing a more-skilled job earned more points. Each week they received a "company" check and they deposited it in the bank. First Union National Bank in North Carolina gave us a check posting machine, printed company (Central Prison Bank) checks and personalized checks for each inmate. For most of them, this was the first checkbook they ever had – at least with their name on it.

Of course, there had to be a way to spend the points or it would all be meaningless. The inmates lived in four dormitories. We made one a "luxury" dorm, one a "quality" dorm, one a "standard" dorm and the last, an "efficiency" dorm. We charged rent. We were the only prison in the country to charge rent – the more luxury, the higher the rent. We also charged for movies, using games and anything else that was desirable. Just like in the real world! Therefore, the inmates who gained the most skills and did the most skilled jobs got to live in "luxury" (believe me, it wasn't really that luxurious!). Now, if an inmate lost his job it had real consequences.

But, we hadn't really figured out what we would do with someone who lost his job. You can't kick him out! And, you can't be homeless in prison. When the first inmate lost his job, we were suddenly confronted with this problem. We realized that we had to give him enough points to pay for his rent in the bottom dorm, the efficiency dorm.

It didn't take long for other inmates to come to us and complain and it was the inmates living in the efficiency dorm who had the complaint. "Hey, what's the deal, were bustin' our butts workin' and this guy ain't doin' nothing. Where does he get the points from to pay his rent?"

We had to confess, "Well, we just give him 43 points a week, just enough for his rent. We can't kick him out, you know!"

"You can't just give him points! Where do you get the points from?" Now, we really hadn't thought about this one. Where do we get the points from?

"We just make them up"

With his voice rising, the inmate replied, "You can't just 'make up' points!" he said incredulously. How could we just make up points? The world didn't work like that. This inmate intuitively recognized that if you can just make up points, print money, it de-values everything, and that's not fair to those working.

So, back to the drawing board – we had to modify the system. Of course, where do points come from in the real world to pay for those who aren't working? They come from those who are working. Taxes, a brilliant idea! So the next week, when all the inmates got their pay checks on Friday afternoon, there was a line item deduction on the check "minus two points – unemployment tax."

That was the nearest we came to a riot. You had to be there to appreciate it. The inmates protested loudly and with passion that taxes were unfair, and they didn't want to pay for anyone who wasn't willing to work, and my goodness, it sounded like a gathering of young Republicans!

You have often heard the expression that attitudes can't change overnight. Not true. The next morning the inmate who had been fired, appeared at our office door with a very changed attitude. He wanted to work, swore he would never be fired again, and definitely did not want to be on unemployment! Miraculous! He must have seen a vision overnight. The angel of work had spoketh unto him and said, "thou shalt work!" And he did. And it was good.

During the course of this experimental program, we kept extensive data on inmate behavior. Virtually all indicators of good behavior improved and rule violations went down. The guards acquired the habit of saying appreciative things to inmates who were studying or helping other inmates. The entire climate of the prison changed.

Emotional Spirals and Why They Matter

You have just worked for a month on an important project and turned it in to your boss. Your poor boss had a hard day. While leaving the office you see him looking at you and it is not a particularly friendly stare. And you say to yourself, "Oh, crap! He didn't like what I handed in, and I worked so hard on it, and I have a performance review coming up, and I really need a raise, and my wife wants to enroll one of our kids in another expensive dance class or something which we can't afford, and my wife never understands the pressure I'm under." Other than that, everything is fine.

Then you drive home and imagine all the rotten things that may follow. Coming into your house the dog runs to meet you, you bark at the dog not to jump up, and the dog, possessing strong emotional intelligence, runs for cover. Noticing the dog's retreat, you say to yourself, "See, even the dog doesn't appreciate me."

Going into the kitchen, you are dispirited already, but your wife is all smiles. She is just delighted to see you because she has a great story to tell you about one of the neighbors' misadventures. You attempt to listen but you can only think, "If she really knew what's going on at work..." Naturally, she soon notices that you aren't paying any attention and she says, "You never listen to me," and this results in you experiencing another series of unpleasant emotions. All of this because the boss had an unfriendly stare, when, he didn't even have time to look at your project!

This sequence of events is a negative emotional spiral that now includes you, your dog and your wife. An emotional spiral is a sequence of behaviors and emotions. One behavioral event (the boss staring), triggers an emotion that produces another behavior, and this behavior causes a response by someone else, which reinforces the emotion. Such spirals can be either positive or negative. You can imagine a similar sequence when an expression of appreciation results in a positive emotion, then behavior, then response by someone else. Research has demonstrated that positive emotional spirals not only have positive effects on individuals, but on the performance of organizations. Barbara L. Frederickson, in a review of the research concluded, "These findings lay the groundwork for the hypothesis that positive emotions generate "upward spirals" toward optimal functioning and enhanced emotional well-being." "As this cycle continues, positive emotions transform individuals into more resilient, socially integrated, and capable versions of themselves. So, positive emotions not only make people feel good in the present, but they also increase the likelihood that people will function well and feel good in the future."[40]

Research has shown that positive emotions, particularly expressed by a leader, produce positive emotions in employees. These positive emotions may be subtly expressed through facial expressions, even without any verbal comment. A group leader's positive emotions accurately predict the performance of their entire group. Studies have shown that the more salespeople experience positive emotions, the more helpful they are towards their customers – resulting in higher sales. This upward spiraling also increases creativity, individual initiative and job satisfaction.[41] The positive and negative spirals are easily generated by leaders, although often unwittingly. It is one way to understand how appreciation expressed by leaders or managers increases performance with a powerful multiplying effect.

Appreciation as a System

In all organizations, there is a system of reinforcement or appreciation. In the society, there is a similar system. Why does Congress constantly change the tax code to provide a deduction for investments in oil drilling, or research, or education? Because tax deductions are a form of positive reinforcement and the government uses this to strengthen effort in that direction. At work, we reinforce good performance with compensation increases, bonuses, and dozens of forms of recognition. We create a climate, a culture, through our personal behavior by either focusing on desired performance or expressing appreciation; or, we create a climate of fear and alienation by looking for the negative case to punish.

Children who are successful in school and later in life have generally come from homes in which at least one of the parents

---

[40] Frederickson, Barbara. Positive "Emotions and Upward Spirals in Organizations", in *Positive Organizational Scholarship,* by Cameron, Kim S., Dutton Jane E., and Quinn, Robert E. San Francisco, Barrett-Kohler Publishers, Inc. 2003.

[41] Ibid, P. 172-173.

consciously taught positive values by showing appreciation for behavior representing those values. Studying my inmates' background, I discovered, not surprisingly, that these young men had never experienced the praise or appreciation of parents who valued reading and success in school or other positive values. They were starved for appreciation and they found it where it was available.

When the first of our three children reached the age when she began to think about driving, and began to make suggestive comments about what would be a nice first car, my devious mind went to work. Give her a car? I don't think so. Earn it!

My wife and I constructed a little game – you get what you want, if we get what we want. We agreed on a contract. We told our daughter "You read the front page of the Sunday New York Times each week for eighty weeks and we will buy your first car." The contract was specific – she had to read one lead international story and one lead domestic story and one book review. She had to discuss each article with Daddy (that would be me). We made a big graph that went from zero to eighty and put it in her room. She could plot her progress each week. Another part of the contract was that we wouldn't bug her. She could do it or not, it was her problem, but if she didn't do it – no car.

She did it. Not only did she do it, but also in the process, she developed a genuine understanding and interest in international relations. Some may fear that if they reinforce behavior it is a "bribe" and the behavior will stop once the deliberate reinforcement stops. That is only true if there is no natural reinforcement, no natural appreciation, associated with the behavior. Soon, our daughter was able to discuss these same articles and the events around the fall of the Soviet Union for example, in her classes in school. The teachers were impressed with her understanding and the simple fact that she was reading the Sunday N.Y. Times. She was able to put her knowledge to work. This led to her traveling overseas each summer, her law degree, and her founding what is now the leading agency in Washington, D.C., that is assisting women who are fleeing human rights abuse.

We did the same "earn your car" program with each of our three children and it generally worked the same each time. Rather than complain about what they were doing wrong or "bug them" to do the right thing, we were very deliberate in showing our appreciation, our value, for positive learning. Our children knew that this wasn't fake; we honestly do value the ability to discuss world affairs accurately and intelligently. We valued this and because we demonstrated our appreciation, we instilled the same value in our children.

Managers convey their values to their employees in the same way. When you demonstrate interest and appreciation to members of the organization, they quickly learn what is important. Every member of the organization has radar, scanning for what really matters most, and it is not what is written down in formal objectives, but rather those things to which the manager pays attention.

Managing Performance Problems

Every manager has the job of creating a learning environment and the most powerful force in that environment is his or her own tendency to find the positive examples, the good performance, and sincerely demonstrate appreciation.

Many years ago, Robert Mager devised a model for analyzing performance problems that is still extremely useful.[42] This model is valuable because, even though it does focus on problems, it asks questions that lead to positive, appreciative, solutions. The model essentially begins by asking the question – "Is it a can't do; or won't do problem?" You will know this if you ask, "If his/her life depended on it, could he/she do it now?" If you ask me to sing opera, or play concert piano, or hit a round of golf like Tiger Woods, and you told me my life depended on it, I am dead! It isn't a "want to" issue. I just cannot do those things. It does not matter how big the reward or how big the threat, I simply don't have the skills. Maybe I could have developed these skills if my parents had trained me to sing, or play golf at an early age, but it is unlikely even with training. I wasn't genetically endowed with those capabilities. Therefore, any effort to motivate me toward those types of performance would have been a waste of time and would have only produce frustration. These are "can't do" rather than "won't do" problems.

---

[42] Mager, Robert F. and Pipe, Peter. *Analyzing Performance Problems or You Really Oughta Wanna.* Atlanta, CEP Press, 1997.

In the work setting, most "can't do" performance problems, problems of knowledge or skill, are not like singing opera. They don't require unusual genetic material and they don't have to be developed in early childhood. They simply require training. Operating equipment, computer programming or using computer programs, making an effective sales presentation, or giving an effective public talk, are all skills, which individuals can learn with training and practice. It is the responsibility of the manager to know which skills and knowledge are required for each job and to provide the necessary training.

Many of the performance problems in a work setting are within the capability of employees, they just haven't been "made to matter" in a way that creates the necessary motivation. Many years ago, I was working in a textile mill in South Carolina. There was an older woman who had been there for a long time. She was known to be slow in her work, but always reliable. Her rate of performance was thirty-five percent of what was called "standard-operating-efficiency." We worked with the supervisor to graph her daily performance and then suggested that he show her the graph, which was very stable, and ask her, "Mary, what do you think you could do?"

When someone is asked, in a non-threatening and positive way if they can improve, they will usually say yes. And when most people are shown data on their performance and asked, they will almost always set a higher goal. When Mary was shown her graph and she was asked what she could do, she said she thought she could do forty percent. A week later, the supervisor brought the graph back, showed it to her, and congratulated her. She was doing forty percent. Again, he asked her what she thought she could do in the next week or two. She said fifty percent. She did. Gradually, week after week, she improved her performance. To make a long story short, she got up to a steady rate of one hundred and twenty percent of standard operating efficiency. No one had ever given her specific feedback, asked her to set goals, and demonstrated sincere appreciation for her effort.

Mary's performance was not a "can't do" problem, it was a "won't do" that became a "will do," with a bit of gentle feedback and appreciation. She was capable of far more than she or anyone else, would have thought. Most of us, and most teams, are capable of far more than we do.

If a problem is a "can't do" problem, it then requires the development of new skills through training, rather than motivation. If the problem is "won't do," a motivation problem, then the techniques of positive appreciation, or positive reinforcement, can strengthen that performance.

Some years ago, Dr. Ogden Lindsley, one of the pioneers of learning theory and the science of human behavior, did a research project to determine the optimum ratio of positive to negative consequences in the classroom. The results may be a bit of trivia, but the significance of the results is profound common sense - 3.57 to 1. When teachers, on the average, praised children more than three and half times as often as they criticized, they achieved the highest performance from their students. One need not meditate for long to recognize the importance of this. Adults are not very different from children in their reaction to positive consequences.

When managers are asked to measure their interactions with employees, from a positive-negative perspective, they often find that the negatives far outweigh the positives. When managers are encouraged to strive for a 4 to 1 ratio of positive to negative interactions with their employees, performance accelerates. Seek four to one! Seek four to one with your children, your team members, your employees; even seek four to one when talking to yourself! High performers have positive thoughts about themselves and do not indulge in negative self-talk or self-pity.

How to Improve Performance with Appreciation

What are the keys to effective appreciation to improve individual performance?

1. Shape Behavior:

All complex behaviors are learned in a series of approximations; each step reinforces and leads to the next. The approximations need to be reinforced, not just the final performance. I remember when my second daughter was taking "keyboard" lessons and she called me into her room and said "Daddy listen to this." It was Three Blind Mice, or something, but I couldn't really tell. It was an effort, but it was not exactly a concert performance. I could have said, "Well that is not what I was hoping to get when I paid for those lessons. Call me when you can play something well!" If I had, it would have been the end of those lessons and probably any motivation for her to learn music. No! Daddy knows his job. Of course I said, "That's wonderful, it sounds like you are really learning some good songs!" and she smiled.

All parents know that you must reinforce approximations (shaping) toward a goal performance if you are going to motivate a child to learn. We are all the same. You and I need reinforcement for our efforts, for making improvement, for trying.

2. **Do It Immediately and Frequently**:

There is a lot of research that proves that the longer the delay, the less impact the reinforcement will have on strengthening a behavior it follows. If you reinforce immediately, the value of the reinforcement is greatest. Have you ever handed in work and waited months for feedback? When it came, you probably didn't feel any great joy.

Because immediacy matters, we need systems and habits of reinforcement that provide many opportunities for earning recognition or rewards. If there is only the monthly paycheck and an annual bonus or review, there are simply not enough opportunities to provide frequent and immediate reinforcement. Motivation depends on the immediacy and frequency of reinforcement.

3. **Personalize It**:

What may be experienced as reinforcing by one person may not be by another. Some individuals may love to be recognized and applauded in a public gathering, while that same recognition may make others feel extremely uncomfortable. Some may consider time off from work a great reward while others would rather be rewarded with an additional assignment. Just as you think about the personal interests when buying a birthday present for someone, consider the personal interests of the individual you are encouraging in the work setting.

4. **Use Variety**:

We love variety in most aspects of our lives. If the same thing, words or events are used repeatedly, they will become less meaningful. The best reinforcement is the surprise, delivered when least expected or spontaneously. When and how reinforcement is scheduled is an entire field of study in itself. In short, reinforcing events can occur on a regular, fixed and predictable schedule (once a week, month, or year) or, on a variable schedule (once during a time period, but you don't know when). Variable schedules tend to produce stronger and more sustainable behavior. I have worked with sales organization with fixed schedules, which have taught their customers to wait until the end of the month in order to get the best price (auto dealerships are a good example – end of month, end of year equals best price). The effect of reinforcement schedules can vibrate all the way through a supply chain with negative effects. Simply varying the schedule on which reinforcement is delivered can greatly increase overall performance, with no additional costs.

You can vary both the type of reinforcement (what) and the schedule (when). The knowledge to vary both will significantly raise the effectiveness of your performance improvement efforts.

5. **Be Consistent**:

A sense of fairness and justice, results from the consistency with which reinforcement is delivered. Inconsistent use of reinforcement creates disunity. Consistency does not mean not varying reinforcement. It means providing equality of reinforcement to different people or at different times. Just as parents teach values by consistently approving behavior, managers teach values by the consistency in their expressions of appreciation. By rewarding improvement consistently, members of the organization gain confidence in the values represented by that appreciation. With consistency come confidence and the elimination of fear. If employees can see that you are consistent in your approval or disapproval, they will come to trust that value.

Appreciation and Organizational Learning

Many improvement efforts have begun with a search for the guilty, to be followed by a good hanging, and a sigh of relief. In short order, it will be time to search again. Nothing systemic has changed. Most change efforts over the past few decades have been problem centered. The nature of change efforts both reflect the current culture, and have an impact on the subsequent culture. It is certainly desirable that a change process reflects the type of culture it is seeking to create. The way by which one goes about creating change, even at the outset of the process, will create and reinforce expectations. A search for the guilty obviously increases fear and reduces participation in that improvement. A positive approach does the opposite.

In the last few years, a new approach to change has emerged called *appreciative inquiry*. The method is entirely consistent with everything I have said above regarding the importance of appreciation, a positive approach, rather than a problem-centered approach. However, we should not dismiss the fact that many of these problem-centered methods improved much of our lives. The incredibly improved quality of our cars, appliances or computers is largely due to efforts to eliminate waste from processes and to reduce defects. So, before advocating a positive approach, I want to be clear that I appreciate all of the good that has come from previous approaches.

Appreciative inquiry is *"the study and exploration of what gives life to human systems when they function at their best. This approach to personal change and organization change is based on the assumption that questions and dialogue about strengths, successes, values, hopes and dreams are themselves transformational."*[43]

Just as the field of positive psychology has argued that more may be gained by studying those who are mentally and emotionally healthy, and focusing on strengthening those competencies and behavior that represent well-being, appreciative inquiry approach focuses on strengths and positive characteristics and seeks to increase those.

Some years ago, I participated in the development of a program for Met Life called *Achieving Personal Quality*. This series of videos and workbooks focused on effective models, examples of personal

---

[43] Whitney, Diana & Trosten-Bloom, Amanda. *The Power of Appreciative Inquiry: A Practical Guide to Positive Change.* San Francisco, Barrett-Koehler Publishers, Inc. 2003.

quality within Met Life. They video-taped interviews of individual Met Life employees who were examples of excellence or quality in their lives. The individuals represented many different functions and levels in the organization. I remember watching the video of a carpenter who worked in the maintenance area of the Met Life building. He spoke with great passion about his apprenticeship as a young boy in Italy with a cabinetmaker. With great emphasis, he distinguished between a "cabinet maker" and a carpenter. He emphasized the skill and attention to detail of a cabinetmaker, and one could tell by watching this how this cabinetmaker had instilled in his young apprentice the pride of workmanship. Met Life was not trying to train cabinetmakers. But observing and understanding this positive model, and discussing, meditating on the personal qualities of this individual and how those qualities might be important in your own life, was a powerful learning experience. Although at the time no one had ever used the term *appreciative inquiry*, this was an example of it. The inquiry focused on the personal performance of an effective individual, his qualities, and how these were achieved.

When Inquiry is Appreciated

Each of the two words, *Appreciation* and *Inquiry*, has important meaning. We have already discussed the power of appreciation, and the ways in which it can effectively change both personal habits and a culture. The word inquiry is important because it implies that the change agents, whether external consultants or internal change agents, are not presenting themselves as those who know the answers. Rather, it implies that through the process of asking questions, of shared discovery, all participants will learn and all will benefit.

The nature of questions is important. At the dinner table in the evening, a parent may ask her children "Have you done your homework yet?" I think we can all remember questions like that in which you felt as though the police were stopping you and asking, "Have any illegal drugs on you?" The question leaves an expectation that punishment may follow if the answer is wrong. Obviously, this creates fear and hesitancy. On the other hand, the parent may ask the question, "What interesting things were in your reading today?" This question has two very different effects. First, it does not imply a judgment and does not induce the fear of punishment. In fact, it makes a positive assumption, the assumption that you have read something and that you will have found something interesting. Second, this is an "open-ended" question rather than a "closed-ended" question. It can't be answered yes or no. The son or daughter will answer with some more thoughtful answer, and that answer can lead to another question, and a positive affirmation. The child may say, "Well, I read in the newspaper about this change in the weather patterns." And the parent might reply with, "What are those different weather patterns?" Or, "What do you think are causing those changes?" After a series of inquiries and the child sharing his or her knowledge and opinions the parent my close the conversation by saying "I think it's great that you are interested in that. It is an important issue."

What has the parent done in this interaction that will have an influence on the child's behavior and learning? By inquiring positively, the parent has demonstrated his or her belief that the child is capable of thinking and reading about things that are important. This will increase the probability of similar reading in the future. The child will want to spend more time reading. The parent is instilling a value into reading and thinking about similar things. In fact, the parent is learning positive things about his or her child. At the same time, think of all the possible negative behaviors that may be reduced. To the degree that children are interested in reading and studying about things they learn, they do not have time for watching so much MTV! They are more likely to choose friends with similar interests and values. They are more likely to have good relationships with their teachers. There are all kinds of unintentional and secondary positive effects from this interaction.

The nature of inquiry is inseparable from the change process itself. What you ask and how you ask it, even in a very preliminary stage of a change process, may determine its outcome. If a process of improvement begins by exploring those things that individuals and organizations do well, those good characteristics will spread like a virus.

How to Begin a Process of Appreciative inquiry

Appreciative inquiry begins with choosing an "affirmative topic," one that lends itself to an exploration of positive qualities. The Met Life program of Achieving Personal Quality began with an inquiry into "what does personal excellence or personal quality look like at Met Life?"

I studied the dozen most successful salesmen selling Mack Trucks and asked the question "to what characteristics or behavior do the best salesmen attribute their success." We interviewed and video taped these salesmen and presented a summary of The Habits of Highly Successful Sales Professionals at Mack Trucks as a video to all eight hundred salesmen and women. This served to reinforce those qualities in the sales force as a group.

In the course of my work with Honda America Manufacturing, they used the metaphor of the "The Racing Spirit." This was particularly appropriate since Honda was successfully involved in several different types of racing. The Racing Spirit was promoted throughout the company with a set of principles and the inquiry, "how can you apply the racing spirit in your work area?" Examples of the racing spirit were discussed, which led to a continuous process and thinking about speed of teamwork, cycle times, and the rate of improvement – all very analogous to how you win races. Imagine the difference when the focus is on exploring this kind of affirmative topic, rather than the search for ways to "cut costs," or "eliminate quality problems."

In the second part of the book, I will share a process for improving organization performance that will include elements of appreciative inquiry as well as other techniques. However, here are a few of the basic steps that distinguish appreciative inquiry and that are worth pointing out here. The purpose of this process is to design the ideal future of the organization by looking at what *is* and what *could be*.

Generally, there is a steering team of senior managers who provide a mandate for the process, and a design team of employees who spend the time and effort to work through the design and develop a set of recommendations for the future.

After identifying an affirmative topic, there are generally four steps to the process. These are *Discover*, appreciating what is; *Dream*, imagining what might be; *Design*, determining what should be; and

Develop, creating what will be. These four steps are similar to steps in other change processes; however, they are all shaped by the underlying values of Appreciative inquiry.

Discovery involves as many members of the organization as possible. Consultants may facilitate and guide the process; however, when you recognize that the act of asking questions changes both the person asking and the person answering, the involvement of internal managers and employees is essential. The purpose of *Discovery* is to search for best practices, best characteristics, best processes or anything that has led in the past or is currently resulting in success. No matter how many problems an organization confronts, there are examples of strength within from which greater strength can be built.

Discovery is the search of examples of high performance both within and outside the organization. I have always encouraged clients to look outside their own organization for best practices. It is even useful to look at companies that are entirely different from your own to find best practices. For example, a corporation might look carefully at the U.S. Army's training and development practices in order to find ideas that could be incorporated into their own training and development. Many companies looked at Federal Express and found ideas that could be integrated into their own efforts to speed cycle times, although these companies were not in the shipping business. Don't look at another company with the assumption that you want to be like them; rather, examine what they do best, and ask "what are the lessons we learned that might be applied to our work?"

The **Dream** stage is an opportunity to brainstorm and imagine the *ideal state*. Asking a person or a group, "If you had a magic wand, and you could make any changes you want in order to create the ideal process or culture, what would that ideal look like?" After having engaged in the discovery process, many of the ideas that were discovered will now be reflected in the ideal state.

One of the difficulties of imagining an ideal state is that most of us, after years immersed in organization life, have become very practical. Skeptical is probably a more accurate description. We are more comfortable when imagining small changes, changes that are likely, rather than imagining an ideal that may involve a major change. My consultants and I have facilitated many dozens of organization change processes in which a design team was assigned to go through these stages and design an ideal process and other systems of the organization.

When facilitating a group who are engaged in the process of imagining an ideal, it is very helpful to review and have a very clear understanding of the organization's purpose; its values; and its business strategy. All of these condition the ideal. The search for the ideal state must be based on an ideal for customers. It may also be a search for the ideal place to work.

The **Design** stage is where the current state *discovery*, and the ideal state *dream* come together to form a specific proposal or design for the future organization. This design can be done in a design team, or in a search conference, or some combination of both. Our experience is that in a large conference, many great design ideas can be generated and enthusiasm created, but a small design team is the best place to work out the details of the proposed future state.

This design will generally include a process analysis of the current core-work process; and a design of the future work process; and then, a design of the enabling systems in the organization. The enabling systems are the information systems, the training and human resource systems, financial information and any other systems or processes that enable the core work process. The design of the future core-work process comes first because that will determine the information needs, training needs, etc.

The **Develop** stage is a process of building action and commitment to move the organization toward fulfillment of the new design. Generally, a steering team of senior managers will review and give general approval to move forward with the new design. It is best that the implementation process be as participatory as possible, and involve as many, perhaps all the members of the organization. However, there will be times when senior management approval is required. Some designs in which I have been involved included moving around all of the equipment of a manufacturing facility, getting rid of some equipment and buying new equipment. Millions of dollars in capital expense were required to implement the ideal state as it was proposed. This may also have required a certain sequencing of implementation steps.

To the degree possible, involving everyone in the planning of implementation greatly speeds the process. Without any direct instructions, employees will start doing things on their own that are consistent with the ideal state design. If they are not involved and are surprised by the design, there is a natural tendency to resist the change.

It is not my recommendation that Appreciative inquiry be employed as a single method for improvement in the organization. My experience says that it works best when incorporated into a process of what I call Whole-System Design, as well as quality management and building the lean team-based organization. Every organization is different and there is no one right plan that can simply be copied from one organization to another. Some judgment and wisdom is required for the best results. But, there is no doubt that an approach to change, whether with individuals or with organizations, is best when it is approached with a strong dose of appreciation for what has come before and the efforts of those in the organization.

Appreciation is not dependent on any formal process. The above description is a formal process by which appreciation can be incorporated into a process of large-scale organization improvement. However, the more important thing is to incorporate appreciation into our daily way of life at work (and at home!). The most important appreciation is that which is serendipitous, the unplanned and spontaneous expression of appreciation. Sincerity, authenticity, in expressing appreciation is an important competence of any leader or manager.

Personal Appreciation:

Personal Action Agenda	I do	I don't	I will
1. I have identified some behavior I wish to learn and I am seeking training or education to learn this skill or knowledge.			
2. I have pinpointed behavior that I would like to improve and that will contribute to my achieving my goals.			
3. I am recording the frequency of the behavior I want to improve.			
4. I have identified reinforcing events that I make contingent (if-then) on the performance of this behavior.			
5. I am appreciating approximations (shaping) the behavior I want to encourage.			
6. I have planned both immediate and longer range rewards that will come from this performance.			
7. The planned reinforcement is personalized to my interests.			
8. I am effective at managing my own performance.			

Summary of what I will do to increase my expression of appreciation:

Team Appreciation:

Team Action Agenda	We do	We don't	We will
1. My team has analyzed its performance and we have identified some behavior we wish to learn.			
2. We have pinpointed behavior that we would like to improve and that will contribute to achieving our goals.			
3. We have looked for positive examples of this performance that we can appreciate in others.			
4. We are recording the frequency of this behavior, or its results in performance.			
5. We have identified reinforcing events that we have made contingent (if-then) on the performance of this behavior.			
6. We are appreciating approximations to the behavior we want to encourage.			
7. We have planned both short-term reinforcement and longer range rewards that will come from this performance.			
8. The planned reinforcement is personalized to our interests.			
9. We are effective at managing our own performance.			
Summary of what we agree to do to improve performance on our team:			

Appreciation in the Organization:

Organization Action Agenda	We do	We don't	We will
1. The desired performances in this organization are systematically reinforced.			
2. The reinforcement systems provide for both immediate and long-term reinforcement.			
3. When objectives or goals are established the accomplishment of those goals results in recognition or some other reward.			
4. Some part of the compensation system is designed to reward successful performance to clear objectives.			
5. We have a culture in which there is more expectation of reward than fear of punishment.			
6. There is a process by which we seek out positive examples to appreciate and from which we can learn.			
7. We seek positive examples both within the organization and from external sources.			
8. Effort, improvement, and progress toward learning and achieving high performance is rewarded (shaping), not only final performance.			
9. I believe that members of the organization are rewarded in a consistent, fair, manner.			

Summary of what we agree to do to improve appreciation throughout the organization:

Chapter 8

When Work Becomes a Game
The Currency of Scorekeeping

"It doesn't matter who scores the points, it's who can get the ball to the scorer.." Larry Bird

Keeping score, taking a count, must be the oldest of all practices of management. Everything that works is not new, and is usually old. Why then is it included as a currency of the new capitalism? There are three answers.

First, one of the reasons organizations are so focused on financial capital and financial accounting, is because it is obviously the easiest thing to account for. And, because money is, in the perception of many, the final result of the entire process of business, there is a great deal of motivation to keep account of money. Having managed my own business for many years, I fully appreciate the desire to know how much money is coming in, going out, and will remain after the bottom line. None of the comments that follow are intended to in any way diminish the importance and need for financial accounting.

If we accept that the future of an organization is also determined by other forms of capital, and if we want to generate effort to increase social and human capital, for example, we will have to develop some form of scorekeeping that reflect, even imperfectly, the degree to which we possess those forms of capital. Do I intend to present an accounting system for these forms of capital? No. Others have attempted to present methods of accounting for human capital, but these have not been widely adopted.[44] This would not only require another entire volume, it is a task I do not feel confident doing. I do not believe anyone, at this point in time has the tools to develop a reliable system of measurement for each of the five forms of capital. That does not mean the reader should not attempt to find ways to account for these assets.

Our culture, particularly our business culture, ascribes a validation to those things that can be accounted for on a scorecard and displayed on a graph. But, we should distinguish our own conditioned response, from our ability to make judgments about those things which are important.

When we raise our children, we know that the degree to which they develop moral judgment and social skills, for example, will be important factors in their success in life. These issues of character will be more important than whether they remember the date of the Treaty of Paris or the functions of calculus. Yet, we have probably never asked, how do we measure moral judgment or social skills? We react to reinforce specific instances of good or bad moral judgment and we show approval when they display social skills, despite the absence of accounting. The same should be true in our organizations.

There are ways to measure other forms of capital, although very little has been done to apply these to corporations or other organizations. Francis Fukuyama has written on the subject of measuring social capital and has presented a number of metrics that can be applied to a larger society. He also suggests that social and human capital can be measured by the differential in market capitalization of a company relative to financial assets.[45] This, however, is not particularly useful in the management of a firm. It is far too encompassing to point to any useful action. It will be more useful to break social capital down into its component parts and measure those.

---

[44] Fitz-enz. Jac. The ROI of Human Capital: Measuring the Economic Value of Employee Performance. New York, AMACOM, 2000.

[45] Fukuyama, Francis. Social Capital and Civil Society, Institute of Public Policy, paper presented October 1, 1999 to the International Monetary Fund.

In Chapter 11, I have defined social capital as the quality of both internal and external relations: internally the degree of trust and sociability; externally the market capital or brand equity. Each of these can be defined and measured by their specific components. The challenges of measuring spiritual capital are even more difficult and some have made the mistake, in my opinion of confusing the issue by equating membership in a religious group with spirituality.[46]

For each of the five forms of capital, in Chapter 11, 12, and 13, I have proposed *critical success indicators* for the organization, team and individual. It is my hope that these will be a useful starting point for developing measures; or, more simply, for the discussion, reflection and judgment that will lead to action to improve in each of these areas.

A second reason to include scorekeeping as a currency of the new capitalism is linked to the concept of *broad-slicing* discussed in the first chapter. The three levels of broad-slicing each serve to unite energy and effort in the organization toward common strategic purpose. The strength of that energy and the direction toward which energy is exerted are directly linked to the nature of scorekeeping. This is particularly true at the second and third levels – strategy and process.

Each unit of an organization should include on its scorecard measures of progress toward common strategic goals. If a strategic goal is to achieve x position in a given market, that goal and the celebration of success toward that goal, will serve to unite effort across units of the organization.

Process measures, particularly the cycle-time of product development through to delivery to end use customers, serves to focus energy in a way that is unifying. If members of the organization are only focused on process measures within the boundaries of their unit of the organization, it is likely that they will not optimize the flow-through to other units.

The third reason to include scorekeeping as a currency of the new economy is the importance of scorekeeping in human motivation.

---

[46] See the Spiritual Capital Research Program funded by the Tempelton Foundation. http://www.metanexus.net/spiritual_capital/index.asp.

Since the development of all forms of capital requires human motivation, the absence of effective scorekeeping would lead to failure. Despite the long experience in the use of measurement in organizations, we are still not very good at understanding how scorekeeping affects human performance.

So you are about to land from Mars, or from some more exotic extra-terrestrial homeland. As your ship descends, you scout around for a good landing site and find an area of relatively flat low cut grass, and although occasionally marked by sand pits, it appears they can be avoided. Your telescope detects people walking around the landing site, sometimes in small motor driven carts. They carry sticks and appear to be waving them at little balls they have just placed on the ground, hitting them toward small holes and occasionally they succeed and the ball disappears in the hole. Like little children, they wave their hands in the air or they may slam their sticks into the ground.

Since it is your mission to study these humanoids, their work and their motivation, you are curious why they seem to be so diligently engaged in such monotonous a task. It must have some productive purpose, perhaps the balls multiply in the ground, or somehow transform so they become valuable in some way.

As you get closer, you notice that many of these workers are hot and perspiring, and even when rain appears they continue working through the rain. Your understanding of work and motivation on this planet, tells you that workers must do work that is very interesting, requiring great mental activity, *or* they must be well paid. This work certainly appears to involve little mental activity since it is so simple and repetitious. Therefore, you assume they must be well paid. You also assume these workers must be at the very lowest end of the intelligence and income scale.

When your ship lands, you capture a few of these workers and interrogate them. You are dumbfounded to discover that they are not paid at all, even though they confess that no great mental activity is required to do this job and they are often tired and frustrated, sometimes causing them to use words they call "swearing," a clear sign that they are angry. You wonder why they would do something that makes them angry so often, with no pay. You are even more bewildered when you discover that they actually must pay with their money to do this, and they do this in addition to their regular job, and some of them have very good regular jobs! When you ask them about their motivation, they stumble and appear confused, but mumble something about enjoying their friend's company and being outdoors. It seems to you that they could accomplish the same, swearing a lot less, by sitting on their back porch. You conclude that humans are even stranger than you first expected. You now think that your briefing on humanoid motivation must not have been accurate. You will file a report on this when you get back.

Of course, you say golf is a game and not work. Yet, it looks a lot like work. In fact many things we do on our own time, most hobbies (gardening, woodwork, sewing) look a lot like work and would no doubt confuse our aliens. What is the difference between golf and work? Almost any job, even the simplest, presents more intellectual challenges than walking around a field hitting a ball in a hole. Obviously, it is not the material reward system because there is none.

Quick, Get the Computer and Destroy Golf!

Imagine now that golf is a business. Perhaps your corporation has acquired golf. And now you want to implement modern management practice to improve efficiency and accountability. The workers will no longer be allowed to carry scorecards, which we have good reason to believe are unreliable, and we place great value in reliability. A computer will be purchased and sensors placed in each cup, signals will be sent from the balls to the sensors indicating how many times they were hit by the sticks. Then the computer will be able to add up, reliably, how many times each worker hit the ball. It is important that this information be analyzed properly so the workers performance can be properly judged. We, therefore, hire a manager to take responsibility for this analysis. The manager now will be able to evaluate and motivate the workers properly by occasionally giving them words of encouragement and by an annual performance review. He will also set goals for each worker so they have clear expectations.

And, what will be the result of this new system of computerized measurement and management? The effect will be that no one will play the game, unless of course, you pay the players well. Now it is work. Imagine the costs of the manager, the computer, compensation, hiring costs, etc.

Keeping score on our own performance creates ownership and personal responsibility. The score, the work, the decisions, are all our own. This connection "keeps it together" for us – a unified logic to the activity from which we derive pleasure. We pay and play for the pleasure, which comes from this connection. The moment the connection is broken, the moment you don't keep score while someone else does, you don't own the work, it is not your game, and you don't derive the same pleasure. In so many work settings, we have destroyed the natural motivation by breaking up this internal unity.

It is true that the scorekeeping on the golf course is not reliable. You cannot trust the crummy little scorecards that the workers carry in their back pockets, because they do sometimes cheat! But is reliability the most important thing? Or is motivation more important.

Scorekeeping is the System of Motivation

Dr. Deming used to say that when he visited a manufacturing plant he wanted to see graphs posted and he wanted to see the workers dirty fingerprints on the graph. No fingerprints – no good! Why? He wanted to know that those doing the work were literally in touch with the results of their work, their score. Many thought this was a simplistic and foolish idea, but perhaps Dr. Deming understood the same common sense that golfers understand.

Scorekeeping is also a system that creates unity in groups. Imagine the scoreboard at a basketball or football game – everyone watches it, everyone cheers when it changes, and without it there would be no fans in the stands. What is the magic of the scoreboard? If you understand this then you understand how to create great scorekeeping systems at work. Something about the way we are internally wired causes us to derive great pleasure in seeing the numbers change; watching the ball go through the hoop; everyone cheers; then their eyes turn to the scoreboard and they are pleased with the change in score. The entire process helps to bond the team and fans together.

Even those who have no reason to motivate others, but only to motivate themselves, create scorekeeping systems. As the lonely runners – those who are able to maintain this behavior for years, almost all have established a scorekeeping system that keeps them going. Minutes per mile; miles per day, week and month; pulse rate after one or five miles. There are dozens of ways to keep score and those who maintain their motivation, maintain a scorekeeping system. It is the single most obvious essence of self-management.

Even writers keep score. Ernest Hemingway measured the number of words he wrote per day. Only after completing an acceptable number of words in the morning did he allow himself to go deep-sea fishing in the afternoon. Scorekeeping is not something for only those who do production work. The principle of good scorekeeping applies to all human beings, in every culture. It is why sports can be found in every culture. There is intrinsic pleasure in scorekeeping.

Scorekeeping has gone through numerous iterations and fads. From the management-by-objectives of the 1950's and 60's to the current statistical standards of quality, there have been numerous techniques that have derived much of their power from the simple impact of feedback and knowledge of performance. The famous Hawthorne studies of Elton Mayo, which were purported to have demonstrated the effect of simply paying attention to workers, actually demonstrated the impact of knowledge of performance and giving a team ownership of their work and their results.[47] The results that have been achieved from Total Quality Management, statistical process control, or Six Sigma are not only the result of computing statistic. The majority of the effect is the feedback effect and it comes from the simple practice of creating systematic scorekeeping.

How to Design the Game of Business Success

Every business manager is driven by the "game" of business, watching scores such as sales, costs and performance relative to the competition. In many ways owning a company, being a business

---

[47] Parsons, H. M. (1992). Hawthorne: An early OBM experiment. Journal of Organizational Behavior Management, 12(1), 27–43

manager, is fun. It is fun, not because of the actual work, but because of the game aspect, the scoreboard, the wins and losses. Why can't every employee experience the same joy of the game? They can. The purpose of *team management* is to create the structure by which every individual in the organization has the opportunity to play the business game.

Here are the keys to scorekeeping that will create the game:

1. Immediacy and Frequency:

It is as simple as tampering with the scoreboard in any sport. Delay how long it takes to change the scoreboard. In basketball, the fans look up at the scoreboard and expect to see a change in one to three seconds after the ball goes through the hoop. In baseball, perhaps because they don't score that often, they have from two to ten seconds. After that amount of time, in either sport, the fans get itchy and may start to show their frustration. If it took an hour to get the score up on the board, how would the fans and players feel? Quickly they would loose motivation and would not show up for the game. How long do your employees, or team members wait? The speed and frequency of feedback both increase motivation and increase the effect of a shared experience, and bonding.

Almost every organization can improve motivation simply by increasing the rate and frequency of feedback. In most organizations, the only reason why feedback is delayed is that no one has worked at creating a frequent and immediate feedback system. Investors watch the "real time" ticker and graphs of their investments as they change by the minute or second. With computer technology, creating this kind of feedback is not difficult; we simply need to determine to do it.

Some may fear that this kind of feedback will cause employees to loss sight of longer-term goals and may be distracted by random fluctuations in data. It is for this reason that all feedback systems should not overly focus on one variable, but should present a data array, five to eight variables that vary in type of data and frequency.

2. Variety:

Of course, not all scores can be delivered in seconds. Some scores (monthly sales, quarterly financials) can only be computed in much longer cycles. This is also true in sports. Sit and watch baseball with a pad of paper in your hand. Write down every type of score that is mentioned and its time frame. Note whether it is for an individual or the team. You will notice that there are probably a hundred different types of scores mentioned during a game. Some are annual or career numbers (earned run average over years or career; annual batting average and current batting average, etc.) and many other scores are for that day's game. This is characteristic of all effective motivational systems. Design your scorekeeping system to include individual and team, short and long range, scores. But, be sure that the information is delivered as quickly as possible to those who perform. Remember, it is not just the fans in the stand (stockholders, analysts, management) that need the information; it is those on the playing field.

3. Visibility

The United Way gets it. Big thermometer graphs, right at the entrance to the building where you cannot possibly miss it. And every day as you pass it, you don't know why, but you get some little satisfaction in seeing it move up toward its goal. United Way understands the power of good scorekeeping – or good feedback systems.

Visiting the Honda America Manufacturing plant for the first time about ten or twelve years ago, I noticed the complete lack of artwork on the walls. Just as well – there was little room on the walls for artwork – they were almost all covered with charts and graphs! They know feedback systems. We think about what we see. We see data, we think about data. We see our scores going up; we react to those scores going up, or down!

Beginning in the early 1970's I was involved in implementing behavior change and performance improvement programs in manufacturing plants. The idea of graphing and charting performance, visually displaying the ups and downs of a team's performance was a new thing in most manufacturing plants. Virtually every time performance, and variations in it, was visually graphed for a team to see, and understand, performance improved. It is the "no-brainer" of performance improvement. Blitz almost any group with feedback and performance will improve. Simplistic? Yes, but effective. Everything that works does not have to be complicated.

Providing graphic feedback has advanced in recent years with the addition of web based graphics and reporting. Root Learning[48] has done a particularly excellent job of creating highly attractive graphics of work processes, particularly the core process through an organization and then linking the graphic presentation to financial reporting data, enabling employees to understand visually where the money comes from and where it is going.

4. Ownership

We are excited by a change in numbers when we feel those numbers are for "my team," when we have ownership of that performance, even if it isn't a direct reflection of our own performance. We don't have to be the athlete, but we do have to feel that it is *our team*. And, if we are the athlete, the one performing, we bloody well want measures of our performance, and not someone else's.

Several years ago, my consultants and I were implementing a team process at Eastman Chemicals in Kingsport, Tennessee. I remember vividly a discussion with a department manager. We suggested that financial information should be shared with all of the employees. We asked him to share information so the employees could take responsibility for their contribution to business performance. The department manager thought that was ridiculous. He said with great authority, "You don't understand these people. These people don't care about that information. They work here just to get their paycheck and go home. In fact, you ought to know that most of them consider this their second job."

This was puzzling since this "second job" was eight hours a day at least five days a week. I asked, "So what do they consider their first job, if this is their second job?"

He replied, "Well, most of them have their own farms, or some other business. That's what they really care about."

---

[48] Note: See www.rootlearning.com to see their visual presentation of processes and financial data.

This raised a disturbing question, "What causes these employees to feel more motivation about their own farms or small company then working at Eastman Chemicals?"

That led me to ask this department manager, "Do you think they look at the income or revenue numbers at their first job?"

"Of course, most of them do their own accounting. They know exactly how well they are doing," he replied.

"Do you think they talk to their customers and are concerned about their satisfaction?" I asked.

"Of course, they make darn sure they can sell their produce or product, it's their business."

So these same employees who consider this their "second job" don't care about the numbers and just want to collect their paycheck and go home. But in their first job, they run the business, do the accounting; take responsibility for sales, marketing, quality management, process improvement and everything else that goes into running a business. This only proves that most often motivation is not simply in the person, but is in the system that surrounds the person.

Hundreds, if not thousands of times I have seen the person change from someone who "just wants a paycheck" to someone who feels and acts like a business owner and manager, not because they received a personality transplant, but because of relatively simple changes in the nature of the system that surrounds them. The essence of that change has always been giving them genuine responsibility for managing a piece of the business, with the information on *their business*, the authority to make decisions, and the accountability for performance inherent in the assumption of being a business manager.

Imagine any environment in which individuals or teams put forth maximum effort, achieve maximum results, and have fun while they are at it. Inevitably, there will be extremely clear scorekeeping, immediate feedback and visual display of the score.

5. Balanced

We have come a long way. There was a time when some managers felt that the only thing that mattered were financial results. Those who wanted to elevate the importance of quality measures, customer satisfaction, or the performance of processes had to do battle (and usually lost!) with the financial types.

Two things have worked to alter the view of most managers today. The first is the surge by Japanese car companies and the adoption of the quest for quality by most major U.S. corporations. These have elevated the understanding of quality and process measures. Almost all managers understand that the way to achieve financial performance is through effective processes and quality. The second is the book by Kaplan & Norton[49] that promoted the idea of a balanced scorecard, which was popular and succeeded in arguing for a system of balanced measures in the organization.

There is nothing complicated about creating a balanced scorecard, the value is more in the process then the "thing". Kaplan and Norton emphasize that their model and definition of a balanced scorecard is not something fixed in stone, but a proposal that they expect others to modify, adapt, and evolve with their own needs and experience.

Any scorekeeping process should enhance learning. When developing a scorekeeping process, the team should identify those questions that will lead to learning and development. For an athletic team, for example, they might ask, "How many seconds does the quarterback take to release the ball? How many seconds does it take the receivers to run the twenty yard dash down field?" The answers to these questions will provide the specific feedback that will promote learning. Learning will not result from looking at the team score at the end of the game. The learning will come from the components of team performance.

At work, both people and processes should be developed as a result of the scorekeeping process. However, in order to develop people and processes, there must be a plan, a process of improvement. Teams must be formed to own processes and those teams must have and understand the scores, and engage in regular problem solving to find ways to improve the process. They must also look at how their own skills and knowledge affects their performance. Questions such as

---

[49] Kaplan, Robert S., Norton, David P. *The Balanced Scorecard: Translating Strategy into Action.* Harvard Business School Press, Boston, 1997.

- why are customers not satisfied, what can we do to improve that satisfaction, and what skills do we lack – must be the subject of open dialogue within the team as they review their scorecard. When does this conversation take place? Who is having this conversation? Whose job is it to find the answers? The answers to these questions must be designed into the regular management process or system of the organization.

It isn't the purpose of this book to go into great detail about building a balanced scorecard, however, your team should consult together on the three categories of scores and be sure that you have at least two scores in each category. You should have two scores that reflect, as directly as possible, customer satisfaction. You should have two scores that reflect the quality, productivity, costs and speed of your work processes. And, you should have at least two financial measures that may include revenue growth, costs and return on assets.

If you take these measures and be sure that they are visible, immediate and frequent, you will have a pretty good scorekeeping system. Be sure to develop a systematic plan for developing processes and people based on a scorecard that is immediate and frequent, is visible, and includes a variety of balanced measures.

Creating Personal Scorekeeping:

Personal Action Agenda	I do	I don't	I will
1. I have personal measures of my own performance.			
2. I have measures that I graph so they are visible and I can easily see my progress (or lack of it).			
3. I review my personal performance measures to see how I can improve.			
4. I make plans for my own learning based on my own measures of my performance.			
5. I have personal financial measures that I review.			
6. I have measures of the work, the process for which I am responsible.			
7. I get feedback and review information from those who are my customers.			
8. I maintain my personal scorekeeping system on a regular basis.			

Summary of what I will do to improve my personal scorekeeping:

Creating Team Scorekeeping:

Team Action Agenda	We do	We don't	We will
1. My team has a scorekeeping system.			
2. We have a visual display that is our scoreboard, reflecting the four to eight key variables for our team.			
3. Some of these measures are updated immediately (within the day.)			
4. Some of these measures are weekly or monthly.			
5. We have financial measures for revenue, costs or return on the assets we employ.			
6. We have measures that reflect how well our process is performing – cycle time, quality, output/input (productivity).			
7. We have measures of customer satisfaction.			
8. We discuss and make plans to improve our process based on the measures we review.			
9. We discuss and make plans for improving our skills or knowledge based on the measures we review.			
Summary of what we agree to do to improve scorekeeping in our team:			

Creating Organizational Scorekeeping:

Organization Action Agenda	We do	We don't	We will
1. We have an organization wide balanced scorecard.			
2. We assure that associates have immediate measures of performance to which they contribute.			
3. We have visual scoreboards that reflect the performance of our organization toward its goals.			
4. We assure that measures are reviewed in order to improve the critical processes.			
5. We plan learning and development activities based on our review of our performance.			
6. We assure that all associates and managers review feedback and systematic scores from our customers.			
7. We share financial information so all members of our organization participate in understanding our financial performance.			
8. The measures of our processes include quality, productivity, speed and costs.			
9. Our score keeping system is maintained in a systematic manner.			
Summary of what we agree to do to improve scorekeeping throughout the organization:			

Chapter 9

The Habit of Process Thinking
The Currency of Flow

"If you can't describe what you are doing as a process, you don't know what you're doing." W. Edwards Deming

Among the five forms of capital that comprise the wealth of your organization is technology or *process capital*. When we worked on the family farm, every farmer had the same technology and employed the same process. There was no differentiation in value based on process or technology. Factories changed that. The big change was the development of mass production. Henry Ford gained a very significant competitive advantage by redefining the processes from those employed in craft shops to what became known as mass production. Mass production required new technologies, new equipment and methods. For the past one hundred years, work processes and technologies have increasingly been a form of competitive advantage and it is long past time we recognized these as assets of the firm.

This chapter is about the single most important discipline in developing process or technology capital. This is the ability to look horizontally through a process and create, what in human performance, is called *flow*.

High performing teams or individuals appear *natural* when their performance flows with the seemingly little effort. Athletes experience *flow*, or what they may call, "being in the zone." A musician may say she is in "the groove." Flow for an individual is complete focus, absorption in a task, when all energies move with ease and without interruption, and rather than feeling like great exertion, it feels natural and exhilarating. Mihaly Csikszentmihalyi described flow as the psychology of optimal experience. *"It is what the sailor holding a tight course feels when the wind whips through her hair, when the boat lunges through the waves like a colt – sail, hull, wind, and sea humming in a harmony that vibrates in the sailor's veins. It is what the painter feels when the colors on the canvas begin to set up a magnetic tension with each other, and a new thing, a living form, takes shape in front of the astonished creator."*[50]

If you have ever watched a great basketball team run the court with each player having perfect confidence in the other, looking one way and passing the ball another with certainty that the teammate will be there, and three quick passes around and over defenders ends in what looks like an effortless dunk through the hoop, you have observed flow.

This experience of flow is not a serendipitous surprise. The sailor has studied her course and angle to the wind, has set the right sail for the conditions, has practiced her hand on the tiller, and knows how her boat responds to this wind and these waves. The appearance of natural or effortless performance is the result of trained competence. The basketball team has practiced each motion a thousand times, knows that when it is two-on-one, or three-on-two, or whatever other combination, there are set patterns to run and each player trusts the other only because they have practiced this repeatedly. In each of these cases, the flow is a well-managed process, a series of steps that fit perfectly together and are acted out in perfect coordination. It is this studied combination of parts, which fit perfectly in a unified whole and their perfect execution creates the sense of flow.

Processes at work rarely provide a similar sense of exhilaration. Notice that processes that are exhilarating, that flow, are without interruption; have an efficiency of no unnecessary steps; and those who are engaged in the process are in control. Processes are a horizontal flow through the source of interruptions we call organization. In a high performance organization, the process controls

---

[50] Csikszentmihalyi, Mihaly. Flow: The Psychology of Optimal Experience. New York. Harper Perennial, 1990. p. 3.

the organization, not the other way around. Customers pay for the output of the process, not any artificial requirement of vertical approvals or orders issued *up the line*. Why shouldn't the organization be ordered to serve the needs of the flow of the process; to support and enable the process; rather than the other way around?

Death by Process!

Processes can kill you, and often do. I don't know how many coroners' reports have said "Death by Process" but many should have.

My consultants and I were working with a large healthcare provider and had been given the assignment to "re-engineer" the core process in the organization. Of course, the core process was providing health care solutions to individuals and insurance clients. A design team was formed to study the core process and develop an improved solution to eliminate many well-known problems. The seriousness of those problems was sometimes buried under the routine of daily work.

The design team, after several months of work analyzing the process and developing a solution, made a presentation to the senior Executive Committee that included the company President. Because they were about to propose some fairly radical solutions they were concerned that they get the executives' attention in a dramatic way. So, they dramatized a patient experience. They role-played a scenario in which one of their client members develops an unexplained stomach pain.

Her first stop is to her general practitioner and after filling out forms and sitting for an hour in the waiting room, she is told that she needs to see a specialist and is given a list of several specialists whom she could then call.

Of course, she has taken off from work for her appointment.

She goes home and gets on the phone. It will be a month before any of the specialists can see her. She makes an appointment.

She shows up a month later at the specialist's office. The specialist immediately tells her that he wants her to take a series of tests and she is referred to a clinic that provides the necessary tests. She calls and makes an appointment for two weeks later.

When she shows up at the clinic she is informed that she has to get pre-approval from her insurance provider before they can administer these tests.

She goes home and calls the insurance provider.

You get the picture. The story was detailed and frustrating just listening to it; let alone if you had to go through it. The story ends; after months of wrong appointments, delays, and re-routing, in the doctors office she finds out that she has cancer and the doctor informs her that treatment could have been much more successful if she had come in sooner. She dies. In effect, *the process* murdered her.

The leader of the design team, to lighten up the somewhat somber mood in the meeting with the executives said, "Of course that story may be a bit exaggerated. Perhaps we don't kill people, but people do suffer through our system."

With that the President of the company, a doctor and healthcare executive for many years, interrupts. "Excuse me, but there is nothing exaggerated about that. That was my mother! That is exactly what happened to my mother."

A long and tense silence followed as everyone tried to figure out how to respond to that revelation. The President broke the silence and said, "Well, let's fix it!" Not surprisingly, they approved implementation of the redesigned process.

Isn't it odd that we handle packages with more efficiency and care than we handle patients?

Lean Production is Optimum Flow

Managers today are a hundred times more aware of their processes than they were twenty years ago. Several crisis, trends and techniques have forced the managers' awareness and understanding. The most powerful of those is the pure economic, good old free enterprise necessity, of competing with Toyota and Honda and their suppliers. Ford, General Motors and Chrysler are all implementing a version of the *Toyota Production System* [51], or what some prefer to call, *Lean Manufacturing.* [52] There are many aspects to this, including a major cultural shift, a redefinition of who makes decisions, and how we view employees, customers and suppliers. However, all of these changes center on the unified flow of the process.

Lean Production, the Theory of Constraints [53], re-engineering, Six-Sigma and Total Quality Management all seek improvement by redefining work processes to eliminate the cause of variations (defects), reduce waste, friction, cycle-time and costs in the process. I fear that of the packaging of these programs managers have come to see these as different things. They are not different things. You have one core work process. If you apply lean production thinking, re-engineering, apply the Theory of Constraints, and continuously improve the process with Six-Sigma or TQM, you will be doing the same things, with slight differences in thinking or language (mostly language).

Process thinking becomes a way of life. Process thinking is learning to look horizontally through the organization as work flows. Those who are trained in lean processes can walk through a work setting and immediately see piles that signify process delays, interruptions in the form of pallets or in-boxes on the desk, or hear questions about "who owns the problem" all of which indicate process problems. You should work on developing your automatic, habitual thoughts about process. Developing this competence will serve you well. Some people don't have a good sense of the process.

This Darwin Award presents a clear case for the need of a sense of process (and a sense of humor!). This man was in an accident, so he filled out an insurance claim. The insurance company contacted him and asked for more information. This was his response:

---

[51] Liker, Jeffrey K. The Toyota Way – 14 Management Principles from The World's Greatest Manufacturer. New York, McGraw-Hill. 2004.
[52] Womack, James P., et al. *The Machine That Changed the World.* New York, Rawson Associates, 1990.
[53] Goldratt, Eliyahu M. *The Goal*, Great Barrington, MA: North River Press, 1984.

"I am writing in response to your request for additional information, for block number 3 of the accident reporting form. I put 'poor planning' as the cause of my accident. You said in your letter that I should explain more fully and I trust the following detail will be sufficient. I am an amateur radio operator and on the day of the accident, I was working alone on the top section of my new 80-foot tower. When I had completed my work, I discovered that I had, over the course of several trips up the tower, brought up about 300 pounds of tools and spare hardware. Rather than carry the now unneeded tools and material down by hand, I decided to lower the items down in a small barrel by using the pulley attached to the gin pole at the top of the tower. Securing the rope at ground level, I went to the top of the tower and loaded the tools and material into the barrel. Then I went back to the ground and untied the rope, holding it tightly to ensure a slow decent of the 300 pounds of tools.

"You will note in block number 11 of the accident reporting form that I weigh only 155 pounds. Due to my surprise of being jerked off the ground so suddenly, I lost my presence of mind and forgot to let go of the rope. Needless to say, I proceeded at a rather rapid rate of speed up the side of the tower. In the vicinity of the 40-foot level, I met the barrel coming down. This explains my fractured skull and broken collarbone. Slowed only slightly, I continued my rapid ascent, not stopping until the fingers of my right hand were two knuckles deep into the pulley. Fortunately, by this time, I had regained my presence of mind and was able to hold onto the rope in spite of my pain. At approximately the same time, however, the barrel of tools hit the ground and the bottom fell out of the barrel.

"Devoid of the weight of the tools, the barrel now weighed approximately 20 pounds. I refer you again to my weight in block number 11. As you might imagine, I began a rapid descent down the side of the tower. In the vicinity of the 40-foot level, I met the barrel coming up. This accounts for the two fractured ankles, and the lacerations of my legs and lower body. The encounter with the barrel slowed me enough to lessen *my injuries when I fell onto the pile of tools and, fortunately, only three vertebrae were cracked.*

"I am sorry to report, however, that as I lay there on the tools, in pain, unable to stand and watching the empty barrel 80 feet above me, I again lost my presence of mind. I let go of the rope and the barrel began its rapid descent..."[54]

I suppose this incident can be recorded as another case in which a bad process was almost lethal. Deficient processes have been lethal to many corporations and products, and often because the managers didn't have any more sense of process than our friend above.

How to Turn Processes into Flow

This writer has been involved in improving processes; both macro and micro, for many years and there are a few practices that very consistently lead to optimum flow-through. These are the essence of what works.

1. Focus on the Core Process

Before diving into details of improving cycle time or other goals, one should ask the most fundamental of all questions: "What business are we in?" This business definition should determine the *core work process*, required *capabilities* of that process, and the *core competencies* that are required to excel in that process. Too many organizations spend a great deal of time and effort improving processes that they should eliminate entirely. Whenever a process is not a core process, two questions should be asked; first, "is this process essential to enabling the core process?" and; second, "should we do this at all?" In many cases in is far better to contract with someone who is expert in that process, rather than spending your energies trying to improve something that is not your core competence.

---

[54] See www.darwinawards.com/legends/.

178 *Competing in the New Capitalism*

If you imagine two restaurants, a business we all understand, you may be able to imagine the core work process, the capabilities of that process, and the core competencies required. Imagine a fine French restaurant with a highly paid French chef, which has only a dozen tables and with an average meal price, around one hundred dollars. Now imagine your favorite fast food restaurant. Think about the work process, which begins as the customer walks in the door and ends when the customer walks out the door. Imagine the different steps in the process. Now imagine the capabilities this process requires. Now imagine the human competencies, the skills and knowledge of the participants. You can easily see that these two restaurants are in entirely different businesses. Customers come to them for entirely different reasons, with different requirements, and will be satisfied by entirely different types of performance. Everything about the process is conditioned by those customer requirements. Both may be equally successful, they may make the same amount of money, but they are in very different businesses.

Core and Enabling Business Processes

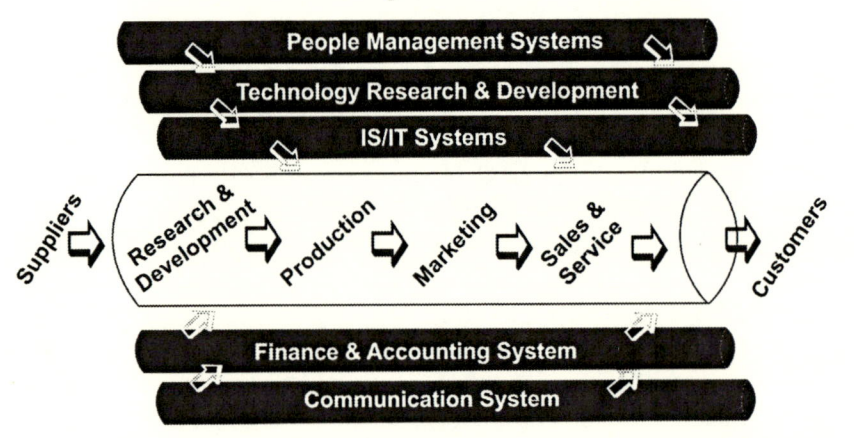

People Management Systems
Technology Research & Development
IS/IT Systems

Suppliers → Research & Development → Production → Marketing → Sales & Service → Customers

Finance & Accounting System
Communication System

Many companies that we think make a product, such as Apple Computer, do little manufacturing. They are not a manufacturing company. Their core process is software development, technology innovation, product design and marketing – not manufacturing. It is a general rule that higher gross margins are assigned to work that has higher intellectual property value. If a company can migrate up the intellectual property chain, from making things to engineering, to software design or marketing innovation, they will return more value to their shareholders relative to financial assets. In other words, the greater the human and technology capital employed, the greater the return on financial assets.

It is, therefore, important to ask, "How do we allocate our investment capital and are we doing it to maximize value to shareholders?" This can help clarify which are the core processes of *your* company.

Generally, the core process is the process that causes customers to write you a check. The core process produces the revenue and the revenue should pull the process through the system of the organization; or, the process should be designed to maximize revenue flow, and maximize customer satisfaction, while minimizing costs. Obstacles, detours, constraints, interruptions and waste in the process should be eliminated.

We have to do some things that are not our core processes. Accounting, for example; managing and developing human resources; managing information systems. These are necessary, but they are not core for most companies. They are *enabling*; they enable the core process. They are valuable to the degree that they enable the core process. Of course, your company may be an accounting firm, in which case accounting is your core process.

Why does it matter which processes are core and enabling? Because the flow through the core process is how you serve your customers, and how you make money. The priority is to optimize that process. That process becomes the customer; it sets the requirements for the enabling processes. In many companies, the tail is wagging the dog and core processes are forced to conform to the limitations or constraints of the enabling processes. Let the dog wag the tail!

2. Assign Process Owners

Who *owned* the process of caring for the cancer patient at the health care provider? Who felt bad and recognized that they didn't do their job when she died? In the original process no one did! And there is half of the problem. Fix this and you already have half of the solution to every other process problem!

Too often, and it is certainly the case in health care, individuals or teams feel ownership for only one narrow piece of the process. The clinic administering tests certainly felt responsible for that narrow function, but certainly not for the health of the patient. The insurance company has vested interest in the patient *not* seeking help, the sooner the patient dies, the better for the insurance company.

Working with a major oil company, my consultants were helping to design the organization that would be responsible for deep water drilling in the Gulf of Mexico. All organization design should begin with the core process. The organization should be structured for the purpose of optimizing the core process and you can't do that if you don't know what it is.

As the design team studied the process and sought to cut the cycle time, from beginning to end, from eight years to four, they recognized that no one owned or was responsible for the process from beginning to end. A piece of property would be leased, explored and a well drilled, then oil produced. But each step in the process was the responsibility of a different function in the organization. One group would do their work and it would then be handed off to the next, and sometimes recycled. They concluded that one of the big reasons for the eight-year cycle was the simple fact that no one was held accountable for how long it took. And, you could not hold anyone accountable if no one owned the whole process from beginning to end.

That process now takes less than half the time it did before the redesign. The two keys to this were the assignment of a "business team" who owned the project as an entrepreneur would own a new business. The second key was employing concurrent rather than consecutive process steps.

Walk through your core process as if you were the thing being made, or the patient or customer being served. Who is responsible for your experience? Who cares about the entire experience from beginning to end? Are they accountable for the quality and speed of that process? If you answer these questions you will have already gone a long way to improving the process.

3. Map It! You Don't Know It if You Can't See It

We are visual creatures. Most human beings understand pictures far more quickly and clearly than they do words or numbers. Every investor looks at graphs of stock price, revenues and earnings, rather than a long list of numbers. Similarly, a map of a process is a far more useful way to communicate and understand the process. This is the beginning of improvement. This book is not intended to be a workbook to provide detailed tools, so I will not attempt to describe all the different types of maps and mapping processes. However, just a couple simple illustrations: Mapping begins with understanding what the system of the organization looks like, from input to output. Some refer to this as SIPOC (Supplier, Input, Process, Output, and Customer).

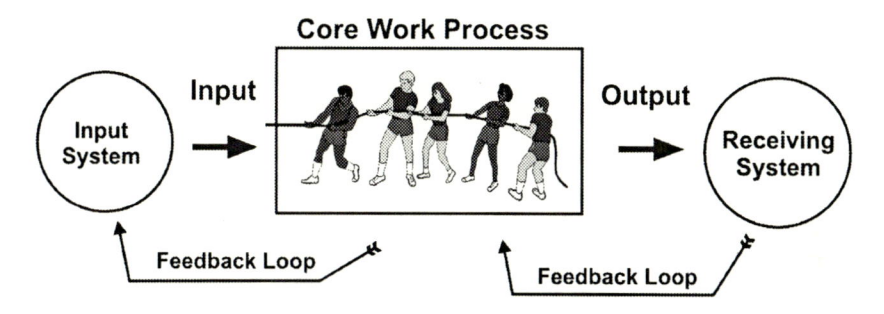

Core Work Process

Input System → Input → [Core Work Process] → Output → Receiving System

Feedback Loop

Feedback Loop

This map raises obvious questions that every process owner should be able to answer:
- What are the inputs into your work process (include materials, information, capital, people)? What are the requirements for each of these inputs?
- Who are the suppliers who provide input? What capabilities are needed on the part of suppliers in order to meet these requirements?
- What are the feedback loops from us to our suppliers and how do they function (speed, quality of information)?
- What are the outputs of your work system (include things, information, service, money, and people)?
- Who are the customers, and what are their requirements, which will satisfy their need for your output?
- Given the above, what are the requirements for your work process?
- What are the feedback loops that inform us of customer satisfaction and how do they function (speed, quality of information)?

This basic idea of a system applies to all work. An individual cooking a meal for someone else can be viewed this way. A university or university course can be viewed this way. And, every business, government department, or not-for-profit agency has the same key ingredients in its system. In my opinion, every manager should be familiar with the answers to these obvious questions.

Once you can answer the above, the next task is to map the work process and continuously improve that work process. There are many ways to do this, with varying degrees of detail. However, just one example – the following map is called a "relationship map" because it illustrates not only the chronological steps in a process, but also who the players are and what their roles are in the process.

Every work team should have a process map of how they do their work. Even senior management teams should have maps of their critical work. When coaching the senior management of one large corporation the annual strategic planning process came to the agenda. They started to talk about who would do it, what meetings would be held and so forth. They seemed to be making this process up on the spot, without considering how they had done it in the past. As the coach, I asked them how they had done it last year and were there any lessons they wanted to consider from that experience? They didn't remember how they did it last year; they only remembered that it didn't work very well.

We then went to the flip chart and started to a) map out last years process as best it could be remembered; b) identified the points of failure in that process; c) mapped out the ideal process for this year; and d) agreed to revisit the map after this years experience to identify improvement points for next year.

Even at the most senior levels of our organizations, some managers don't know how they do their work. As Dr. Deming said, *"If you can't describe what you are doing as a process, you don't know what you're doing."* Therefore, they are doomed to repeat their mistakes. Mapping the process is the beginning of improvement. If, as Dr. Deming has said, managers are responsible for the design of the system, managers are certainly responsible for the design of their own system of management work and decision-making. Most quality problems are system problems. Some of the worst work processes are those among managers and professionals.

4. Eliminate Waste:

For more than thirty years, Toyota has worked to improve the process of designing and building cars by focusing on the elimination of waste. They continually gain market share, are the most profitable car company in the world and are at the top of quality surveys. However, contrary to the understanding of many, the primary focus of improvement at Toyota has not been making more money or managing quality, although both have been the result. The primary driver for improvement at Toyota has been the elimination of waste. It is not cost reduction!

Most companies cut costs, usually meaning cutting people, and leave the waste. The waste is in the process, not the person. If you eliminate the waste in the process, you can then redeploy the person, and other assets, to "value-adding" work and thereby increase value to customers. That is how you make money. Company after company has gone out of business cutting costs, which results in worse products, worse service, fearful employees who loose their creativity, and the inevitable loss of customers. You stay in business by maximizing value to customers.

What is waste? Any activity that does not directly contribute to producing the product or service is probably waste. Warehouses do not directly contribute to productive work. Pallets, bins, empty space, any area where re-work is done, people who do re-work, unnecessary supervision, control and management are all waste.

One good exercise to think about eliminating waste is to play the "Win a Million" game. Assume it currently takes two weeks, for example, from the time materials come in at the beginning of a process, to the time the product is shipped to the customer. With a sample of the people who "play" in the process from the beginning to the end, ask, "If you could win a million dollars, could you complete this process, from beginning to end within twenty four hours?" There is usually an "Oh, that's impossible" first reaction. What they are actually saying is that "It is impossible the way we do things now." True enough. Now, consider how you would do it, if you could change anything and everything.

Soon enough you will find the group eliminating steps, combining tasks, doing tasks concurrently rather than consecutively, and finding ways to speed the remaining steps. Take them seriously. They have probably just eliminated 30% of the costs in the process, cut cycle time, improved quality and eliminated waste, all at the same time.

5. Speed: You Are In A Race and Turtles Don't Win:

Waste slows things down. Interruptions slow things down. If you eliminate them, you will speed the cycle time. The old paradigm said if you speed things up, you would cause quality problems. The mindset was one of forcing people to work faster without changing the job. I am always amazed when I see the Rolex Watch ad that proclaims proudly, "It takes a full year to make a Rolex!" I always wonder, "So, when are you going to learn how?" The assumption that longer is better, is nonsense. Either you know how to make a quality watch or you don't and taking a year proves you don't. But, it does prove you spend a lot of money doing it!

We are a speed-addicted culture. Blame McDonald's. Blame your television's remote control. Blame the Internet for giving us almost any information we want at any time. Now many of us have wireless broadband in our homes and sit in front of the television and when the announcer mentions a person or event, we immediately "Google" it and access most information available. We are rich, rich in information, rich in access, and rich in speed. We aren't going backwards. To compete you have to be fast, in virtually any business.

Test your team or organizations speed savvy. Quickly ask yourself, what is our core process? What is the average cycle time from beginning to the end of the process? Now, what was it a year ago or a month ago? You don't know? You aren't speed savvy. Imagine you manage a NASCAR racing team. Do you know what your lap times were at a given circuit last year? This year? Do you know your average pit stop time to change four tires, and only two? Of course you do! These are the basic, most essential processes and because you are competing, and winning or losing is defined in fractions of seconds lost or gained, you know the answers to these questions.

Your team, even though it may not be as obvious to you, is competing for time, just like a NASCAR team. How long it takes you to develop and new product; how long it takes to test the product and get it to market; how long it takes to delivery; how long it takes to answer the customer's phone-call are all pit stops. You win or lose by your timed performance on these processes.

6. Knock the Walls Down – Interruption Free Wins!

Customers don't care about your walls. If you go to Best Buys, and buy a computer or television, it either works or it doesn't. If it doesn't, you are unhappy with Best Buys, not HP who may have their label on the computer, although they probably didn't manufacture it. And the problem may be one chip or hard drive in the computer that wasn't manufactured by the company that assembled the computer, but by a disk drive or chip manufacturer. But, the customer doesn't care about any of that. Next time, they will go to Circuit City.

Customers look horizontally through a process. It is all one flow to them and the customer is always right. Do you remember our patient who died trying to jump over walls and hurdles in the health care system, all the system of one company? Banging into walls killed her. It is our responsibility to create a "seamless" or "boundary-less" process flow. Interruptions cost money, increase inventory costs, increase the cost of quality, slow cycle times and result in poor service. Interrupted processes are killing companies.

One way to address this is to "flow" through the process personally and "be" the thing being made. It may sound a bit silly, but try it and you will be amazed. Pretend that you are incoming material supply. Get off the truck. Go to the warehouse. Sit on a shelf. How do you like it so far? How long do you sit there? When you go to the next stop (notice the word stop!) in the process, how long do you sit (interruption) there? How often are you recycled? It is probably very frustrating. As you walk through this process, have a pad of paper and pencil handy. Write down every possible improvement, every possible elimination of a wall or interruption. Now ask yourself, if I were this thing, how would I like to be treated? What would I like the process to be in order to help me become the best end-product I can become in the shortest period of time?

The worst walls and interruptions in most processes, are jumping over the legal walls we call companies. Things don't care about companies. Customers don't care about companies. But we are obsessed with them. When a customer buys a car, it is one whole car, although fifty different companies have contributed parts to the final product. The degree to which the primary manufacturer works closely as one process team, managing the horizontal flow and final quality, with all the suppliers is the degree to which they will produce a car that satisfies their customers. For more than twenty years, the U.S. auto companies have been struggling to compete with, and adopt Toyota Production System practices. While they have had many success and improvements in their production process, they still have difficulty jumping over the corporate walls.

The first criteria in selecting a supplier should be whether they are willing to work with you in a seamless, interruption free manner. Are they willing to serve on a team that designs the process? Are they willing to work with you to minimize in-process inventory? Are they willing to respond to quality issues within hours, not days, weeks or months? Are they willing to share financial and quality data in a completely transparent manner? These are the issues that create competitive advantage and result in lower total costs.

7. Design Processes to Principles:

You can't claim to be principle-centered if your processes do not conform to your principles. Your processes are what you do, not what you say.

If you say that you believe in "decision-making at the lowest possible level" for example, look at your process and ask whether it conforms to this principle. If you say you believe in continuous improvement, are your processes designed to incorporate the mechanisms of continuous improvement?

Almost every company has developed a statement of values or principles that hangs on the walls of the company. Unfortunately, employees walk by, and some of them actually stop and read it. Then they often say to them self "Sounds great, I wish I worked there!" Many employees become skeptical and de-motivated by witnessing behavior and processes that contradict the principles or values. Involve them in analyzing those processes and assessing their conformance to principles. To the degree that they are involved in this analysis and they work, to align process to principles, they will have respect for their company and its management.

My Personal Contribution to Improving the Flow:

Personal Action Agenda	I do	I don't	I will
1. I know what processes are my responsibilities.			
2. I am able to analyze and improve those processes.			
3. I know which process(s) is the core process.			
4. I am familiar with a visual map of the process for which I am responsible.			
5. I believe my team and I have successfully eliminated waste from this process.			
6. I know the flow-through speed, the cycle time, of this process.			
7. Interruptions and delays have been eliminated and do not hinder our process.			
8. My process is consistent with my values and principles.			
9. I continually try to find improvements in this process.			
Summary of what I will do to improve my management of processes:			

My Team's Process Flow:

Team Action Agenda	We do	We don't	We will
1. My team knows what processes are our responsibilities.			
2. We are able to analyze and improve those processes.			
3. We know which process(s) is the core process.			
4. We have a visual map of the process for which we are responsible, posted for display in our work area.			
5. Our team has successfully eliminated waste from this process.			
6. We know the flow-through speed, the cycle time, of this process.			
7. Interruptions and delays have been eliminated and do not hinder our process.			
8. Our process is consistent with our values and principles.			
9. We continually try to find improvements in this process.			
Summary of what we agree to do to improve our processes:			

The Flow through the Organization:

Organization Action Agenda	We do	We don't	We will
1. Managing processes is a priority in this organization.			
2. This organization has sought to eliminate walls between divisions, offices, or other internal barriers that might interrupt our core work process.			
3. We know what the core work of the organization is.			
4. The organization works with suppliers and customers to create a "seamless" flow through to the end use customer.			
5. We measure the cycle time of this process through the organization.			
6. The organization encourages the continual elimination of waste from processes.			
7. Our processes have been designed to optimize the customer experience.			
8. We seek to make these processes consistent with our values.			
9. Process improvement is measured and rewarded in the organization.			
Summary of what we agree can improve the effectiveness of processes in the organization.			

Part Two

A Strategy for Creating Value

Chapter 10

Organizational Strategy

A Plan for Building the Five Forms of Capital: Whole-System Design

This chapter provides a roadmap for designing the future, the ideal organization that will unite energy and effort toward a common strategy. There are two sections in this chapter: the first defines the *what*, the five forms of capital that are the wealth of any organization; the second defines the *how*, a process of design based on high involvement of the managers and employees who must be responsible for implementing any change.

The process of designing the future is a strategic process. There are two kinds of strategy, externally focused (business strategy) and internally focused (organizational strategy). Business strategy, defines the future relationships with the outside world, with customers, shareholders, the community, etc. What markets will you sell to in the future? What products and services will meet the needs of your customers? What will the financial return be if you are successful? What return is necessitated by the capital markets? All these questions comprise business strategy and the answers must precede the development of internal or organizational strategy.

Unfortunately, it is too common for organizations to develop elaborate *business strategies*, yet spend no time defining the internal capabilities, the nature of the organization – *organizational strategy*. It is this organizational strategy that will enable them to achieve their business strategy. For example, it would be very easy for a pharmaceutical company to develop a business strategy with a goal to discover five major new drugs over the next ten years in the area of oncology. However, simply stating that goal does nothing to achieve it. To discover new drugs requires, first and foremost, human capital. It requires researchers who are capable of drug discovery in this area. It requires technologies, equipment, processes, and money. If there is not a clear assessment of the capabilities within the organization and specific plans to design the organization around the business strategy, that strategy is hollow.

Defining the Wealth of an Organization

This is the new capitalism. Financial assets cannot define the means of production and distribution. In the days of Andrew Carnegie, J.P. Morgan and Karl Marx money could buy virtually every tool of production. Money was power. Today knowledge, relationships, character, and technology all represent power and production capabilities that are at least as important as money.

In order to design the best possible organizational system, you must know what you have and what you lack that would enable performance. You need to know your assets and liabilities. Traditionally managers have looked at the balance sheet and considered their financial assets to be the real assets of the company. The real value of an organization, just as the real value of an individual, is not in their bank account alone. Financial assets are important. But the real value that will determine competitive success, particularly in the knowledge and global economy, are assets other than the financial assets.

Organizations are designed to be capable of meeting the needs of their customers and achieving strategic goals. This capability resides within the following five forms of capital. Each of these assets are affected by systems and processes. You will first analyze the assets and liabilities, then the systems and processes that must be changed in order to improve the asset.

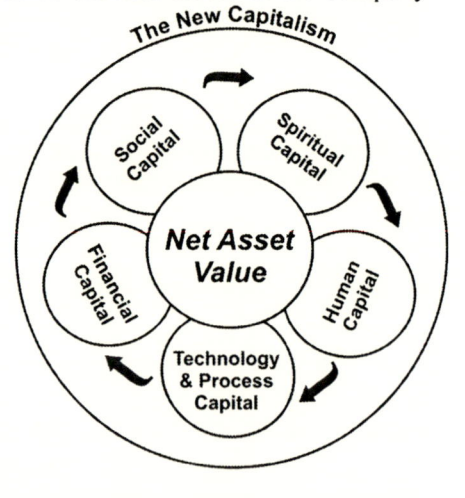

Social Capital

Social Capital is the value of trust. The degree, to which other people trust you, will determine the likelihood of their purchasing your products or services. Social networks, norms of reciprocity, trustworthiness all are forms of social capital.

The World Bank, recognizing the importance of social capital in economic development, has said, *"Social capital refers to the institutions, relationships, and norms that shape the quality and quantity of a society's social interactions... Social capital is not just the sum of the institutions which underpin a society – it is the glue that holds them together."* [55] In a society, there is a great deal of evidence that social capital is a critical force for development. The number of parents who participate in school activities is directly related to the quality of education and further economic success. There is even a demonstrated relationship between social capital and health. *"As a rough rule of thumb, if you belong to no groups but decide to join one, you cut your risk of dying over the next year in half. If you smoke and belong to no groups, it's a toss-up statistically whether you should stop smoking or start joining.'"*[56] Social capital, the quality of our relationships, interacts with our physical well-being.

If, as the World Bank and others have concluded, the quality of social capital in a society has a positive effect on all measures of social and economic development, it is logical that these same qualities of sociability have a similarly positive effect within the mini-society of an organization, as well as its relationships with other organizations and the market place.

There is increasing research, which demonstrates that the strength of social networks, particularly voluntary networks, within an organization correlate positively with higher rates of productivity. *"A social environment rich of participation opportunities, allowing people to meet frequently, is a fertile ground for nurturing shared values and social norms of trust and reciprocity. Where such values*

---

[55] The World Bank 1999: *What is Social Capital?*
[56] Putnam, R. D. (1995) 'Bowling Alone: America's Declining Social Capital', *Journal of Democracy* 6:1, Jan, 65-78.

and norms develop, the likelihood of cooperative behaviors is higher, and workers may be more motivated and not inclined to shirking behaviors."[57]

To analyze the current state of social capital and plan the future, it is important to drill down to a more functional level. There are two types of social capital that may be assessed: internal sociability or trust, and external market capital or brand equity.

The chapters on trust and dialogue in the first part of this book address key elements of internal social capital. To the degree that members of the organization trust leaders and co-workers, they are likely to engage in voluntary problem solving and engage in the discretionary effort (thinking about the problem while driving in the car, or during other personal time). This discretionary effort is critical to competitive success in the knowledge work organization.

Internal social capital is also indicated by the soft desire of individuals to join the organization or sacrifice greater financial rewards to stay with the organization. All choices made by employees are the result of a "balance of consequences," weighing one type of reward against another. Social capital has immediate financial consequences in that it acts as a form of payment, an incentive to remain a member of the organization despite what may be real or perceived lower financial rewards.

But, internal sociability probably has its greatest impact in the ability to solve problems. All organizations are a continual stew of problem solving. Whether it is solving the problems presented by a customer, a new technology, or a competitor, business is a game of constant adaptation to a changing environment. The apparently small act of walking down the hall to an associate's office and sharing a problem, casually brainstorming without regard to who gets credit, or who bears what responsibility, is the most frequent, and probably the most effective way to solve problems. These encounters may escalate into a formal meeting or problem solving process. Whether the interaction remains highly informal or becomes more formal, the

---

[57] Sabatini, Fabio (2006) *Does Social Capital Improve Labour Productivity in Small and Medium Enterprises?* Working Paper, Dipartmento Di Economia Pubblica, Rome.

critical ingredient is the simple willingness to be engaged, to care about the problem, to listen deeply, think together, and brainstorm solutions.

The following are some *critical success indicators* of internal sociability:[58]

- Do you feel that your manager cares about your personal well-being?
- How many groups comprised of other members of the organization do you meet with weekly?
- Do you volunteer to participate on groups that solve problems at work?
- If you are sick or absent from work for a period of time, do you believe co-workers will express concern and sympathy?
- I am confident that my voice will be heard when solving problems.

Market capital is the recognition and respect in the market place. It is brand equity, which is almost as good as money in the bank. Some have measured market capital by subtracting the financial value of all material and cash assets from the firm's market capitalization. In other words, if the stock market values the total equity of the firm at $1 billion, and the firm has cash, accounts receivables, building, equipment, and other balance sheet items worth $500 million, it is logical to assume that the value of the brand, the trust of the marketplace represents the other $500 million. Of course, it can also be argued that this value may represent future cash flows.

No one has defined a single or accurate way to measure the value of reputation, trust or loyalty toward a firm's brands in the market place. But the absence of a definitive measure in no way diminishes the power of brand or market capital.

---

[58] Similar indicators will be presented with each asset class. It is not intended that these be used as a formal survey. Rather, they are simply indicators of the issues that define this form of capital. Neither is it intended that the five indicators in each area be considered comprehensive. These may, however, be a starting point for group discussion, self-evaluation and measurement.

If Honda produces a new car, without any direct knowledge of that car, it will have a high degree of respect, simply because Honda, which has developed a strong image for quality and performance, produces it. This is market capital. Recent studies of brand loyalty indicated that the experience of Honda car owners led to the highest probability that they would buy another Honda product. This brand loyalty reduces the marketing cost of each sale. The dollars that would otherwise be spent on marketing to acquire a new customer can be invested in new product development. Similarly, if Pixar comes out with a new movie, even without any reviews or promotion, families will have a positive bias that this will be a good movie to see with their children. This brand equity has direct monetary value.

Arthur Andersen, the major accounting firm that sank in the Enron scandal, went out of business not because they lost financial assets or human capital; rather, they completely lost the trust of those who read financial statements. They lost their market capital. This quickly translated into bankruptcy as customers fled to other accounting firms.

The following are some *critical success indicators* of market capital:

- Our customer's loyalty to our products or brand is the highest in our market.
- Our brand is associated with quality and excellent customer service.
- If we introduce a new product, we can expect a positive reception in the market even prior to evaluation.
- Research indicates that repeat buying by our customers is in the top quartile of competitors.
- When considered against our competitors we are the employer of choice for professionals in our market.

Human Capital:

Human capital is the sum of all of the skills or competencies of the people within the organization. Human capital has always been a critical component of the performance of any business, but in a modern economy in which technology and creativity produce competitive advantage, human capital has become ever more important.

Human capital can be divided into two major areas: first, the *competencies* that allow an individual to perform; and second, all of the forces that result in *motivation* to perform.

Many years ago, when helping clients address human performance problems I came to rely on the very simple, yet logical, distinction made by Robert Mager.[59] A critical step in *performance analysis* was the distinction between "can't do" and "won't do." Ask your self, "If this individual was offered one million dollars to perform as desired, could they?

If you offered me one million dollars to stand up in front of an audience and sing opera in an acceptable way, you would produce nothing but frustration and a very unhappy audience! Yes, I would be motivated to perform; however, I still could not do it. The competence to sing opera is not within my capabilities, nor will it ever be.

Some human competencies are linked to inherited qualities, as singing opera. However, most human competencies are the result of education and training. Training priorities are developed by defining those competencies required to fulfill the work process. Most of those competencies can be developed, rather than inherited.

There are times when attempts to increase motivation actually hinder performance. If one does not have the skill to perform, motivational exhortations or incentives produce only frustration. A critical function of management is to make the distinction between situations that require the development of new skills and those that require greater motivation.

Motivation has been the subject of hundreds, if not thousands of books for managers. When all is said and done, the keys to motivation are relatively simple: work that is interesting and ennobling; sincere recognition by both peers and superiors; opportunities for career advancement; positive feedback that can guide performance; strong and supportive social interaction by a team; and, oh, did I forget? – fair and attractive financial rewards. There is little reason to waste time in

---

[59] Mager, Robert F. and Pipe, Peter. Analyzing Performance Problems or You Really Oughta Wanna, CEP Press, Atlanta, Georgia, 1997.

the endless debates about money versus recognition, versus enriching work. They are all motivating, and different personalities are more or less, influenced by different types of incentives. The job of designing an organizational system is to optimize all of the various forms of motivation. Over-reliance on any one form is a prescription for poor performance.

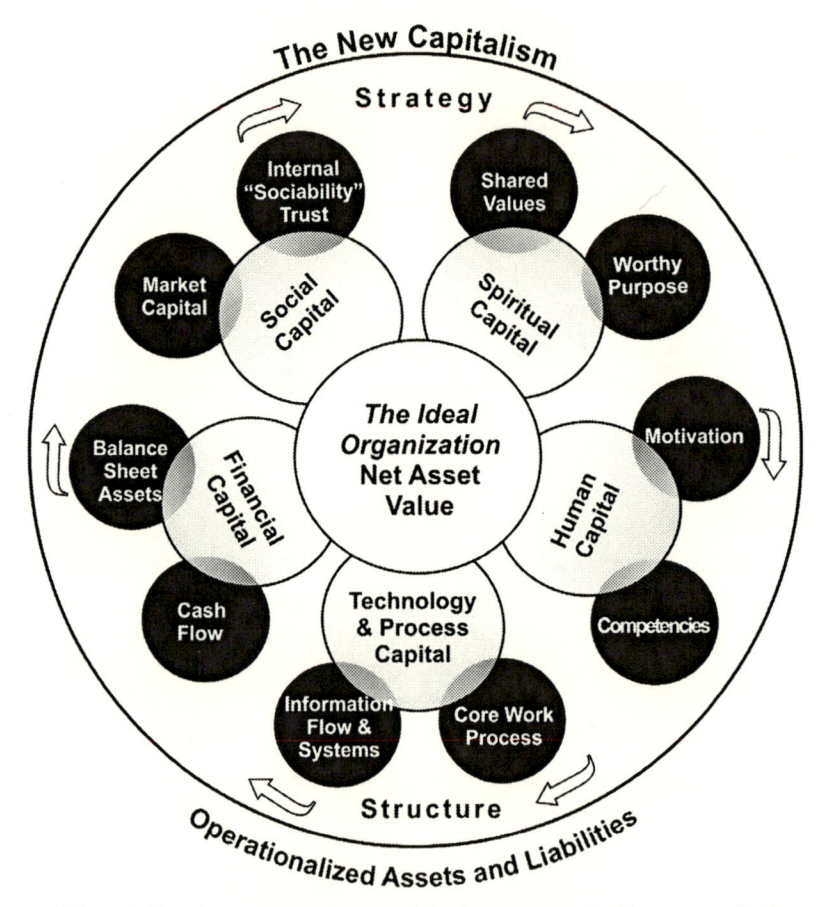

The New Capitalism

Strategy

- Internal "Sociability" Trust
- Shared Values
- Market Capital
- Social Capital
- Spiritual Capital
- Worthy Purpose
- Balance Sheet Assets
- Financial Capital
- **The Ideal Organization Net Asset Value**
- Human Capital
- Motivation
- Cash Flow
- Technology & Process Capital
- Competencies
- Information Flow & Systems
- Core Work Process

Structure

Operationalized Assets and Liabilities

The following are some *critical success indicators* of the motivational component of human capital:

- Members of the organization are specifically recognized or rewarded for progress in the development of their professional competencies.

- Individuals share, in some form, in the business success of the organization and receive regular (weekly, monthly or quarterly) reports that inform them of business success.
- Members of the organization are members of work groups or teams that control their own process and regularly consult together on how to improve that process.
- Work groups have public celebrations of business success.
- Our rate of turnover of valued employees is lower than comparable organizations.

Human competence is the only modern parallel to production technology of the past century. Modern production most often occurs in the mind, or the collective mind of a small work group. If you have highly trained marketing professionals, skilled sales men and women, great engineers and brilliant financial managers you have an important form of capital. These competencies are a foundation of performance. Investment in these assets is likely to pay off in the creation of other classes of assets.

Those organizations that have exhibited the greatest dedication to the development of human competence have consistently outperformed those who have only given lip service to training and development. General Electric, Microsoft and other companies that have grown into the great economic powers have done so as a result of both attracting and developing the most competent people.

Competence can loosely be divided into the function skills, managerial skills and social skills. While there are many important functional skills, the most important are those that enable the core work process in the organization. If the organization is a software development company, the competence of software design and engineering are the core competencies. Managerial skills – decision-making, planning, project management, etc., are all critical to every organization, as are the social skills of communication.

The following are some *critical success indicators* for human competence:

- We have identified the *core competencies* that enable the *core processes* within our organization.

- We benchmark our process of training and development against our industry competitors.
- We provide world-class training in management skills to our managers.
- We provide world-class training, or encourage our professionals to seek external training in the areas of our core competence.
- Members of the organization consider one of the attractive features of working in this organization the learning and development process.

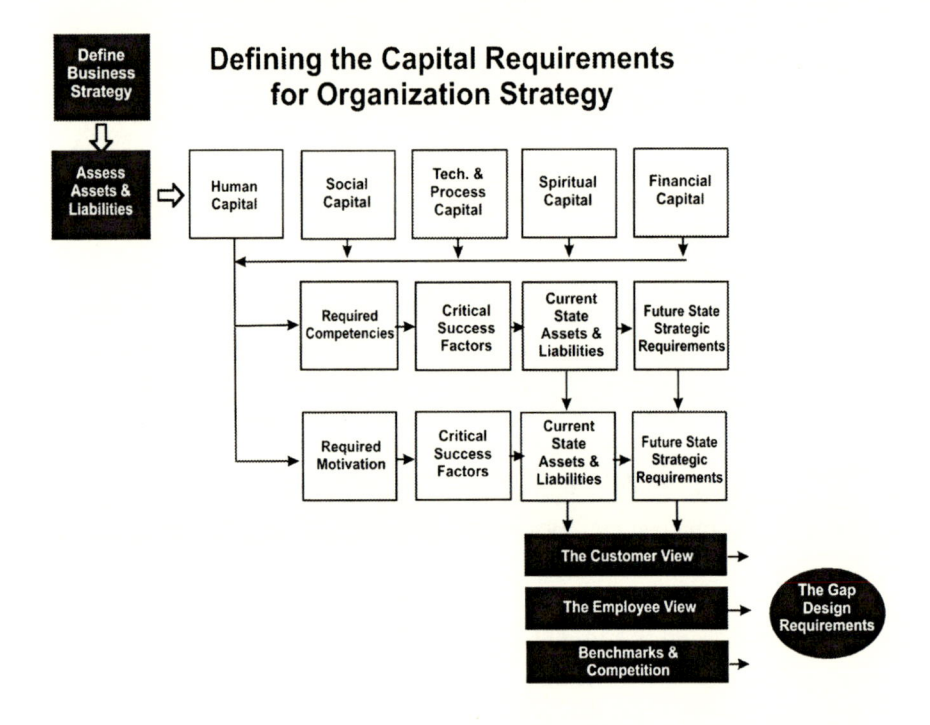

Defining the Capital Requirements for Organization Strategy

Define Business Strategy ⇨ Assess Assets & Liabilities ⇨ Human Capital | Social Capital | Tech. & Process Capital | Spiritual Capital | Financial Capital

- Required Competencies → Critical Success Factors → Current State Assets & Liabilities → Future State Strategic Requirements
- Required Motivation → Critical Success Factors → Current State Assets & Liabilities → Future State Strategic Requirements

The Customer View
The Employee View
Benchmarks & Competition

→ The Gap Design Requirements

Note: The above diagram describes the first part of an organization design process – defining design requirements. This should be done for each of the five asset classes. The second part of the process is designing the ideal future state – as described in the second section of this chapter.

Spiritual Capital:

I am fully aware that to many ears, the word *spiritual* may sound incongruous in the context of a discussion of business or capitalism. However, the perceived division between work life and spiritual life is both false and impossible. A high percentage of our social interactions occur at work. Many of our anxieties, ambitions, passions and fears center on our work life. The nature of the organization in which we work has a profound effect on our spiritual life.

I will not take the reader's time at this point for a lengthy discussion of the meaning of the word *spiritual* or *spirituality*. It simply refers to our aspirations, our guidance, our connections that are not founded in the material world, but rather from some source, we regard as more noble. Every religion seeks to strengthen our spirituality, the inner strength and serenity, which come from knowing of a higher source of authority. Those who do not believe in God may also seek spirituality in the power and perfection of nature or through meditation.

I am also not suggesting that work organizations should in any way engage in the practice of religion or interfere in the religious life of their members. This, I believe, should remain entirely personal and voluntary. Business organizations however, can create a cultural environment that supports religious and spiritual values and that does no harm to the inner spiritual well-being of the individual.

To the degree that an organization can enable, support, or encourage a depth of personal morality and dedication to a noble purpose, it possesses spiritual capital. I sincerely believe that this form of wealth accrues both to the organization and to the individual. It will interact and support every other form of capital and ultimately, will have its effect on the actual bottom line.

In practice, many organizations have done great harm to the spiritual life of their members, even while the leaders may profess loudly their religious commitments. The reader no doubt has sufficient examples without the author providing depressing illustrations. If not, simply watch Arthur Miller's *Death of a Salesman* and know that the graveyard is well populated by kindred spirits of Willy Loman.

I believe that spiritual capital has two most significant components: first, the degree to which members of the organization are committed to an ennobling purpose; and second, the degree to which shared values serve to guide ethical behavior.

The pursuit of **worthy purpose** was the subject of an earlier chapter of this book and is the primary means of achieving *energy* in an organization. Human beings are energized by, and will sacrifice for that which they believe to be noble, and therefore ennobling of them. Any manager who believes that only technical processes, human skills or financial capital are required for competitive success is much like the racing team that spends a million dollars for the latest racecar but then hires a driver who doesn't care about winning. Purpose matters. Ennobling purpose matters most.

The following are some *critical success indicators* of worthy purpose:

- When asked, "Why do you work for this organization?" individuals tend to reply with answers other than one of simple personal gain.
- Our orientation for new employees seeks to instill a sense of *calling*, or dedication, to a noble purpose to which the organization is committed.
- An examination of presentations made by the leaders of the organization will reveal regular references to the worthy purpose of the organization.
- Individuals decide to work for our organization while accepting compensation that may be less than other companies offer.
- We make business decisions, decisions regarding products, services or markets, in part based on their contribution to our worthy purpose.

Shared values are the basis for trustworthy relationships and sociability. We all have beliefs about human nature and ourselves that guide our behavior. When someone holds the belief that human beings are created evil and are naturally devious than it is logical to assume that they must be watched and controlled. However, if we believe that people are essentially created noble and worthy, we treat them with an assumption of trust. Business partners, fellow managers and employees all have a tendency to conform to our beliefs about them. These belief systems have enormous impact on the culture of organizations and it is the function of leaders to exert efforts intentionally to shape these beliefs.

Countries that are unified have a clearly articulated set of values stated in a constitution or "Bill of Rights" that form the basis for relationships. We know that (in the United States) we believe in freedom of speech, press and religion. We know that one is innocent until proven guilty. And, we know that everyone is entitled to equal treatment and opportunity regardless of race, religion or gender. These values are not innate. We were not born with them. Certainly, many people are born with contrary views. These values must be taught.

The fundamental values of religion must be taught. To *"do unto others as you would have them do to you"* is not a response with which we are born. It is why religions "beat the drum" with weekly discipline as discussed in a previous chapter. It is the human condition to require disciplined training.

Because of our humble human condition, business and other organizations, which desire a high level of sociability or trust, internally and with external customers and partners, must clearly articulate their values, demonstrate adherence to those values, and hold all members accountable for their compliance.

The following are some *critical success indicators* for shared values:

- All employees have a written document that defines the core values and principles of the organization.
- When making decisions about human resource practices, hiring, or incentives, these values are frequently a factor in our decision-making.
- We can all remember a case in which leaders of the organization made a decision to adhere to our shared values despite sacrificing personal or business gain.
- Most employees believe that this is a "high trust" organization.
- The anxiety most likely to be experienced by employees concerns customer satisfaction, and not the internal support of co-workers or managers.

Technology and Process Capital

The success of Dell is in their manufacturing and distribution processes. The success of Wal-Mart, Home Depot, L. L. Bean or McDonald's is all about process. Processes either create or minimize cost. They assure either consistency and reliability, or the unfortunate alternative. Like other forms of capital value, the quality of the work process, and particularly any technological breakthrough that creates distinction with customers, is a significant asset.

Organization design begins, not with the design of levels or division in the organization, but with a clear definition of the future *core work process*. Many processes in an organization are not core processes. The core process is the input-to-output flow that causes a customer to write you a check. It is that simple. If customers write you a check because of the quality of your accounting then accounting is a core work process (which it is not, unless you are an accounting firm).

The core work process is generally designing or engineering what you sell; making it; and marketing and selling it. Every other process in the organization is an enabling process. Training, accounting, information systems and others exist to enable the work of the core process that serves your customers. Enabling processes should be designed only after designing the ideal core work process because the core work determines the requirements for the enabling processes.

Structure follows and should enable the core work process. Information systems should enable process. But first one must examine the flow of the work, eliminate unnecessary steps, reduce all in-process inventories to a minimum, and eliminate all other forms of waste. Toyota worked for thirty years on the elimination of waste and that effort was the motivating force behind the development of the Toyota Production System. The innovation that was the competitive advantage of McDonald's was one of work process, the application of manufacturing process techniques to restaurants. Wal-Mart has taken this a step further in their supply-chain management. All of these companies have built their enabling processes to support their core work process.

The following are some *critical success indicators* for the core work process:

- We have clearly defined our core work process.
- We have measured and benchmarked the cycle time of the core work process.
- Our cycle times are the best among our competitors.
- Our process is distinguishing us from our competitors and is creating a unique competitive advantage.
- Our process has provided a reliability that has given us a quality advantage in the market place.

Information flow and technology are key enablers of performance. Information systems should not only be considered a decision-making tool, but also a key ingredient in the motivational system. How information is presented and used can create the element of a great business game that motivates everyone to play; or, it can be a cause of fear and surprise punishment.

Information systems are often changed without carefully analyzing the work system or who makes what decisions, therefore who needs what information. Information systems should be designed after the definition of the best possible work process; otherwise, the information system may actually inhibit improvement in the work.

The following are some *critical success indicators* for information systems and technology:

- Our information systems enable data driven decision-making at every level of the organization.
- Our information systems create a sense of personal or team ownership at the first level of the organization.
- Our information systems allow us to monitor customer satisfaction and respond to customer needs almost immediately.
- Our information systems easily adapt to changes in work process, customer needs or organization.
- We have developed unique information technology applications that have given us a competitive advantage.

Financial Capital

Needless to say, when the word capital is used the first thought among business managers, is the "cap ex" budget and the corporate balance sheet. It might be assumed that the discussion of social, human and spiritual capital in some way minimize the importance of financial capital. As a business owner, manager, and now private investor, the author fully appreciates the value of financial capital. I want a return on my investment, like every other investor and I have read hundreds of 10K's and 10Q's.

When designing the ideal future organization, there is a bias, which I try to insert in the conversation. That bias is simply to manage the flow of money in a way that causes every employee in the organization to feel a part of the business game. This may simply involve education and frequent information sharing; or, it may involve sharing a bonus based on the utilization of financial capital (return on operating assets) and profitability.

The *financial system* is the totality of the movement of money in and out of the organization. A key issue is "who has what information about costs and revenues?" Who needs to know? Financial transparency, making known the real costs, the real revenues and the true financial status of the organization to all those who participate in achieving its financial success, is an increasingly well-accepted principle.

Financial targets motivate most organizations and most individuals. There is nothing wrong with this, as long as financial targets are complimented by larger purpose. Financial targets alone soon become a hollow and repetitive exercise. However, managers are often hesitant to be forthright in the necessity of achieving financial targets, and many organization design processes are clearly intended to achieve these targets.

It would be wonderful if every manager and employee were provided the monthly income statement and the balance sheet. If every employee was asked, every month, "how can you improve cash flow and how can you improve return on the assets we use," it would not be long before every employee would feel like a business manager and would be making decisions to improve financial performance.

The following are some *critical success indicators* for the utilization of assets, or the balance sheet:

- We are able to access capital markets at a highly competitive rate if or when we need additional investment capital.
- Our return-on-operating-assets is among the top quartile of our competitors.
- Our debt-to-equity ratio is in the top quartile of our competition.
- First line managers and associates know the financial value of the assets they employ and measure the return on those assets.
- Improving return-on-assets is an objective at every level of the organization.

The following are some *critical success indicators* for current cash flow or the income statement:

- Our cash flow generates an operating profit margin in the top quartile of our competitors.
- Our capital expenditure needs, are met from internal returns.
- Year after year revenue growth is in the top ten percent of our competition.
- Year after year return-on-equity growth is in the top ten percent of our competitors.
- Our costs of sales, or costs associated with delivering our services, are below average among our competitors.

The Extended Environment

In this age of lean manufacturing and Six Sigma quality management, it may seem trite to say that organizations must be designed to meet the needs of their customers. Yet, it is equally true that the processes of the organization must be designed to extend to partners and suppliers, and to enable them to be effective in their support of your work.

I have led several design projects in which representatives of both supplier and customer organizations served on the design team, to create a seamless flow of work from one to another.

We are used to thinking of those *within* the legal boundaries of our organizations and then of those *outside* the boundaries such as customers and suppliers. However, the reality of life in organizations today is not so simple. Work is often done through a network of people who share knowledge, or of customers and suppliers who cooperate on the design of a solution. This is the extended environment, an extension of our work and organization, our partners who help us succeed and without whom our performance would be impossible. The ability to manage our relationships with these partners, to create trust and loyalty, is a key to our own success.

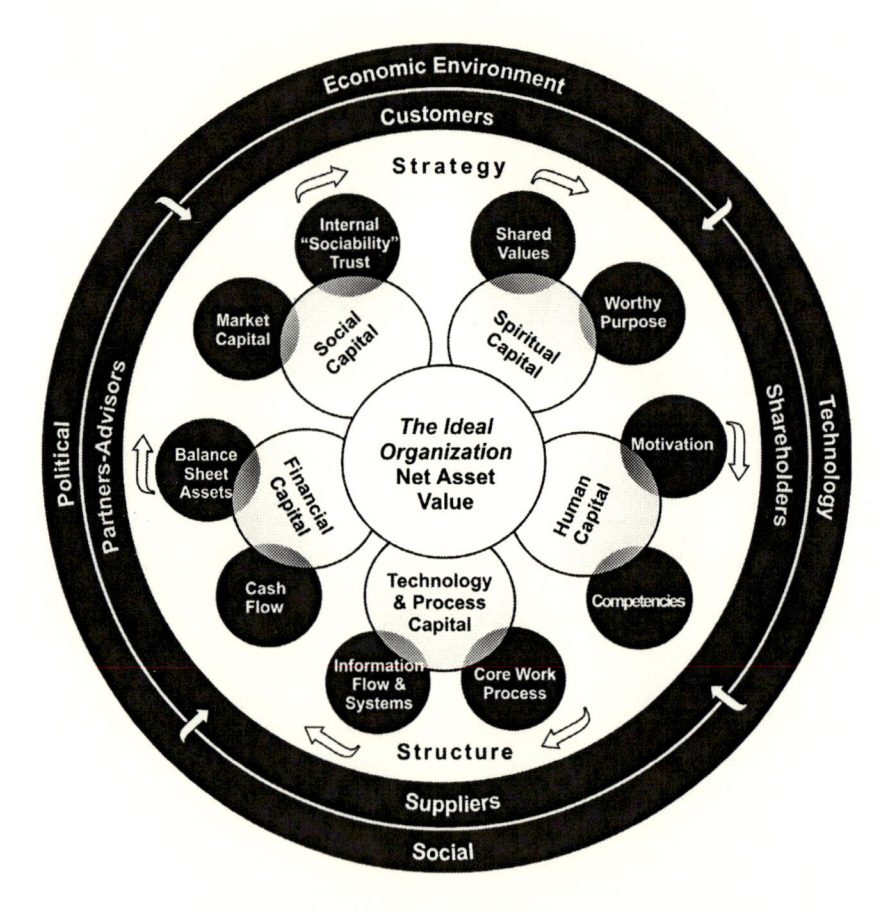

Diagram: Concentric wheel showing "The Ideal Organization Net Asset Value" at center, surrounded by capitals (Social, Spiritual, Human, Technology & Process, Financial, Market) with elements (Internal "Sociability" Trust, Shared Values, Worthy Purpose, Motivation, Competencies, Core Work Process, Information Flow & Systems, Cash Flow, Balance Sheet Assets, Market Capital). Outer rings labeled Strategy, Structure, and surrounded by Customers, Shareholders, Technology, Suppliers, Social, Political, Partners-Advisors, Economic Environment.

Virtually no one works alone. Even the individual artist working in his own studio must find a gallery interested in his work. He needs a source of supplies, clay or paint or canvas. He also needs critics, friends whom he trusts to give him feedback on his work. In a sense, these are all partners, whether paid or not, who help him do his work. In a large organization, the network of partners, customers or suppliers is even more extensive. Every team depends on other teams to supply information, resources or materials.

All these close relationships upon which we depend are the extended environment. They are not "external" because they are *inside* the work system or process, *not outside*. In most organizations, the design efforts ignore these relationships, which are so critical to success. The flow of work and the system that supports this work must be designed because it may well be a cause of either competitive advantage or disadvantage.

The process of quality management should define not only the requirements of effective process, but where organizational boundaries, competencies, information flow, and other operations inhibit achieving the highest quality standards. This should all be represented in the room when the future process and organization are designed.

The External Environment – The Big System

Every system is a sub-system of a larger system. The Earth is a sub-system of the solar system. The oceans are a sub-system of the larger eco-system of the planet. And in the same way, every company is a sub-system of the economy and of an industry. This larger system defines the external environment in which a company must operate.

We are all influenced or have constraints imposed by the larger system. For example, a family in a village in Tibet gives birth to a child. No matter what DNA in their genetic code, no matter how determined they may be, their learning and development will be dramatically different (not necessarily worse) than the average citizen of the United States or Europe. The system imposes constraints. Similarly, a company born during the Internet technology explosion of the 1990's had to be influenced by the free flow of capital, the assumptions of rapid growth, and the virtual discounting of normal market economics. A company born in the year 2005 was born into an entirely different social and economic system and their operations adjust to this different environment.

Organizations often fail because they do not respond to changes in the external environment, changes beyond their control. If you produced typewriters and the market for typewriters is disappearing because of the advancing technology of the semiconductor, you have no choice but to respond to these changes.

The external environment includes not only technology, but also economic, political and social forces. Sensing and responding are keys to survival. It is why we have eyes, ears and a sense of smell. But we often fail to use our senses because we fall into predictable patterns and habits. It is helpful to plan a scan of the environment systematically, turning on the radar to sense what is out there, enabling a sensible response.

Anticipating and defining changes and requirements imposed by the external environment are a key component of both business strategy and organizational strategy. If we can anticipate technologies that can dramatically alter decision-making, for example, this may have implications for organization structure. If we can identify political changes that may affect the requirements on a multi-national organization, this may also have significant implications for the organization structure, required competencies or other factors.

Those engaged in organization design must assess both, their internal assets and liabilities as well as the external influences.

The *How* of Strategic Organization Design

There is a long history of improvement theories and practices, beginning with Frederick Taylor one hundred years ago and continuing today. Rather than becoming overly infatuated with one method, it is wise to seek to combine the best practices of a variety of methods. I began my journey on this path infatuated with the potential of positive reinforcement, and then became very involved in employee involvement teams and the quality movement. Socio-technical systems design also influenced my way of thinking to a large extent. My firm and I developed a process we called *whole-system design* or whole-whole system architecture.

The most important single idea underlying whole-system design is the simple idea that an organization is a complex system, like the human body, with different organs and sub-systems, all of which interact and influence each other. Attempts to change one system without considering its interdependence with other systems, frequently lead to failure.

The whole system of the organization includes everything described in the model presented above. What must be designed are the assets. Designing the whole-system does not mean changing everything, but it does mean the ability to discover the relationship between the systems, to find constraints, the sources of interruption in the workflow, and to imagine improvement throughout the whole system.

Socio-technical system design, pioneered by Eric Trist and Fred Emery, which formed the basis for the design of the first "self-managing team" plants at Gains Topeka and Proctor & Gamble, proved to create long lasting and radically different systems. Proctor & Gamble considered this system design such a competitive advantage that they redesigned all of their plants using this methodology, and companies like Corning and Kimberly-Clark followed suit. In the rapid turnover of management fads and theories, much of this good work has been ignored. However, it is a foundation of whole-system design.

Another foundation of whole-system design is the Toyota Production System, or "lean manufacturing." Many years ago, I had the good fortune to be involved with Honda America Manufacturing as they adopted their methods to the American culture. Honda readily admits that their production system is "the Toyota Production System" with their modifications and continual improvements.

When Americans first went to Honda or Toyota to study how they could produce cars at both low cost and high quality, they often came away with superficial understandings. They would see the teams and think, "That's it!" Or, they would see control charts and Kanban, the common uniforms or the small lot inventory system. Often based on the background and biases of the observer, they would conclude that the explanation lay is one or two specific techniques. When they came back and tried to apply these, they would usually fail. They would then conclude, "Japanese management doesn't work in the U.S." But, Honda America Manufacturing and Toyota's Nummi experience, in which they took an old General Motors plant, with older workers and a strong union, and turned it into an effective high quality plant, disproved that nonsense.

You cannot understand lean manufacturing if you think about one technique. It is a whole-system! It is comprised of a hundred different things from the behavior and attitudes of executives to the process of hiring new employees. You can't get there without a redesign of the whole system.

Competing in the New Capitalism

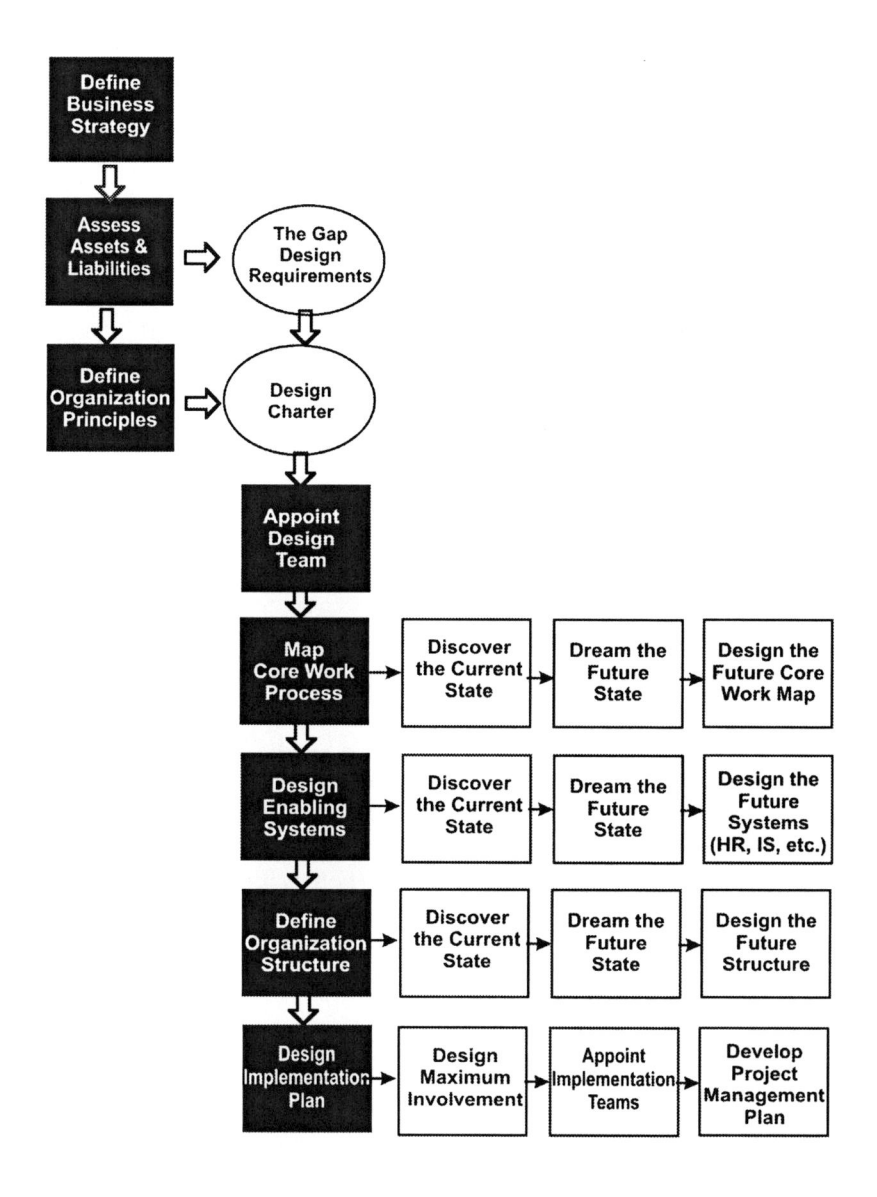

```
Define Business Strategy
    ↓
Assess Assets & Liabilities  ⇒  The Gap Design Requirements
    ↓                                  ↓
Define Organization Principles  ⇒  Design Charter
                                       ↓
                              Appoint Design Team
                                       ↓
Map Core Work Process → Discover the Current State → Dream the Future State → Design the Future Core Work Map
                                       ↓
Design Enabling Systems → Discover the Current State → Dream the Future State → Design the Future Systems (HR, IS, etc.)
                                       ↓
Define Organization Structure → Discover the Current State → Dream the Future State → Design the Future Structure
                                       ↓
Design Implementation Plan → Design Maximum Involvement → Appoint Implementation Teams → Develop Project Management Plan
```

Note: The above diagram is a general workflow for whole-system design. The exact steps and flow depend entirely on the specifics of the organization, its culture and business circumstances.

Principles of Whole-System Design

Experience has shown that the following principles lead to successful whole-system design:

1. Discover Beyond the Village

If you went into a Chinese village, got the ten smartest villagers, and asked them to design the ideal house, what would they design? Would they design a contemporary or a Williamsburg Colonial, even if they were given a blank check and encouraged to design the "ideal" house? No. They would design a house that looked a lot like other Chinese village houses, because their "ideal" house is defined by their mental maps and those maps can only be of Chinese houses. We are all "Chinese villagers" in our tendency to design the future, based on our own maps of our past-experience. This inevitable limitation can be broken by deliberate efforts to "get out of the village" and seek the ideal without boundaries. It is important that the design team benchmark companies who may represent best practices for the process they are redesigning. Often the best practices are found outside of the industry of the company going through a redesign process. A hospital emergency room might find that they could learn a lot from fast food restaurants; government offices can learn a great deal from best practices in private enterprise; and, a taxicab company could learn a lot by studying overnight package delivery companies. It is important to inquire and appreciate the best in nature of the processes, whether the exact business is the same or not.

2. Dream Big

If you aim low, you will not go very high. If you aim high, you may not get there, but you will end up higher than if you had aimed low. When those participating in the change begin to discover best practices within the organization and beyond, they should look for incredible, fantastic, out of this world, examples that at first, may seem impossible to achieve. Look for the WOW! factor; practices that would absolutely delight your customers.

Several times, I have participated in efforts that sought, for example, to reduce the cycle time in half for a process that historically had taken eight years and hundreds of millions of dollars. At the outset, everyone thought it was impossible. But, when they aimed for it, they actually found it could be done in less than four years.

Creative dissatisfaction is the gap between where you are and where you believe you could be. You should not be satisfied with this gap – you are dissatisfied. This dissatisfaction is not a fear or negative feeling; it is the feeling of potential gain, inspired confidence to achieve.

3. Design an Adaptive, Open- System

Open-systems interact and learn from other systems. Imagine the worst dictatorship in the world. That government is most likely a closed system. Closed means that the leaders of that government are all talking to each other, reinforcing the same ideas, and outside views that may disrupt the internal views, are not allowed. Learning rarely takes place in a closed system. Closed systems consume but do not generate new energy and therefore achieve what is called entropy, a process of degradation leading to the disintegration of the system. Many companies have failed because they have developed the competencies of closed systems and were not discovering or imagining based on the exploration of external ideas. As you design changes in the system of an organization, you should look for opportunities to build in learning from external sources deliberately.

Because open systems are constantly impacted by the external environment, there is an element of chaos, an apparent lack of control. But just as in the free economy, the apparent chaos of this constant interaction leads to adaptation and the speed, and ability to adapt leads to durability.

4. Maximize Involvement – Gain Commitment

The success of change efforts is due largely to the enthusiasm to implement the new design on the part of members of the organization. The worst way to do a redesign, is to have consultants do it, then present it to the organization. This kills ownership and enthusiasm. Consultants can be helpful in guiding and facilitating a process, but the members of the organization should be the ones designing "their own house," and in turn, this would create a feeling of ownership and pride in the new design. This is critical to successful implementation.

5. Design for Inherent Stability

We all seek stability and security. We would like our business, government, or home to be stable. There are two types of stability: inherent stability, as result of the design itself; and, dynamic stability that results from movement and energy.

Imagine a bicycle. How would you create the most stable bicycle? First, you might ask, "If you want stability why aren't you designing a tricycle instead of a bicycle?" Good point. The design of something with three points on the ground is inherently more stable than one with only two. The more grounding points, the more stable.

Governments are designed with elements of stability into their system. In the United States a system of three branches, with checks and balances was designed in order to create a more robust or stable system. Without the checks and balances, or with only two branches (bicycle versus tricycle) of government would be less stable. This was the intention of its Founders.

6. Design for Dynamic Stability

Dynamic stability results from motion. A sailboat moving through the water gains stability with speed. An arrow moving quickly forms a straighter path at high speed and becomes less stable at low speeds. Anyone who rides a bicycle has experienced the greater stability at speed. Organizations also become less stable if they are standing still and more stable if they are in motion.

Design the organization for rapid motion in a purposeful direction.

7. Design for Continuous Adaptation

Never think you are designing the definitive system. You will fail if you think you are creating the ultimate end-state. The environment, in which every organization evolves, changes rapidly and requires continual and rapid evolution. When engaging in a redesign project, design the mechanism of continuous improvement into the design. It is much better and more likely to result in success if you say, "Here is the best design we can think of now, and we expect those who start to carry out the process, those who will live in the new design, to find what we missed and make improvements." Again, think of governments. Constitutions usually, and wisely, contain provisions for their amendment and change.

8. Design to Customer Requirements

The beginning of the design process should include a careful assessment of the market and customer requirements, as well as a study of all aspects of the external and extended environment. If it is possible, involve your customers in the actual design of your process and systems. This will strengthen your relationship with your customers and ensure that your process meets their needs.

9. Design to Principles

Organizations are a reflection of values and principles, intentionally or not. The traditional mass production assembly reflected a set of values and assumptions regarding the capability of front line workers. The organization designed to be a lean production, or Toyota Production System, must be designed with very different principles in mind. The leadership team, who will write a design charter, must think through their values and principles and be explicit in calling for the design to reflect those principles.

10. Design with the End in Mind

Assuming your organization is a business; design the organization with its business function in mind. A business has a purpose to meet the needs of its customers and market, as well as to meet the needs of its owners and employees. If you are designing a business system, design its business function into the systems. For example, if you are designing a team structure, design business information and business responsibility into those teams.

The Process of Whole-System Organization Design

No one can define the steps in a process of change without knowing the context - knowing what is going on in the organization, the size, the urgency and priorities, the strengths and weaknesses. In each case, the process should be developed while considering its contextual realities.

Below I describe some of the common steps that have proven successful and point out why. It may appear that these steps are defined in a *linear* manner, meaning that A comes before B that is necessarily followed by C. Surely, when you are discovering best practices it is only natural to be thinking about what the ideal might look like in your organization. It is not necessary that the stages be neatly separated. They are presented in an order that generally makes sense and it will be desirable to plan them in this order. But, it will also be important to let the process flow down a path that unfolds before it.

It is recommended that this process be an "inter-active" planning process with an executive *steering team* who gives the process direction and authority; and *design teams* comprised of members of the organization who are responsible for the following four stages; *Discovery, Dream, Design* and *Development*. These two lead groups will seek ways to involve as many as possible in the organization to gain the broadest possible engagement.

This design team will receive a "charter" from the steering team and this charter will provide clear guidance as to the objectives of their work and the boundaries of what they may and may not redesign. The design team will ultimately report their design and recommendations for implementation.

The design team may do a number of things to gain even greater involvement from the organization, such as hold "design conferences" utilizing the Search Conference methodology developed by Marvin Weisbord[60] and others. These design conferences may involve hundreds of employees, customers, suppliers and other

---

[60] Weisbord, Marvin R. *Discovering Common Ground.* San Francisco: Barret-Koehler Publishers, 1992.

"stakeholders" who have an interest in designing the ideal process. There are often a series of design conferences. The first may be a "Discovery Conference" to search for those things that are done well in the organization and to gain a shared awareness of strengths as well as needs. After the discovery, there may be a "Dream Conference" to imagine the ideal future. It is possible to combine these two in some cases. There may be a third, established to gain broad based engagement in the design phase. Finally, after the significant changes are approved by the steering-team, there may be a "Development Conference" in which large groups become engaged in making plans for the implementation of the new design.

Who Designs The Organizational System?

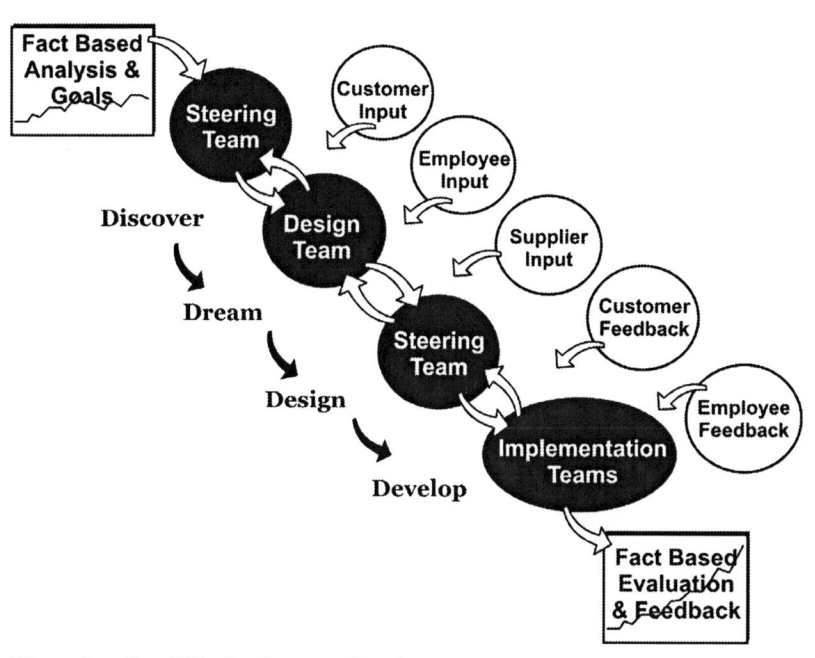

Planning for Whole-System Design

Identify Steering Team: The Steering team is the leadership team of the organization. It is very important that the team that assigns the design teams, and charters the design process, is the group that has the power to decide to implement the design. If the steering team does not have the authority to approve the design, it should not be chartering a design team to study and redesign the organization.

Write a Charter

A design charter is the output of the work of the steering team. This design charter is a very important document and will tell the design team exactly what their mission is, what is expected of their work and what they can and cannot do. Here are the key elements of a design charter.

- Objectives: Why are we doing this and what changes, either in process or performance, are expected?
- Principles: What principles should be considered when designing the organization?
- Timeline and Expectations: How long does the design team have to do their work? What presentations or benchmarks are there in the timeline?
- Boundaries: There are always things that are out of bounds, even though the design team may be charged with redesigning the whole systems. For example, can the design team redesign the compensation system? Whose compensation? You will quickly find a boundary. What are the boundaries of the work process, where does it begin and end? And, are there financial concerns or a budget that must be considered?
- Core and Enabling Processes: The steering team should know which processes are core and enabling and should make this clear to the design team. A design team should start with studying the flow of the core process and redesigning that, and then design the enabling processes.

Appoint a Design Team

It is essential that the members of the design team are expert in the processes they are going to redesign. Only those, who have had their hands on, who have first hand knowledge of a process, are expert in that process. The design team members must also have the respect of both the steering team and the members of the organization if the result is to have credibility and is to be implemented. Design teams should be from eight to twelve members and should be diverse in their experience. They should have good communication and problem-solving skills, should be courageous and creative, and should have the desire to participate in a significant improvement effort.

Stage 1: Discover

Many different activities can be employed during the discovery phase, but you can generally divide them into External and Internal Discovery.

External would include anything happening outside the organization that may affect the organization or that may generate ideas for a better future. In some methodologies, this is called an *environmental scan*, which has nothing to do with the weather! The environment includes the market, the technology environment, social environment and other factors that are external; as well as the extended environment of customers, suppliers and partners all create requirements and opportunities for the organization.

The internal environment begins with clarification of the guiding values, mission, vision and strategy. These principles and ideas should give direction to all of the work of the design process. It is the responsibility of the steering team to provide this guidance.

The next step is mapping the core work process. This is the most important thing that happens in the organization, despite what many people may be thinking or feeling. Getting a solid grasp of this is an essential beginning. It is beyond the scope of this brief introduction to whole-system design to go into various mapping procedures, but the design team and conferences may spend a good bit of time developing this graphic depiction of the work of the organization. As they discover this map, they will want to ask questions about the organizations strengths and discover stories about how individuals or teams have done heroic things to serve their customers and improve the product or service. These stories will be important in developing the dream of the future organization.

The design team will then want to identify all of the enabling processes, those that support and make the core process successful. Depending on the scope of their effort, they may want to map these processes and follow the same steps they did for the core process.

Three different types of discovery activities can be used in this and most of the stages: individual interviews, small focus groups, or large-scale conferences. The design team members may develop a series of interview questions focusing first on the strengths and positive performance of the organization and then on wishes, desires, or needs. They may split up into pairs to go interview customers and suppliers, or they may schedule focus groups. It is desirable to invite customers and suppliers to conferences for employees. I have seen customers speak to conferences of more than a hundred employees at Corning and other companies to give their views on what the company does well and what they would like to see by way of changes or improvements.

Stage 2: Dream

Three BIG questions can help members of the organization develop dreams about their future:

- Considering our mission as an organization, what would be the ideal service or product for our customers? What would this look like, be able to do, and how would it make our customers feel?
- What would make this the world's best place to work while we accomplish our mission? What would it feel like? What work setting would provide the most encouragement and development for the members of our organization?
- How would the first two questions make us a great business, and help us achieve great business results?

Around each of these three big questions, it will not be hard to imagine many other questions. There are numerous exercises and fun ways to explore the dream. For example, you can ask individuals or small groups to write an article for the Wall Street Journal that is doing a story on your company ten years from now. The WSJ is writing an article about your company as a success story that will inspire others. The story should reflect everything you want the company to be, what you hope you will be able to say about the company. You can also call upon the creative imagination of members of your organization by asking them to develop and act-out skits that reflect the dream of your future company. These skits, for example, could be at a cocktail party. The President of the United States, ten years from now, is having a dinner and cocktail party for winners of the National Quality Award. As a member of the team who helped make this happen – you are invited. Now write a script and act out the conversation where you are explaining to others at the cocktail party what you did that made your company worthy to win this award.

These are just examples of some of the fun things you can do to encourage the development of the dream. Remember that people dream in groups. In other words, one person's story stimulates ideas in another. Have you ever watched a group sitting around and imagining what could happen together? They feed on each other, laugh with each other, and from the dialogue comes a collective dream that none of them alone would have imagined.

Out of the discovery and dream stage, it will be desirable to form a "consensus dream." Some elements of this may become clear in large group meetings, but it will probably take shape in meetings by the smaller design team. Out of all the dreams, some of which may be far out into left field, we now need to develop a dream that becomes our real target.

Stage 3: Design

Based on the discovery and the dream, it is now time to begin the design process. While the dream phase put practical concerns and all forms of skepticism aside; now is the time to begin to get practical. Now is the time to say, "Ok, what can we actually do, which will make that dream come true?"

During the Discovery and Dream process, you have generated a long list of things you would like to change. Now you have to organize those and start designing in some logical manner. The beginning point should be the core work process. It is best if they start with a clean sheet of paper and ask themselves the question, "If we were starting a new company and had no restraint, what would we design to be the ideal process?"

This should include the following:

- Cycle time analysis: what would be the fastest, most interruption free path from beginning to end of the process?
- Quality – what do we do well and what are the variance from standards and customer expectations? Along each step in the process, how could we design features that would eliminate or reduce the potential for quality problems?
- Principles – where does the process either reflect or deviate from our principles? How can we design our principles into the process?
- Cost – where are the major costs in the process and how can costs be reduced while improving throughput and quality?
- Eliminate waste – are there any unnecessary steps? Are there ways to combine steps? Does the product or service ever stand still as it makes its way through the process? How can these delays be eliminated?

Since the organization exists for the purpose of creating the output of the core process, the enabling processes (human resources, information systems, etc.) should be designed to support and optimize the core work process. At this stage the design team may either redesign those processes (they may not have the right people on the design team and it may not be within their charter); or, they may create process requirements for the enabling processes. The core work process is the customer of those processes and should be clear in stating what it needs in order to optimize the core work.

Once the core work process is designed into its ideal desired state, the design team begins to address the structure and systems around the process. There is one BIG rule as they begin to do this. Design the organization from the bottom up! In other words, what is the organization of groups at the first level, where the work is done, that will maximize the probability that the work will be done in the best possible way.

This is the beginning of structure. The structure of society begins with the structure of the family. The beginning of organization structure should be the design of the small work groups who will manage and improve their work on a day-to-day basis. After the first level groups are formed, the question is then asked, "What help do they need to do their work in the best possible way?" Think about how this question is different from asking, "How many managers are needed?" If you ask what help is needed you will get a very different answer, and it will be a more "lean" answer. If the right training, information, tools, decision authority, and coaching are provided, you will find that far less management is needed.

Similar questions are then asked about all of the systems in the organization. For example:

- How can the information systems most help those who do the work?
- What method of presentation and delivery of information would be most helpful to the teams?
- What training systems would most enable teams and individuals to do their job in the ideal way?
- What methods and patterns of communication would be most helpful and encouraging to employees?

The design team will identify all of the relevant systems that support the core work, and will then develop a list of questions and issues to be addressed in their design work.

Design teams are always confronted with the issue of details – "how far into detail should we go?" An analogy has proven helpful. You are designing a house. When designing a new house you need to decide where the walls go, where the staircase will be, and where electrical wires need to run. But, you do not need to decide the color of the walls, or the carpet, or where the furniture is going to go. You can leave those decisions to the new owners who will move in. In fact, allowing them to make these decisions will give them a feeling of ownership for the new house, and encourage them to care for it and improve it. Similarly, there are "walls" and then there is "furniture" when doing an organization design. The design team should ask themselves, are we doing furniture or walls, when they begin to feel that they may be descending in to excessive detail.

Stage 4: Develop:

Rather than think of any design as complete, or finished, it is best to acknowledge the inevitable reality that you have only done the best you could do at this time. In short order, as groups set about implementing the new design, they will quickly find ways to improve it. Rather than create any resistance to this, it is best to plan for it, encourage it and hope that the process of implementation is one of on-going development and learning.

Once the design team has completed their work, they will first present that to the steering team for their reactions and approval. They may have a large group conference where they present their design as a proposal, a tentative design, and then get the group to react to this and suggest improvements, point out possible concerns, and suggest ways they can help the implementation of the design. This again, increases the engagement and commitment of the organization.

How the new design is implemented will depend entirely on the nature of the new design. However, it is generally the case that one or more implementation teams are appointed to take responsibility for components of the design. Depending on the specifics of the design, the nature of the implementation and implementation teams will vary. There may need to be an IS/IT implementation team if there are a large number of information system issues. There may be an implementation team to focus solely on the physical relocation and set up of a manufacturing plant if that has been redesigned. Similarly, there may need to be a training implementation team or one for other human resource issues. The steering team should appoint the implementation teams; they should be given a charter based on the design, and should report their progress to the steering team.

Having observed more than one hundred whole-system design projects roughly following this model, it has always surprised me that an enormous amount of energy is put into the process of design, and then there is a let down when it comes to implementation. The value of the design can be lost if similar energy is not invested in the implementation itself. The implementation must be managed. Good project management skills now need to be used.

It is important that everyone involved has an attitude of continuous improvement when implementing the new process, systems or structure. It will never be 100% right! It will be your best shot at this point in time. However, once you start implementing the new design you will start learning. You will find that some of the pieces don't fit together perfectly, or you may find you have not thought of some element of the process, which also needs to be aligned with the new process you have designed. If you view these discoveries as mistakes or failures, you will stifle the learning process. It is much better to understand that these are inevitable and form integral part the natural process of learning, which occurs during implementation.

Chapter 11

Creating High Value – High Performance Teams

The most critical unit of performance in any organization is the work or management team. High performing organizations are comprised of high performing teams. Performance, however, is not merely the number of widgets produced or the measures of quality. Just as in the organization, the team is a whole-system and the five types of capital parallel those of the organization. This defines its value, its true net worth.

The team is also the most essential unit of learning, just as the family is the most essential unit of learning in the larger society. Learning is the lifeblood of the modern organization. Just as the heart pumps life giving oxygen to the muscles and cells of the body - the process of learning will pump energy, creativity and knowledge through the organization.

The nine disciplines, the broad-slices that create unified energy and effort, are the key drivers of building wealth in the team, creating the five types of capital. This is the currency of competition at the team level, just as it is at the organization level.

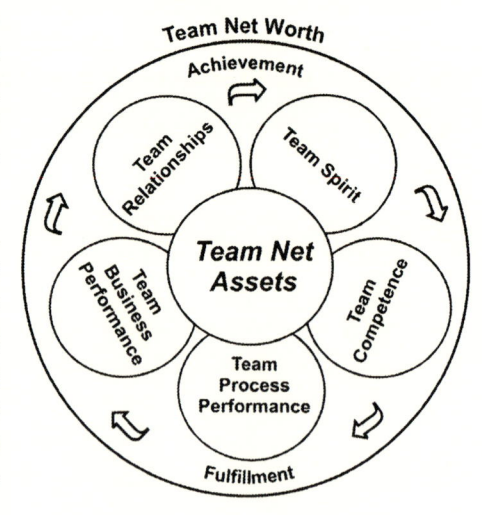

We will use slightly different terminology for the five types of capital to suit the realities of work or management teams. The five types of team capital are *team relationships* (social capital); *team spirit* (spiritual capital); *team knowledge* (intellectual capital) and, *team business performance* (financial capital).

As in the previous chapter, we will review some *critical success indicators* for each of these five forms of capital. In the second half of this chapter, the author will share a process of team development.

Team Relationships:

Effective ***team relationships*** are ***social capital*** and the first requirement of team success. As teams are developed, we typically train them in problem-solving skills, technical skills and process management skills. But failure more often results from poor relationship skills, either within the boundaries of the team or with other teams and managers. Because a work organization is a complex social system, the ability to engage in effective social relationships is the mechanism that enables learning. Learning is the result of dialogue with customers, other teams, and within the team itself.

Anyone who has watched athletic teams understands the importance of chemistry. Chemistry is trust, mutual appreciation, shared purpose, discipline, teamwork and flow. In order to have optimum chemistry in a team it is important to *know* the thoughts and feelings of team members and to trust their values and motivations.

Among the first tasks to improve this chemistry is to create clarity of the team's mission and maintain some consistency in team membership. Families that are constantly breaking up and reforming do not provide the social support to a member that is available in families that are more permanent. Clarity of scorekeeping, an understanding of responsibility to customers, and shared rewards all contribute to close bonds within the team. But, perhaps even more important, teams need to learn to engage in dialogue as discussed in the first section of this book. Most teams do not have the habits required to think together, rather than alone. This requires deliberate training and coaching which we will discuss later in this chapter.

The ability of a team to maintain effective *external relations* is critical to their success. Almost every team in today's business organization is one of many teams, linked together through a process that serves an end-use customer. It is rare for a team to do all of the work that results in customer satisfaction. Similarly, management teams are also linked to other management teams for different functions or units in an organization.

The following are some *critical success indicators* for a team's external relationships:

- The members of the team have defined their customer(s) and have directly communicated, preferably face-to-face, with those customers.
- The team has defined measures of customer satisfaction, which they record, graph, and discuss on a regular basis.
- The team communicates regularly with their suppliers, groups who provide input essential to their work, and they discuss how those groups perform to the team's requirements.
- The work process for which the team is responsible has been designed to optimize the flow (minimize cycle time, inventory, etc.) from suppliers to customers.
- The team gains valuable input and feedback from a coach or team coordinator who helps them solve problems and continually improve.

The *internal relationships* with the team are critical to their ability to solve problems. Just as a dysfunctional family can break down into blaming different members for bad feelings, a team can experience similar internal conflicts that will inhibit their ability to improve their performance. Just as family relationships require deliberate work to maintain its unity, the relationships within a team require attention.

The following are some *critical success indicators* for healthy internal relationships.

- When our team meets to solve problems, the focus is on the facts, the process and the customer, not on personalities.
- We enjoy spending time together outside of the work environment.
- Our team leader or facilitator assures that each member of the team is able to speak freely, in his or her own voice, without any other member dominating the conversation.
- We respect and take into account the opinions of all members of the team.
- Our attitude toward our team's performance is something like a game, where we strive to win, to set new records, to achieve victories that we all celebrate.

Team Spirit:

The term *team spirit* is a genuinely old-fashioned term. But some things that are oldies truly are goodies. The idea that there is a spirit within a team is just as true today as in the past and this spiritual life, is a form of spiritual capital, genuine value to the team, as it is in the organization.

The term *team spirit* will mean different things to different people and the author is not proposing any definition as inclusive or authoritative.

Spiritual capital and social capital are closely linked. The reader will recognize that the idea of team spirit and the internal relationships are inseparable. Just as the relations among its members affect the spiritual life of a family, the same is true of a team. However, there is something deeper implied in the concept of spiritual capital. It is something that transcends the immediacy of personal communication and feelings. If a husband and wife share a deep religious commitment, a commitment to a well-defined set of values, that commitment can overcome or resolve the more transitory personal communication and relationships. Similarly, the spirit of a team is defined by their commitment to both a set of **shared values** and a dedication to a ***worthy purpose***.

A worthy purpose for a team must begin with an understanding of their customers. Team members usually have a desire to improve and meet their customer's needs if provided an effective team system. This team system should include good data to enable scorekeeping and decision-making authority to improve their process. Valuing the customer is the most critical value on most work teams. It is also the first and most important worthy purpose. However, many other values can easily affect the performance of a team.

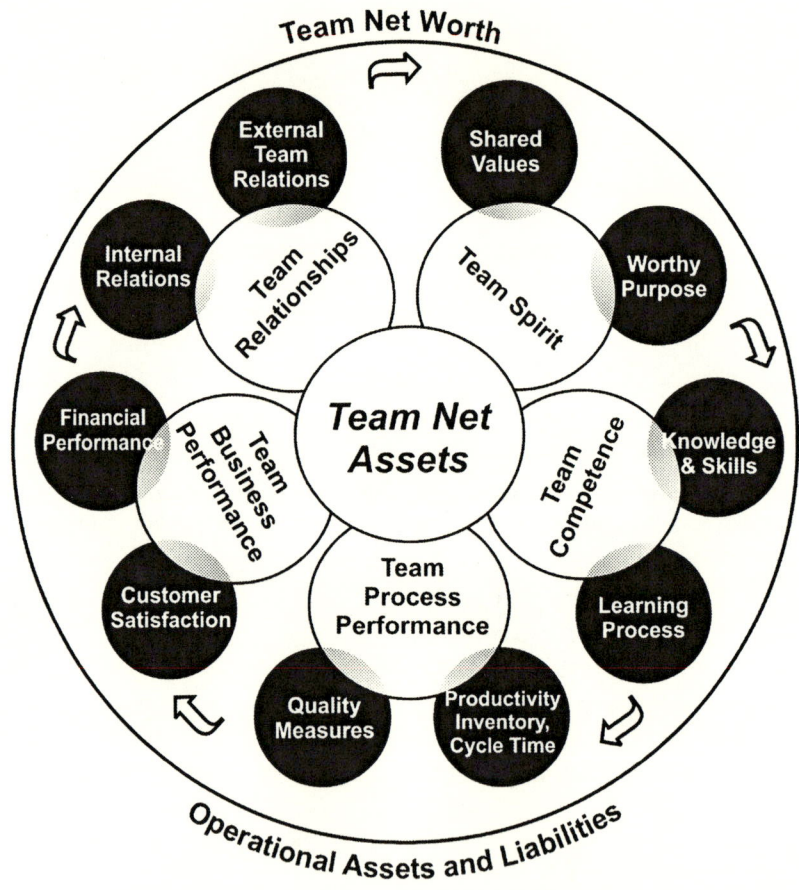

Team Net Worth

- External Team Relations
- Shared Values
- Internal Relations
- Team Relationships
- Team Spirit
- Worthy Purpose
- Financial Performance
- Team Business Performance
- **Team Net Assets**
- Team Competence
- Knowledge & Skills
- Customer Satisfaction
- Team Process Performance
- Learning Process
- Quality Measures
- Productivity Inventory, Cycle Time

Operational Assets and Liabilities

Most of us live in a culture with people of diverse backgrounds, diverse religious beliefs, and differing personal priorities. Some members of a team may feel very strongly about putting their family first and not allowing work meetings or priorities to interfere with their family life. Others may make different choices. The trick in developing shared values is not to force conformity of all personal values, but rather to develop and ethic that will bring together people with differing personal values into a cohesive work unit. This requires a deliberate effort to recognize those values that are shared.

Developing a common value structure and shared motivation is more difficult in professional and management teams. Often members of management teams have competing interests and may be competing for promotion to the next level of management. The most serious case I have seen of competing interests was on the senior team of a health care organization. This organization included hospitals, clinics and insurance. Each of these three divisions had very different interests. It was in the interest of the insurance division for as few of its customers as possible to seek care at the clinics or the hospitals. When a patient sought care at a clinic or hospital, it resulted in a cost to the insurance company. However, it was revenue and profit to the other two divisions. And clinics and hospitals had similar competing interests. It was nearly impossible to develop a unified strategy and common objectives with such contrary interests on this team. This however, is the exception. It is generally possible, with effort to develop a common set of values, belief in the future goals, and a common score card that can unite the team.

The following are some *critical success indicators* for shared values within a team:

- The team has developed a statement of principles or values by which it has agreed to live.
- When solving problems, or seeking improvement, the team refers to its values as a criterion for its decisions.
- We can remember situations in which members of the team were willing to sacrifice their personal interest for the sake of the team's shared values.
- There is a high level of personal trust among the team members.
- We know that members of the team will come to aid of another member who may be having difficulty on the job or in their personal life.

The following are some *critical success indicators* for a common worthy purpose among team members:

- Members of the team feel that the work they do serves a worthy purpose.
- Members of the team feel a genuine empathy for the end-use customer, truly understanding the customer's needs.
- We feel that the work we do makes the work of our internal customers more successful and we constantly think how to be helpful to these internal customers.
- We are proud to tell people that we work for this organization.
- If I were offered a similar job with similar compensation, I would still prefer to work in this organization because of the type of work we do.

Team Competence:

An athletic team succeeds due to the individual skills of each member. Some teams have a unique ability to develop competence in their team members. For many years, the author lived in Atlanta and followed the Atlanta Braves baseball team. While they only won the World Series once, for fourteen years they have won their division. Such consistent performance says something about both their process for selecting players and their process of developing those players. For both companies and teams, the ability to develop the talents, knowledge and skills of their members is a critical form of capital.

Shared team competence is also a factor that unites a team. If a few of the players have outstanding ability, and others have mediocre or less ability, that difference becomes a source of disunity. This is not to say that team members need to have the same abilities. On a baseball team, the pitcher has unique and different abilities than those who play the outfield. It is generally accepted that the best and most valued pitcher on the team may be completely incompetent at swinging the bat. Teams are very capable of appreciating different abilities. However, it is important that team members feel that everyone is seeking to improve his or her skills so that they will make their maximum contribution to team success.

Competence includes many things. It includes more than knowledge. *Competence* can be divided into **knowledge** and **skill**. Knowledge is in the head, while skill is in the performance. I may know how to type a hundred words per minute on a keyboard. I know because I have read every book ever written on the subject of typing. Intellectually, I am a true expert on the subject. Does that necessarily mean that I can type at the rate of one hundred words per minute? No. Knowing and doing are entirely different. A seventy-year-old coach can instruct twenty-year-old basketball players. While the coach has great knowledge, he cannot perform the skill. The athlete may also perform this skill with relatively little intellectual understanding of what he or she is doing.

In today's organization, the knowledge and skill requirements are continually changing. New equipment, new processes, new responsibilities are continually being added to the requirements of a team. For this reason, it is the responsibility of every team to manage their learning. It is also the responsibility of the larger organization to provide the time and tools required for effective learning. Both the learning process and the presence of the needed knowledge and skills comprise the capital of team competence.

The following are *critical success indicators* for team knowledge and skills:

- Our team has defined the specific sets of knowledge and skills that are required for our success.
- Each separate position on our team has a defined set of knowledge or skills.
- We are able to measure our knowledge or skills and we can demonstrate that we possess the required competence.
- Our team has an outstanding reputation as a result of our demonstrated competence.
- We have been able to find creative ways to improve our work, our product or service that has contributed to the performance of the larger organization.

The following are *critical success indicators* for our teams learning process:

- We set aside time for learning each week.
- The organization regularly provides us with outside resources to increase our knowledge or skills.
- One of the best things about being a member of this team is that we are constantly learning.
- We benchmark other teams, both in this organization and in other organizations, to find ideas that can improve our work.
- We have a coach or someone who has the specific job of helping us learn and develop as a team.

Team Process Performance:

In chapter six, we defined teams, not as temporary problem-solving groups, but as permanent groups that take on-going responsibility for business or process performance. Teams are formed around, and take ownership of specific processes. It is their job to manage, to measure and improve those processes. This definition applies whether the team is at the first level of the organization or whether it is the team led by the chief executive officer.

Teams become the "world's greatest experts" as Honda calls them, in their processes. Who else should be more knowledgeable about a process for which a team is responsible than the members of that team?

There are two key elements of process performance for a team: one is the *quality of the process* and the other is *productivity* of the process. The productivity can be measured in terms of input divided by output; the levels of in-process inventory and cycle time through the process.

The quality of the process can be measured both at the customer, how satisfied they are with the product or service; and it can be measured within the work process itself, as each step produces a result that conforms to quality standards.

Although it is a somewhat an arbitrary distinction, we will consider customer satisfaction as a measure of business performance. Here we will consider only the measure of quality within the work process.

The following are *critical success indicators* for the quality of the process:

- Our work process is clearly defined and we can see a visual map of the process.
- We know that we are responsible and are empowered to make changes to improve the process.
- Our team has been trained in statistical methods to ensure that our process is in control and to identify problems that are "special cause" outside of the control limits.
- On a regular basis, such as weekly, we meet to review our process and brainstorm ways to improve our process.
- We cross train members of the team to be able to perform various jobs within the process to enhance both our flexibility and our problem solving ability.

The following are *critical success indicators* for the productivity of our work process:

- We have measures that indicate the ratio of output of our process divided by the input to give us a productivity measure.
- We measure the cycle time from input to output through our work process.
- We measure our in-process inventory levels.
- For each of the above three measures we have goals for improvement.
- We have succeeded in improving our measures of productivity over the past year.

Team Business Performance:

Team business performance is the final form of capital for a team. This is the equivalent of the financial capital for the organization. A team is valuable to the degree that it possesses all the previous capabilities, but in the end, these must result in some type of financial performance if the team is in a business.

Financial performance can be measured directly and ***customer satisfaction*** is the leading indicator of ***financial performance***. For example, if the market place comes to feel that your product or services provide the greatest total satisfaction, you will be able to price that product or service favorably and it will be in sufficient demand. Financial results follow customer satisfaction. Both should be measured.

Nothing enhances the self-esteem, creates a sense of confidence and the motivation to improve, more than the knowledge of business results. In a sense this is the "real-deal" and any team that is deprived of the knowledge of how it is actually producing business results (or not) senses that it is being treated in a somewhat parent-child manner, not completely trusted with the important business of business. When granted knowledge and responsibility for business results teams always perform in a higher manner, seeking to improve those results.

The following are some *critical success indicators* for customer satisfaction:

- We have recently (the past few months) received direct positive feedback from our customers.
- We have data that tells us that our customers prefer our products and services to those of our competition.
- We have data that tells us that our customer satisfaction is in an upward trend.
- We have very specific goals for responding to any request or complaint from customers, and this cycle time usually provides a positive surprise to our customers.
- We have measures of both the reliability of our product or service, and we have measures that tell us the value, from superior features, are both better than our nearest competitor.

Management and work teams are business teams. Just as the family operating a store or a family farm, functions as a business unit, so should every team in the workplace. The family farm was an economic unit that had to make income match or exceed expenses. There is a personal satisfaction, a pride, which comes from managing to the real financial numbers.

In the ideal case, every team would have a balance sheet indicating the operating assets employed in their work; and an income statement that would report their real expenses and their real earned income. Of course, in many organizations creating such a specific system of financial report to each team is not administratively possible or practical. However, it is most often possible to share the real financial reports with the organization and allocate some specific numbers to the teams that contribute to either costs or income.

It is difficult to generalize about the specifics of financial reporting to teams because teams can be very diverse in their structure and responsibilities. However, some time of financial accountability is simple good business and causes team members to feel ownership for the real financial results.

The following are some *critical success indicators* for financial performance at the team level:

- Our team receives reports based on real financial results for which we are, in some way, responsible.
- We measure our financial costs of doing our team's business.
- We have a measure of income that we can compare to our costs.
- We have a measure of the assets we employ doing our work.
- We are able to compute the relationship of our earnings (our income minus our costs) to our assets employed to give us a return-on-operating assets figure.

If any team is measuring and doing well on the above five types of capital they are a high performing team. No team will be able to respond positively to everyone of the critical success indicators given in the previous pages. However, we are working toward these things. Remember that it is valuable to have some idea of an ideal toward which you can strive.

Creating an Effective Team Management Process

The implementation of teams must be an *action-learning process*. You don't become a competent team from a seminar, workshop or book! After a three-day workshop, participants will gain knowledge, some motivation, but will not develop the skills of application or change the habits that are required of an effective team.

What has proven successful is an introductory workshop, but then a process of phased implementation, coaching and feedback are needed to achieve effective team performance. With companies such as Amoco, Shell, Texaco, Coca-Cola, Landmark Communications and a hundred others, my consultants and I have trained internal coaches who literally coach every team. Just as a young person learns to play baseball or football by receiving a very short amount of instruction and then going out on the field and playing, followed by gentle coaching and feedback, we have had great success by applying a similar action learning process.

Action-learning is simply learning by taking actions, in this case, as a team, and experiencing the effects of those actions. Action-learning can be outside the work environment, but most importantly, it must also be in the real world of the team's responsibilities.

A few years ago, I was working with the senior management team of Tarmac in Norfolk, Virginia. We agreed that it might help to build the bonds and improve communication within the team if they did something together outside of their work. One member of the team knew someone who worked with the YM/YWCA and one of the facilities was badly in need of repair. They were looking for help. The members of this team knew about construction, they were guys who built things, real things, roads and buildings. This was right up their alley. As a group, they went to visit the facility, met with the director and some of the children who used the facility. They came back to their usual meeting room, and after months of coaching this team, this was the most enthusiastic discussion I had witnessed.

There is something about doing something for someone else, something about an apparently self-less act, that unites people. When discussing this project, and for the following months as they worked to improve this facility, entirely at their own expense, their communication was freer, unburdened by political pressures and competitive concerns. They were a better team in every respect. With this experience, they could reflect on that communication and ask themselves why it was different.

This is action-learning and it cannot be replicated just sitting in a classroom, or even with experiential games that are used in workshops. While those experiential exercises are also useful, doing something real is a far more enriching experience.

Envisioning the Ideal Team:

Like individuals, teams should have some view of who they want to be "when they grow up" or to put it another way, what is the "ideal-state," the perfect team in their work setting? It would be wise to have a series of team meetings to discuss a self-managed learning and development plan, one that the team itself will take responsibility for managing. The critical success indicators discussed in the previous section will be a good starting point for this discussion.

The process of Appreciative Inquiry is very helpful when thinking about the future "ideal-state" of the team. In every organization, there are well functioning teams. If every team seeking to develop itself engaged in the process of looking for the best, looking for outstanding performance, and asking why? What is it that causes that team to perform so well? What do their team meetings look like? How do they keep score? What training have they had? How are they facilitated? How do they keep track of decisions and follow-up on those decisions? These questions, when asked about a successful team, naturally and inevitably will result in the improvement of the team doing the inquiring. To inquire is to learn.

It is interesting that in sports no one ever goes and studies the worst teams and says, "Let's problem-solve what is wrong with this team?" On the contrary, they are always studying the best players and the best teams. Why in our organizations do we reverse this and focus on the problems? Which one leads to the most effective learning? I believe it is the model of appreciative inquiry.

But the team should discover beyond its own borders. There are two aspects of this: the first is inquiry with customers and others who have knowledge and interest in their performance; and the second is to benchmark other teams in search of best practices.

Customers are usually willing to help their suppliers (whether internal or external to a company) in their quest for improvement. If you go to the next team in the value chain from input to output, and ask how you can serve them better, it is often true that they will be helpful. Those outside of a team, particularly those who receive the work of the team, often have insights into how a team is functioning that it cannot see for itself. For example, you may learn that the customer is much more concerned about *how* something is delivered, instead of *what* is delivered. It is often very important on the receiving end that things are boxed in a particular way, that the delivery is timed or in sizes that match a production process. The customer's needs may be very different from the focus of the team and may result in improvement that would be impossible if viewed from an inside only perspective.

When was the last time your team looked around for the best performing teams in the company? What would happen if your team asked to meet with that team for the sole purpose of inquiring as to what they did well? I think it is important for this process to be encouraged at every level in a company.

Coaching As a Development Aid:

An important component of *Development* is coaching. Consider why every athletic team has a coach. How effectively would the team learn and develop if there was no coach?

A consultant of mine was working in a division of United Technologies that manufactured defense weapons some years ago. The leader of this division, for the sake of this illustration we will call him Steve, was the advocate for our program to improve quality through self-directed work and management teams. My consultant had been working with them for about four months when I received a call telling me that things weren't going well and the difficulty was Steve's team.

It is an axiom in a management/culture change process, that the senior team must be a model, must lead by doing. Steve's team wasn't leading. They were not the model of an effective team. I asked the consultant what he felt was the problem. He had difficulty describing it, but he was continually getting reports from the members of the team that Steve did not allow or encourage participation.

I paid a visit and met with Steve. Steve was positive and supportive as usual. He believed in the effort, yet he acknowledged that his team was a problem. He said he wasn't sure that he had the right people on his team, and he thought he might have to replace some of them because they didn't participate actively in problem-solving. They tended to sit passively rather than engaging in the conversation.

I made my visit on a day I knew Steve was planning to have his weekly team meeting. I met with him in the morning and asked if I could sit in the meeting that afternoon.

Steve was right. The members of the group didn't participate well. Steve did a good job of laying out an agenda, reviewing action plans from previous meetings, reviewing the graphs on past performance, and introducing a topic for discussion. When Steve asked for participation, he was standing up. In his strong, confident and authoritative voice, he described a problem and then, with his arm extended and his finger pointing said, "Joe, what do you think we should do about that?"

Joe did not respond enthusiastically. He paused and then very quietly offered a suggestion. Steve looked at me, as if to say, "See, I told you they were a problem!"

I didn't say anything during the meeting, I waited until Steve and I met to debrief. I asked Steve to sit in his chair and I stood in front of him. I extended my arm and pointed at him saying, "Steve, how do you think that went?" Then I immediately put up my hand as if to say, "No, don't answer." I then brought my arm in closer to me, turned the palm of my hand upward, with no finger pointing and said, "Steve, how did you feel the meeting went?"

Then I asked him how different he felt, when the two questions were put to him, and why.

He got it, immediately. He experienced the difference in how it felt to be on the receiving end, and he recognized that he had just done the same in the meeting. I made a couple other simple suggestions, such as asking other members of the group to share the role of facilitating parts of the meeting, such as when problem-solving particular topics.

Steve thought he was encouraging participation. Steve was not a "bad guy." But, Steve's behavior did the opposite of his intentions. His finger pointing hand discouraged the very thing he wanted to encourage. The difficulty is that the way Steve experienced events, the way he saw himself, and the way others experienced his behavior and saw him, were completely different. We all have a mirror in which we see ourselves, and that mirror is somewhat distorted for all of us. Our self-perceptions are never one hundred percent accurate. Coaching and sensitive feedback can create awareness. But, this must occur in the context of real life events. This is one important form of experiential or action-learning.

The Role of the Leadership Team:

Implementing a team-based organization is an exercise in developing new skills, new habits, and new culture. It will require motivation and discipline. An athletic team does not develop superior performance by practicing simply when it is in the mood, when it "feels" like it. It does not develop by practicing in a random or disconnected manner. It does not develop without a clear sense of roles and responsibilities and a game plan for each position on the team. Similarly, in order to develop the skills and habits of a team based organization there must be a clear plan and a disciplined effort.

The leadership team of an organization must take responsibility for actively managing the process of improvement. Every consultant, regardless of the methodology, has learned the importance of leadership from the top. This was just as true in Total Quality Management as it is in Six Sigma, and was true in reengineering, or at General Electrics "work-out" process. The leaders of the organization, put very simply, must make it important! If not considered important, too many distractions will derail significant changes.

To be an effective team leader or member requires the development of new habits and skills. When these become the norm in the organization, you have changed the culture. However, to establish that change in behavior and culture it is important to come to terms with how individuals actually learn new skills.

We have standard methods of training in our organizations, particularly the two or three day workshop model, which works well to introduce new knowledge or new skills, but is entirely insufficient to actually establish a new set of habits in the organization. Habits are changed over time, often a long time, with repeated practice, feedback and encouragement. There must be a process that provides for this.

The method that has proven most successful involves an introductory workshop, then a six to twelve month period of practice, coaching, feedback, and on-the-job training. During the first year of implementation, every team should have a coach to provide support and guidance through the development process. Coaches should form their own team to process the lessons they are learning, share experience and insights and identify system wide constraints and needs for modification of systems and structures. These coaches can be either internal or external consultants, and a combination often works best.

A Specific Implementation Plan:

The following is a step-by-step map of an implementation process. These steps represent the learning, after much trial and error and expense, in several hundred organizations. My associates and I have implemented team management over a twenty-year period and we have learned many lessons. I have attempted to incorporate several of those lessons in the design of this process. It is certainly not the only way to implement a team system in an organization. Every organization is different and requires modification and customization. However this plan is, at least, a good starting point for developing your own plan.

The left hand columns are the "macro" steps; and, the detailed steps are presented horizontally, from left to right – with a very brief discussion of each step.

248 *Competing in the New Capitalism*

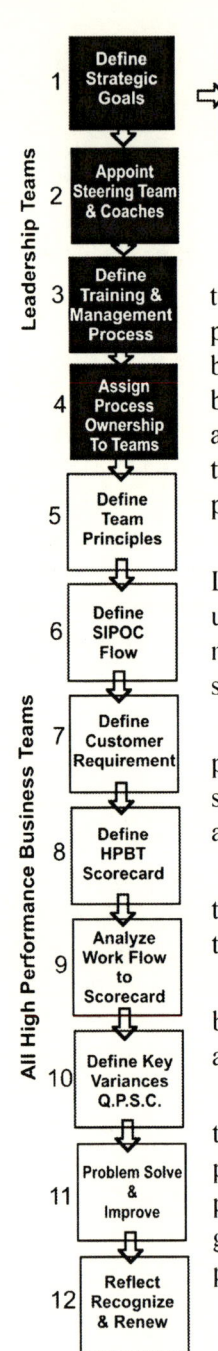

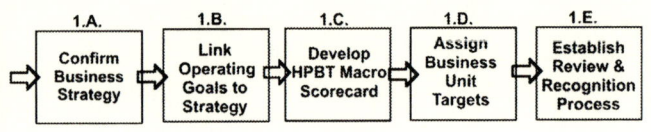

1. Define Strategic Goals:

The leadership team of the organization is the team with overall responsibility for business performance. Their responsibility is to have a business strategy that defines future market position, brand strategy, and the strategic initiatives that will achieve that strategy and financial performance. It is their job to translate that strategy into clear performance targets.

1A. Confirm Business Strategy: The Leadership team should begin by confirming that it understands the business strategy and that it has clear measures of business success that are linked to the strategy.

1B. Operating goals include quality, productivity, cost and speed (QPCS). Virtually every strategy, at the team level, can be measured in the achievement of these four measures.

1C. Develop a macro scorecard, the scores for the entire organization, and this should serve as a template for teams lower in the organization.

1D. Set one or two "challenge goals" for business units. These may be targets such as achieving Six Sigma, or reducing cycle time by 50%.

1E. The leadership team must begin to create team discipline and motivation by establishing clear progress reviews and a recognition and feedback process to reinforce teams who are achieving their goals. This progress review should include both process and results.

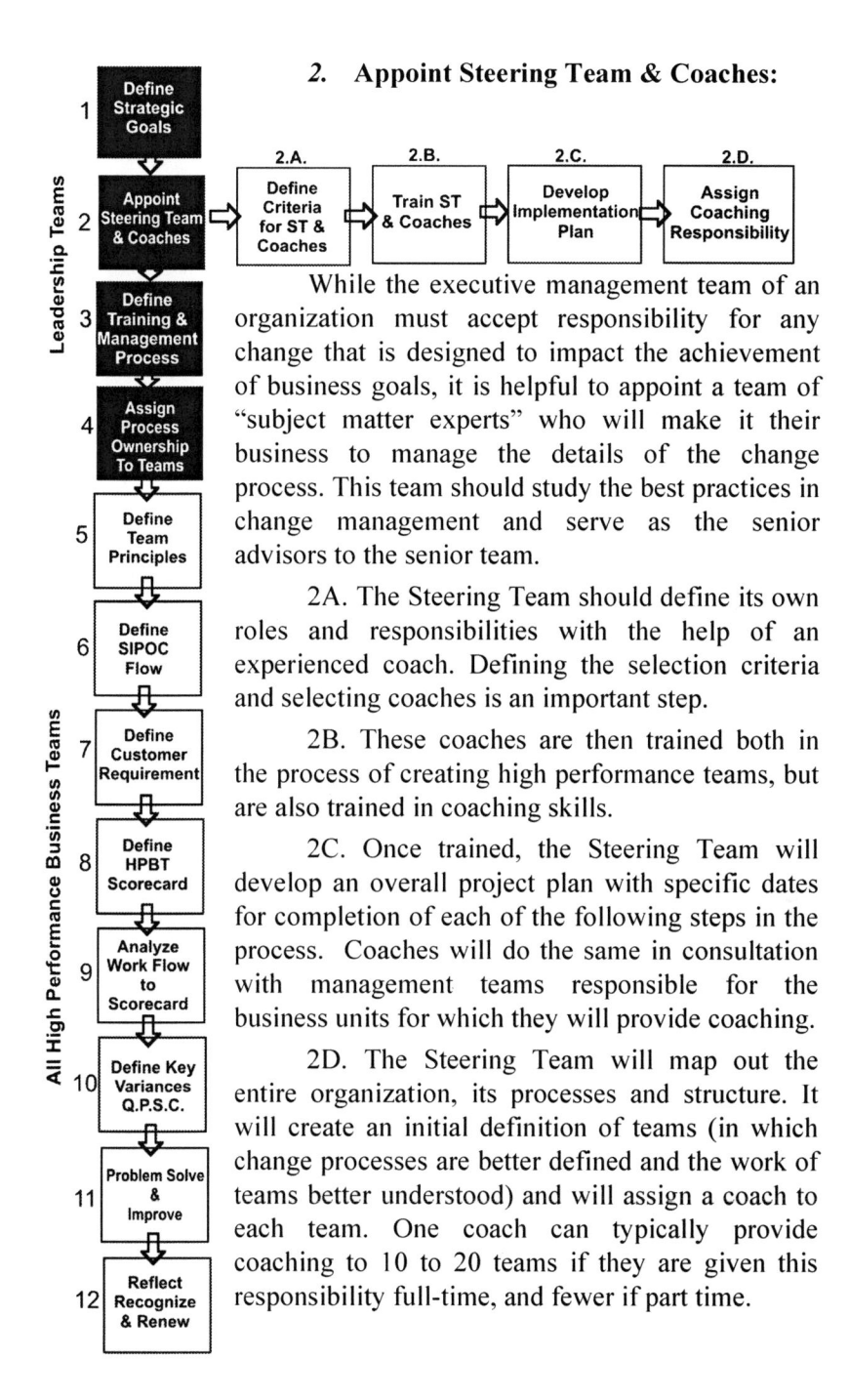

2. Appoint Steering Team & Coaches:

While the executive management team of an organization must accept responsibility for any change that is designed to impact the achievement of business goals, it is helpful to appoint a team of "subject matter experts" who will make it their business to manage the details of the change process. This team should study the best practices in change management and serve as the senior advisors to the senior team.

2A. The Steering Team should define its own roles and responsibilities with the help of an experienced coach. Defining the selection criteria and selecting coaches is an important step.

2B. These coaches are then trained both in the process of creating high performance teams, but are also trained in coaching skills.

2C. Once trained, the Steering Team will develop an overall project plan with specific dates for completion of each of the following steps in the process. Coaches will do the same in consultation with management teams responsible for the business units for which they will provide coaching.

2D. The Steering Team will map out the entire organization, its processes and structure. It will create an initial definition of teams (in which change processes are better defined and the work of teams better understood) and will assign a coach to each team. One coach can typically provide coaching to 10 to 20 teams if they are given this responsibility full-time, and fewer if part time.

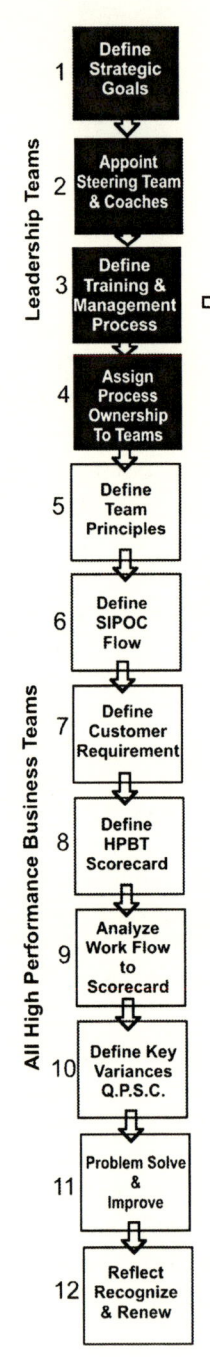

3. Define Training & Management Process:

An important aspect of developing high performance teams is that everyone in the organization should participate in training and in the team process itself. It is an inclusive management system, not simply a training program. Therefore, it is important that all of those who will be expected to participate receive training.

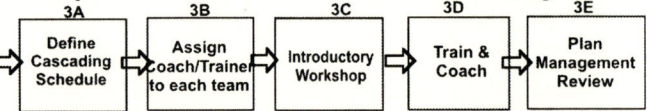

3A. Define Cascading Schedule: It is important the leaders of the organization be among the first to participate in the training so they can begin to serve as a model for the rest of the organization. A schedule should be established starting at the top of the organization and cascading down.

3B. Assign coach to each team.

3C. Present introductory workshop and training materials.

3D. Train and coach on a weekly/bi-weekly or monthly basis.

3E. Plan and assure management review of training and team development process.

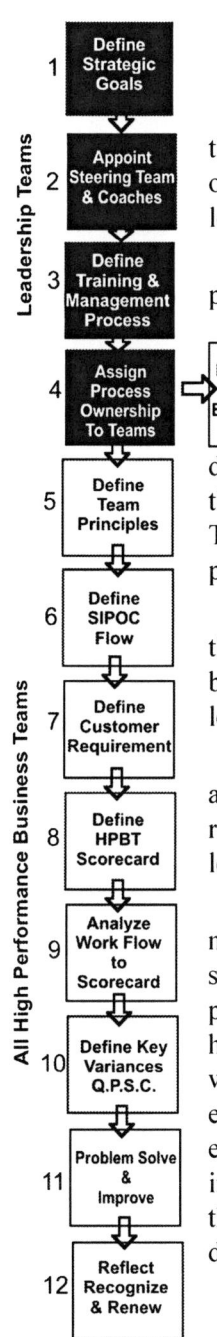

4. Assign Process Ownership to Teams:

The most senior team owns the entire process that flows through the organization. The components of the large process must be broken down into some logical flow, and each component assigned to a team.

4A. The steering team should map the entire process flow from input to output. This should be done first with the "core work" process, that process that directly results in revenue to the organization. Then the "enabling" processes that support the core process should be mapped out.

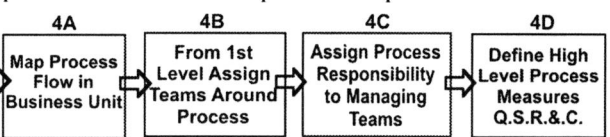

4B. Each component of these processes should then be assigned to a team. Assign team responsibility beginning at the first level of the organization, the level at which the core work is actually performed.

4C. Then assign teams of managers at the level above. The team process should maximize responsibility at the first level, reducing the need for levels of management.

4D. Each team should be responsible for clear measures of performance (quality, productivity, speed, and costs) for their process and/or for the process of a group of teams. In other words, you may have a team whose work is too closely linked to the work of another team for their revenue measure, for example, to be an independent measure. Nevertheless, every team should strive to have measures that include quality, speed, revenue, and costs. These are the four BIG ONES – the four measures that distinguish any another team from a business team.

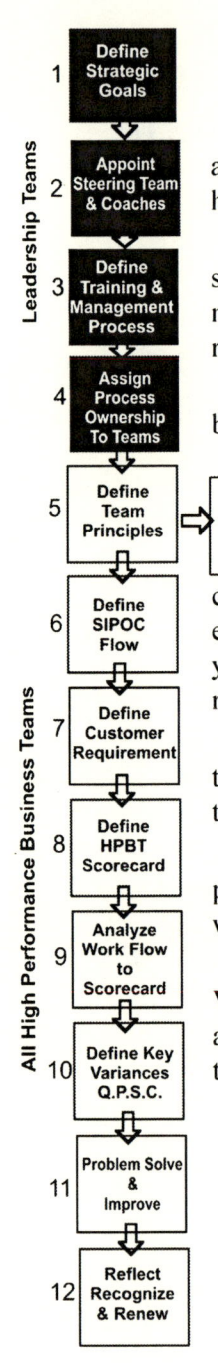

4. Define Your Team's Principles:

All groups, whether families, communities, or work and management teams, perform best when the members have a common understanding of principles.

5A. Frames of Reference: Corporate value statements are one frame of reference. However, you and members of your team may have other frames of reference.

5B. Stakeholders: Who cares about the work done by your team? Anyone who cares is a stakeholder. Your customers, your suppliers, your managers or your employees are all stakeholders. What do they need from you (in general terms, later you will define specific requirements).

5C. Business Purpose: What is the purpose of your team in terms of the business? How do you contribute to the overall success of the business?

5D. Ideal State: Imagine that your team is the perfect, ideal team; performing in the ideal manner. What would this ideal state look and feel like?

5E. Form Consensus on Your Team's Purpose, Vision and Principles: After having brainstormed the above questions, it is time to reach consensus on your team as to your purpose, vision and principles.

Leadership Teams:
1. Define Strategic Goals
2. Appoint Steering Team & Coaches
3. Define Training & Management Process
4. Assign Process Ownership To Teams

All High Performance Business Teams:
5. Define Team Principles
6. Define SIPOC Flow
7. Define Customer Requirement
8. Define HPBT Scorecard
9. Analyze Work Flow to Scorecard
10. Define Key Variances Q.P.S.C.
11. Problem Solve & Improve
12. Reflect Recognize & Renew

Step 5 detail:
- 5A: Study Frames of Reference
- 5B: Define Stakeholders' Needs
- 5C: Brainstorm Business Purpose
- 5D: Define Vision of Ideal Future State
- 5E: Form Consensus Purpose, Vision & Principles

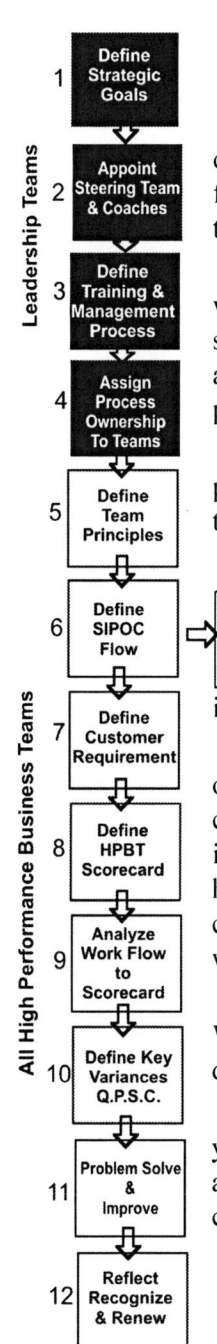

6. Define SIPOC Flow:

Business teams manage a system. It can be defined in a number of different ways, but the most fundamental way is to analyze the flow of work to the customer.

6A. Define Core Work Process: The core work process is the essential work that results in service and satisfaction for your customers. For almost every team there are core and enabling processes.

6B. Define Your Customers: Your work process may be one component of a chain processes that serve and end use customer, as well as an immediate customer who uses your work output.

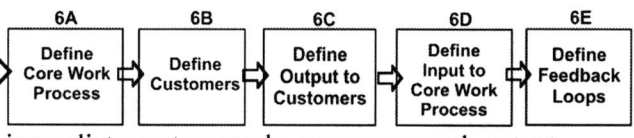

6C. Define Output to Customers: What is the output of your work process that ads value to your customer? This is the product, service, or information that enables the customer to perform his or her work. Your product or service is the critical, measurable item for which the customer is willing to pay.

6D. Define Input to Core Work Process: What do you need to do your work? From whom does it come?

6E. Define Feedback Loops: It is the job of your team to establish sets of feedback loops. First, and most important, define feedback from your customer to you, second, from you to your supplier.

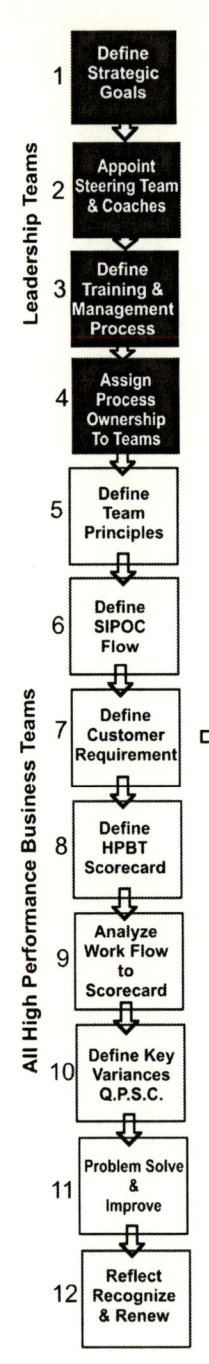

7. Define Customer Requirements:

There is no more important step in developing high performance business teams than clearly and accurately defining customer requirements.

7A. Review & Confirm Customer Relationships: Before proceeding with the following steps, just be certain that you have identified your customers.

7B. Prioritize Customers: Are all customers equal? Sometimes they are and sometimes not. It may be, for example, that your strategy calls for a migration from one group of customers to another.

7C. Know the Facts! It is absolutely normal to think you know what your customers want – and to be entirely wrong. We are often operating on assumptions about our customers without having actually asked them, listened to them, and reflected back our understanding to them to check out the accuracy of our perceptions. It is essential that you go through the process of actually gathering the data on customer perceptions of your work.

7D. Gather the Facts: Now you have to do the actual data gathering. Gathering the facts is not simply a one-time thing but a process that presents facts over time, trends, and variability.

7E. Analyze the Facts: Once the data is gathered it must be given meaning and significance. It is a key function of the team to process those data, assess the meaning of customer's input. Assessing that meaning is the beginning of the improvement process.

8. Define Your Business Team Scorecard:

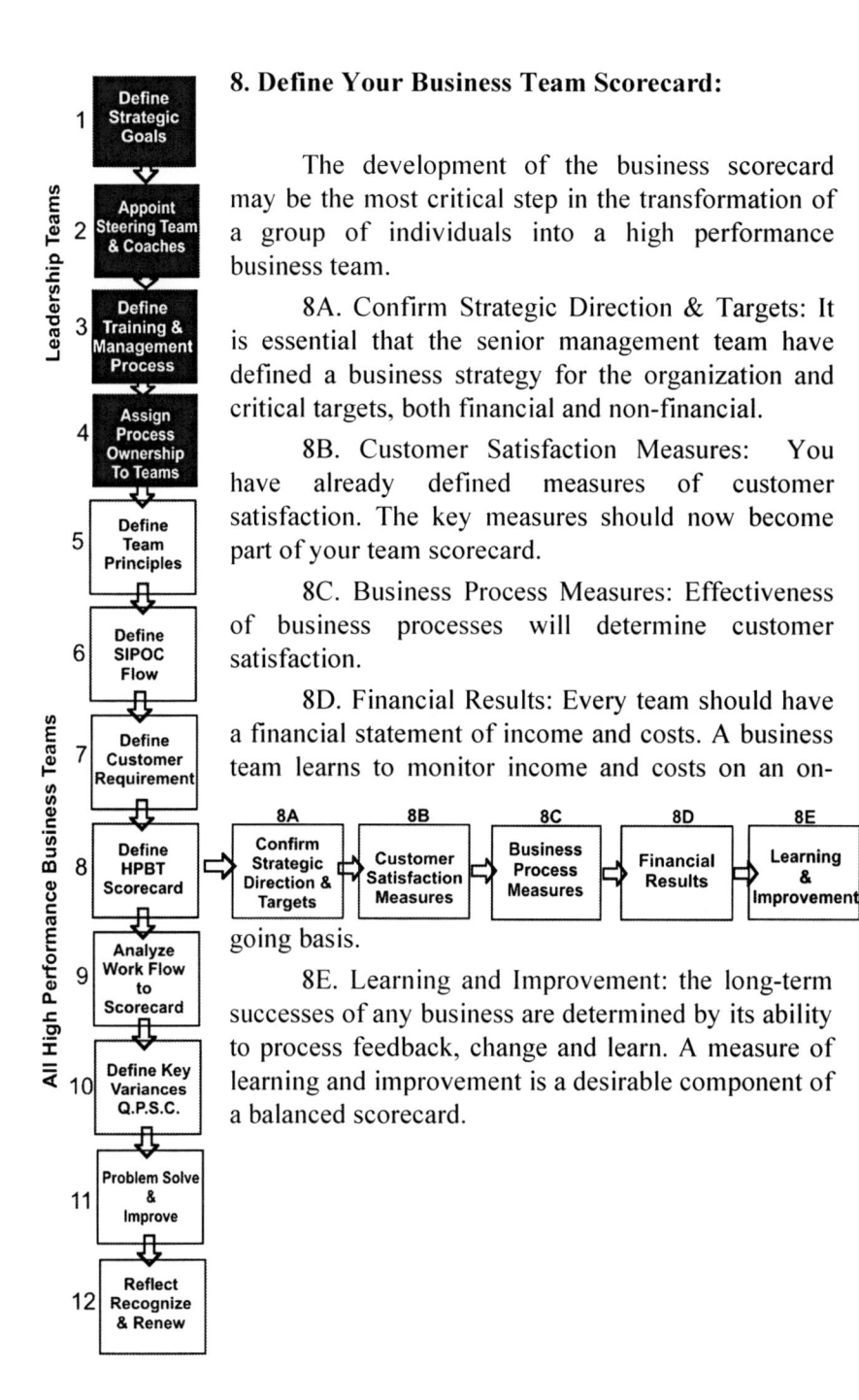

The development of the business scorecard may be the most critical step in the transformation of a group of individuals into a high performance business team.

8A. Confirm Strategic Direction & Targets: It is essential that the senior management team have defined a business strategy for the organization and critical targets, both financial and non-financial.

8B. Customer Satisfaction Measures: You have already defined measures of customer satisfaction. The key measures should now become part of your team scorecard.

8C. Business Process Measures: Effectiveness of business processes will determine customer satisfaction.

8D. Financial Results: Every team should have a financial statement of income and costs. A business team learns to monitor income and costs on an on-going basis.

8E. Learning and Improvement: the long-term successes of any business are determined by its ability to process feedback, change and learn. A measure of learning and improvement is a desirable component of a balanced scorecard.

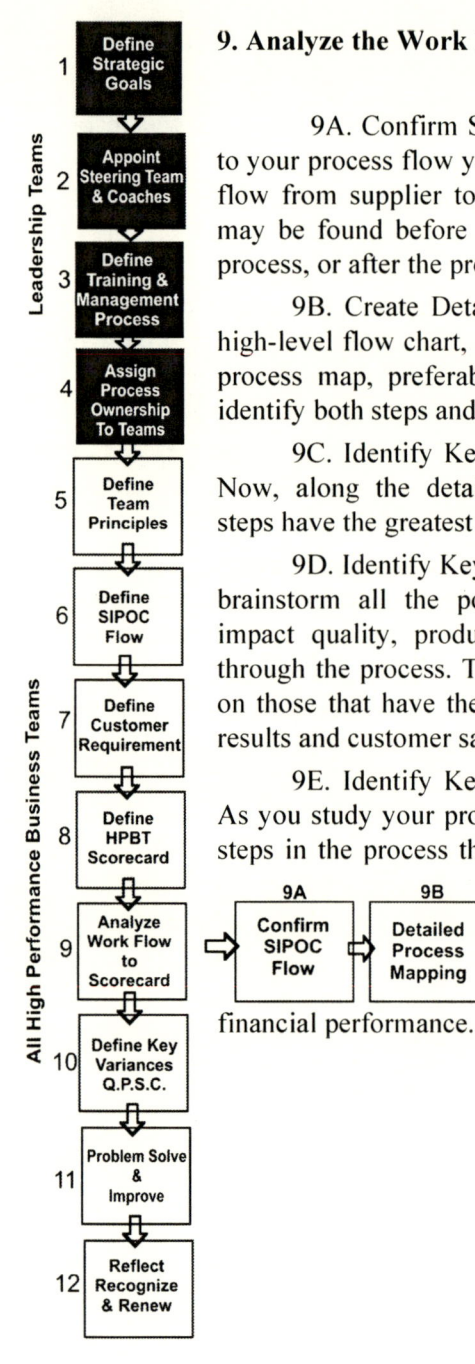

9. Analyze the Work Flow:

9A. Confirm SIPOC Flow: To link the scorecard to your process flow you should first review your process flow from supplier to customer. Links to the scorecard may be found before the core work process, within the process, or after the process.

9B. Create Detailed Process Mapping: An initial, high-level flow chart, should now be turned in a detailed process map, preferably using a "relationship map" to identify both steps and responsibilities.

9C. Identify Key Steps for Customer Satisfaction: Now, along the detailed process map, identify which steps have the greatest impact on customer satisfaction.

9D. Identify Key Q.P.S.C. Measures & Steps: Now brainstorm all the possible steps in the process that impact quality, productivity, speed and costs of flow through the process. Then prioritize and reach consensus on those that have the greatest impact on both financial results and customer satisfaction.

9E. Identify Key Steps to Financial Performance: As you study your process brainstorm and identify those steps in the process that will have the greatest effect on financial performance.

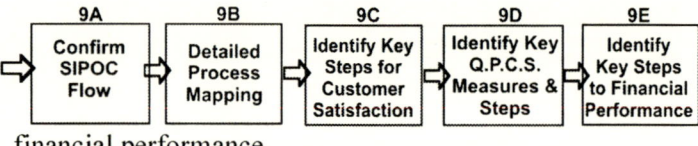

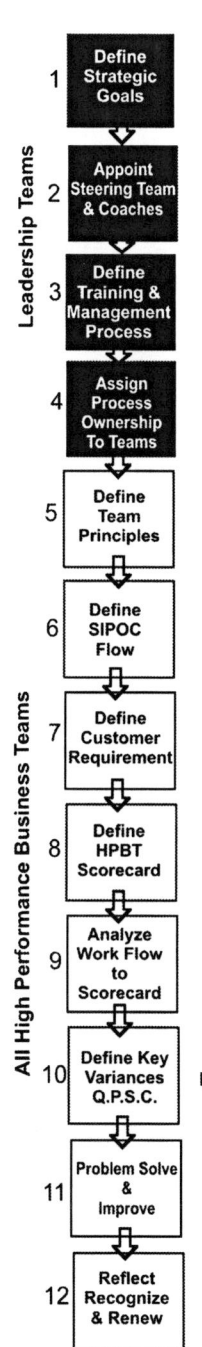

10. Define Key Variances:

A variance is a performance or result that differs from the desired performance or result.

10A. Brainstorm all Variances from steps 7, 8, and 9. When you defined customer requirements, your scorecard, and the workflow you probably thought of ways in which current performance fails to meet those standards. Brainstorm all of the possible ways that the current process varies from standards of quality, productivity, cost and desired cycle times.

10B. Define Key Quality Variances: Now it is time to decide which quality variances are most critical to achieving the results in your balanced scorecard.

10C. Define Key Productivity Variances: Productivity is defined by ratios of input to output. Production units to costs or time spent in production, for example. What are they variances from desired productivity?

10D. Define Key Cost Variances: From your financial statement and from having identified the key financial measures, you can now identify the key variances for desired cost levels.

10E. Define Key Cycle Time Constraints: Speed of flow through the core work process is cycle time. Every team should measure cycle time and be aware of the constraints, the blockages or obstacles, to flow.

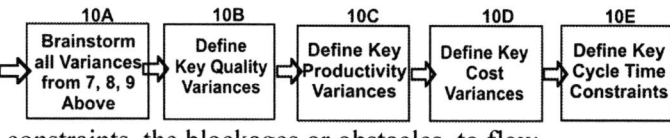

11. Problem Solve and Improve:

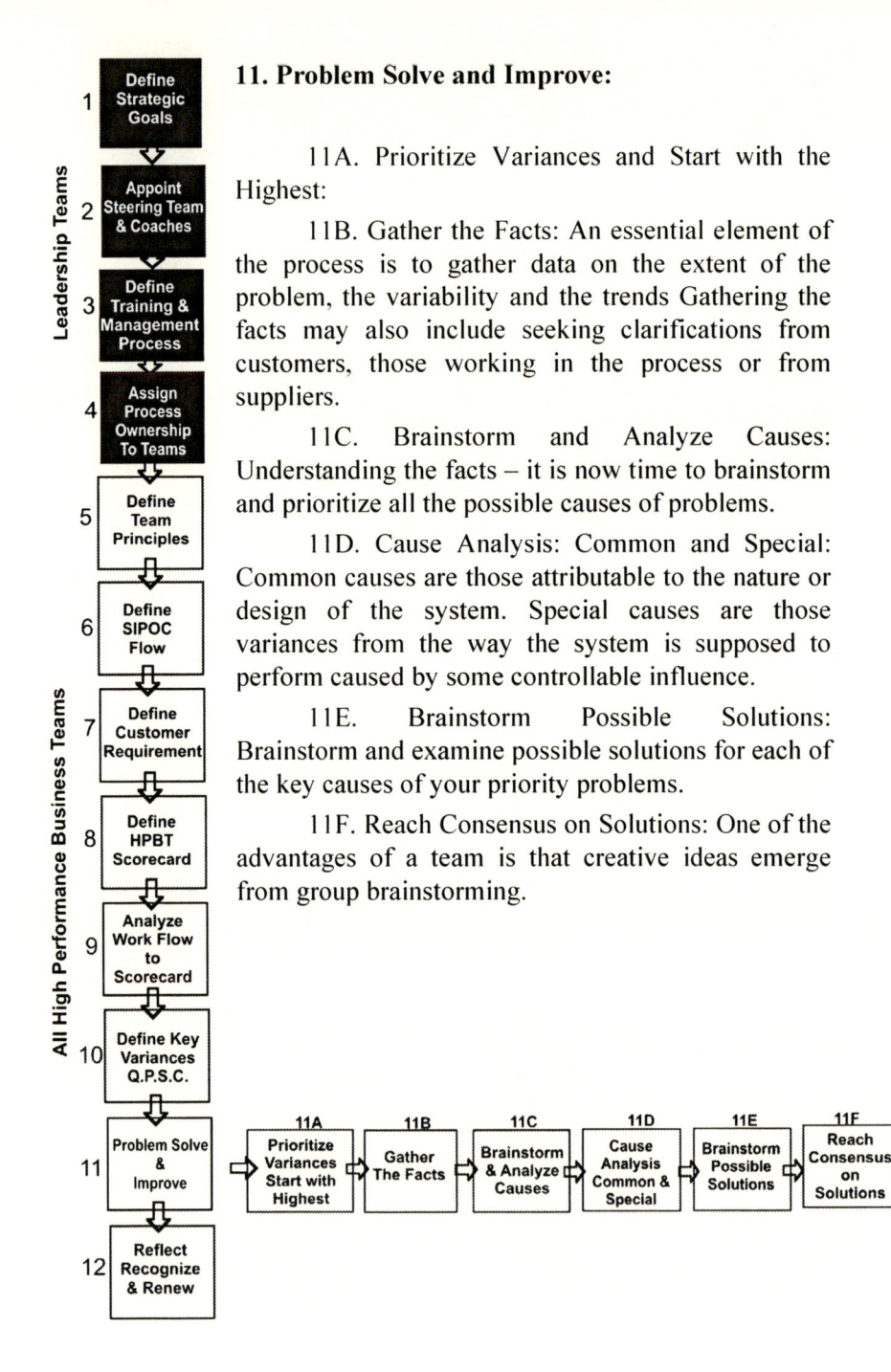

11A. Prioritize Variances and Start with the Highest:

11B. Gather the Facts: An essential element of the process is to gather data on the extent of the problem, the variability and the trends Gathering the facts may also include seeking clarifications from customers, those working in the process or from suppliers.

11C. Brainstorm and Analyze Causes: Understanding the facts – it is now time to brainstorm and prioritize all the possible causes of problems.

11D. Cause Analysis: Common and Special: Common causes are those attributable to the nature or design of the system. Special causes are those variances from the way the system is supposed to perform caused by some controllable influence.

11E. Brainstorm Possible Solutions: Brainstorm and examine possible solutions for each of the key causes of your priority problems.

11F. Reach Consensus on Solutions: One of the advantages of a team is that creative ideas emerge from group brainstorming.

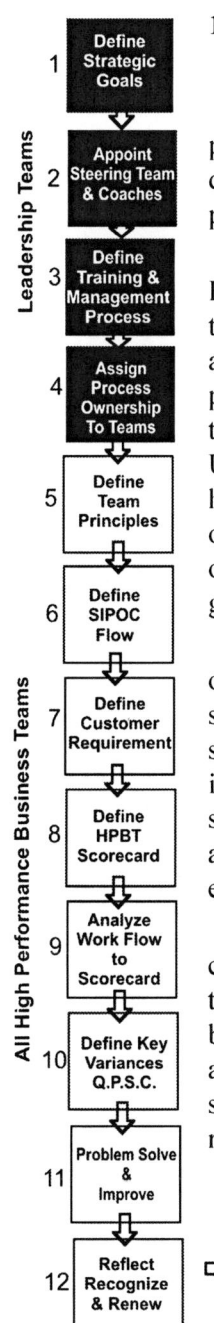

12. Reflect, Recognize and Renew:

12A. Agree on Periodic Process Checks: A process check is a reflection, a period of asking questions about "how it's going" for the people participating in the team.

12B. Reflect on How to Improve the Team Process: Most of what has been presented in the twelve steps in this process involves the steps to achieve improvements in measurable business performance. However, it is also important to improve the quality of team interaction and motivation. Ultimately, business performance is the result of how human beings feel about their work, and about each other. It is therefore, critical to reflect on the quality of dialogue, communications and trust within the group

12C. Plan Recognition for Contributions: One of the keys to motivation is empowerment. Another is simply recognition for effort and contributions to the success of the team. Recognition needs to be a regular item on the agenda of the team. It also needs to be the subject of more periodic reflection on how to show appreciation to those who in some way assist the efforts of the team.

12D. Plan Celebrations & Renewal: In some cultures, it is normal for teams to go on vacation together for the purpose renewing their spirits and bonding as a group. While this is an extreme, there is a fundamentally right idea that teams should take some time together to celebrate their successes and renew their commitment to each other and their work.

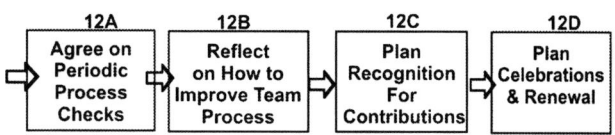

Chapter 12

You're a Business – Build Your Net Worth

Why do we say, "She has her act together?" "Wow, is he coming unglued." "I hope he doesn't fall apart!" "I am feeling very disconnected." "Get it together, man!" In our popular culture, we intuitively recognize the need for internal unity or alignment. Intuitively we know that someone who is *together* will perform better than someone who is *falling apart*. What does it mean to be together? What are the parts that may be falling apart?

Intuitively we recognize that human beings are whole-systems, with different parts that can be either underdeveloped or developed to excess. We all know people who are highly developed in their social relationships but have done little to develop their intellectual capacity. We also know people who are highly intellectual but lack social skills. We also know individuals who are very focused on their material well-being and have ignored their spiritual capacities. Our goal in life should be to develop all of these different aspects of our whole self. The sum of these five forms of capital is our true net worth.

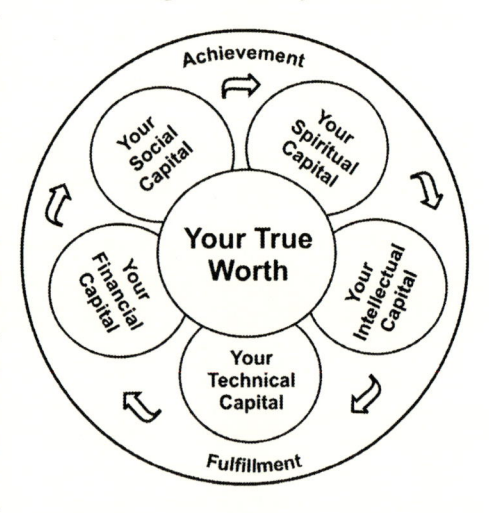

As in the previous two chapters describing the assets of the organization and the team, the same basic model, with some modifications, can be applied to describe the wealth of the individual.

The Five Assets that Make Us Worthy

One way to view our value as a human being is to consider these five different forms of personal capital: *social capital, spiritual capital, financial, intellectual* and *technology capital*. These forms of capital are built by the exercise of the nine disciplines presented in the first part of this book.

The individual is the cell that comprises the building blocks of the team. The teams are the organs that comprise the building blocks of the body of the organization. It is logical that the same DNA runs through each of these inter-connected units. As the author considered the application of this model to the individual, there was one somewhat bothersome concern.

Theoretically, you could have all these capabilities and put them to little use. It is not likely, because most of these assets are only developed through their exercise. However, I still had the concern.

Our worth as human beings is largely from *doing*, not merely *having*. In other words, you might be financially poor, have little education or professional skills, yet you might work in poor neighborhoods to rescue neglected children. I read a story about a very poor woman, a single mother, who had adopted eight children in a high crime neighborhood, all who were abandoned by their birth parents. Her life was dedicated to raising these eight children. She was such a good mother that all of them had completed high school and they were all attending college on scholarships. What is the worth of this loving, sacrificing mother? In truth, I think we have no ability to judge another human being's worth. In my mind, at least, this woman, with little money or education, but with obvious spiritual and social riches, may possess greater true worth than millionaires with graduate degrees. Ultimately, it is a judgment I believe only God can make.

With that note of humility, I will still propose that it is logical and worthy for each of us to strive to develop all of our God given capacities. I also accept that there may be ten other ways to organize our potential other than into the five forms of capital I have proposed.

As is true for all complex systems, the division of one sub-system from another is somewhat arbitrary and only done for convenience.

The Cycle of Life: Hubris and Creative Dissatisfaction

The rise and fall of the human character is a standard plot of Greek tragedy and a valuable lesson. The young hero, perhaps aggrieved from birth, his father killed by an evil enemy, dedicates himself to his learning and growth, rises to become strong and courageous, and then takes on the challenge of defeating his evil nemesis and emerges victorious after a long journey of near defeat and final conquest. Now he settles down to a life of fulfillment, honored and powerful, just and wise. And with the emergence of his power and wealth he grows to assume his position, to become accustomed to the accolades of others, and to be suspicious of those who doubt his power and wisdom. And, in time it will come to pass, with a certainty that is as sure as the rising sun – he will grow to distrust those near to him, to suspect their motives and will eventually act against them. He will be warned that his actions may be unjust, but he trusts his own instincts even when inspired by idle fears. Our once young hero is now a mature King, powerful, but today he is relying on yesterday's tired knowledge and skills in the face of new challenges. From his birth he has always carried an insecurity that once gave energy to his rise and is now clothed in wealth and power but remains the source of his fears. And with his increasingly harsh attacks on others, and his refusal to listen and adopt new ways, increasing numbers of enemies gather around him. Fueled by the King's own pre-emptive strikes, their determination and strength grow until they bring the story to its violent conclusion. The entire cycle of life is played out.

Consider how the nine disciplines presented in the first part of this book are exercised through the development and decline of our hero. In his early days, he must rely on the trust of those with whom he seeks shelter. He builds trust with those who become his followers. Later, with his suspicions, he loses trust with all of those around him and this is the core ingredient in the disintegration of his relationships. In his period of learning and conquest, he is driven by a strong purpose. Once this is accomplished, he has little purpose other than to maintain his position. This cannot inspire either oneself or one's followers. He clearly loses the ability to engage in dialogue with his followers, just as he must have employed effective communication skills in his early days. One can easily imagine how teamwork was essential in this emerging period and absent in its decline. Our hero must have been able to express his appreciation and recognize the positive qualities in others, but that same ability was no doubt lost in the later years.

The tragedy is inevitable and the cause is *hubris*, the excess of pride; a pride that closes the door to new insights. It is the reason most heroes fall. It is the reason great companies reach their zenith and at the very moment of seaming invincibility, begin their decline. And even nations or empires suffer the same fate for the same reasons. It is not hard to find examples of the "fall" from Dennis Kozlowski to Ken Lay; from General Motors to Arthur Andersen; from Rome to Washington. Power and pride lead to blind blunder and the incapacity to learn and think creative thoughts. Hubris is the best poison to defeat learning and creativity. And, hubris requires no plan; no objective for its infusion need be set. It appears naturally and with no effort or intent.

There is an antidote to hubris that should be cultivated within each of us individually and systematically within our organizations. It is what I call *creative dissatisfaction*, the awareness of the gap between who you are and who you could be, between where you are and where you could be, and the passion to close the gap. There is always a gap. The potential is always greater than the present. The only issue is whether satisfaction or dissatisfaction is seen in the gap, and for those who excel, who strive toward the fulfillment of their potential, there is never complete satisfaction.

The reason one should constantly seek improvement, whether in a company or in your personal life, is to avoid the decline that sets in with satisfaction. If we continually seek to practice the nine disciplines in our own life and build the five forms of personal capital, we will experience the most worthy of lives.

The Benjamin Franklin Principle

I love Benjamin Franklin. How could you not love someone who, at the age of eighty was developing a system of self-improvement, nurturing his virtues and attacking his vices, with discipline and determination? For some reason, hubris never overcame Franklin. Franklin said, "I wish to live without committing any fault at any time... As I knew, or thought I knew what was right and wrong, I did not see why I might not always do the one and avoid the other." He recognized the importance of developing or changing his own habits. "...the contrary habits must be broken and good ones acquired and established before we can have any dependence on a steady, uniform rectitude of conduct." [61]

In order to implement his program to acquire good habits and rectitude of conduct, Ben Franklin identified thirteen virtues (similar to our nine disciplines) and wrote a description of each of these virtues. Included in his list were industry, moderation, sincerity, temperance, order and silence. He then devised a feedback system that would have been admired by any modern management consultant or behavioral psychologist. He focused on one virtue each week, for thirteen weeks. "I made a little book in which I allotted a page for each of the virtues. I ruled each page with red ink so as to have seven columns, one for each day of the week, marking each column with a letter for the day." He would then make a mark in the column for each day and each time he violated one of his virtues. "So, I should have (I hoped) the encouraging pleasure of seeing on my pages the progress I made in virtue by clearing successively my lines of their spots... I never arrived at the perfection I had been so ambitious of obtaining but fell far short of it, yet I was by the endeavor a better and happier man."[62]

While Ben Franklin lived with his faults to the end, he never suffered hubris and disgrace as so many great ones did. Perhaps it was because Franklin was never King, never granted an excess of corrupting power, and as one of our Founding Fathers of democracy he lived in a time of limited personal power. Perhaps there is a great lesson in that for the design of our systems of governance, corporate and public. Perhaps systems that grant an excess of power to any individual are inherently corrupting of human nature and destructive of

---

[61] "Ben Franklin's Pursuit of Perfection". John R. Snortum, Psychology Today, April 1976, pp.80-83.
[62] Ibid.

the capacity of the leader. Perhaps an excess of power brings an end to learning, to creative dissatisfaction.

Taking Account of Ourselves

As Ben Franklin did, and as many great religions have taught, it is wise to take account of oneself each day. How have we lived our life this day to exercise virtues and increase our assets? One way to do this is to focus on the nine disciplines in the first part of this book and answer the questions at the end of each of those chapters. Another way is to assess your capital, your acquisition assets that are the true measures of your success.

Building Personal Social Capital:

We all have social or relationship needs and competencies. We have a need to be with, to love and to receive love from friends and family. The quality of our social relationships is the number one factor in achieving authentic happiness. Research has shown that those who are happiest spend the least time alone and the most time socializing and they are rated highest both by themselves and others on their relationship skills.[63] Those who are most successful at work, who are more likely to be promoted and hired as managers, are those with well developed social skills. Effective personal relationships will both make you happy and wealthy.

It is easy to see that the discipline of creating trust, of effective dialogue, teamwork, and creating unity with others are all essential to building your social capital. We are also attracted to others who are dedicated to a worthy purpose and who display discipline.

When thinking about our social capital it is worth considering two dimensions of those relationships: your family relationships and your professional network.

---

[63] Seligman, Martin E.P. *Authentic Happiness,* The Free Press, New York, 2002, p. 56

Family relationships can be both the greatest source of happiness and pain. A bad marriage, undisciplined children, or sick parents are all among the most common sources of stress in our lives. The Christmas holidays have been recognized as the time people are most likely to experience depression as they are confronted by family relationships they have successfully avoided throughout most of the year.

It is impossible to separate our family relationships and our well-being in other aspects of our life. Despite well-publicized exceptions, the most successful executives of the Fortune 500 tend to have long and successful marriages. Why, because they have learned to value their relationships, to nurture them, and they have developed the necessary social skills. Those skills, such as listening, appreciating others, creating unity, all carry over into their relationships at work.

The subject of building family relationships is a topic that is worthy of an entire book and we certainly cannot address it here fully. However, the following are some *critical success indicators*, things you can work on and evaluate when considering your social capital:

- I put aside specific time to invest in my family relationships (such as a *family day*, that we spend together working around the house, going to dinner, etc.).
- My spouse considers me a good listener.
- I have maintained close relationships with my parents and siblings.
- Spending time with my family is fun.
- I am very disciplined in my communication with my family members (for example making a habit of calling home and speaking to each family member each night when traveling for work).

Our ***professional network*** is the single greatest professional asset we have. Different jobs require different degrees of social competence, but the ability to develop and sustain strong personal relationships, is a key factor in any success in management. Anyone in a sales position is no doubt relying on their social skills to help them meet their material needs. Managers and team members all employ their social or relationship skills in their work.

I have spent a lot of time working with youth groups, particularly the global youth leadership organization, AIESEC. I have frequently been asked the question by youth *"What is the one most important key to success."* My answer is always the same – *nurture your network!* Your professional network is your most important professional asset. It is not the "good old boys" network anymore, but it is your network that matters most to your professional advancement. This is particularly true in an age when solo practitioner consulting, frequent job changes and interdependent links between companies all succeed based on personal trust and relationships.

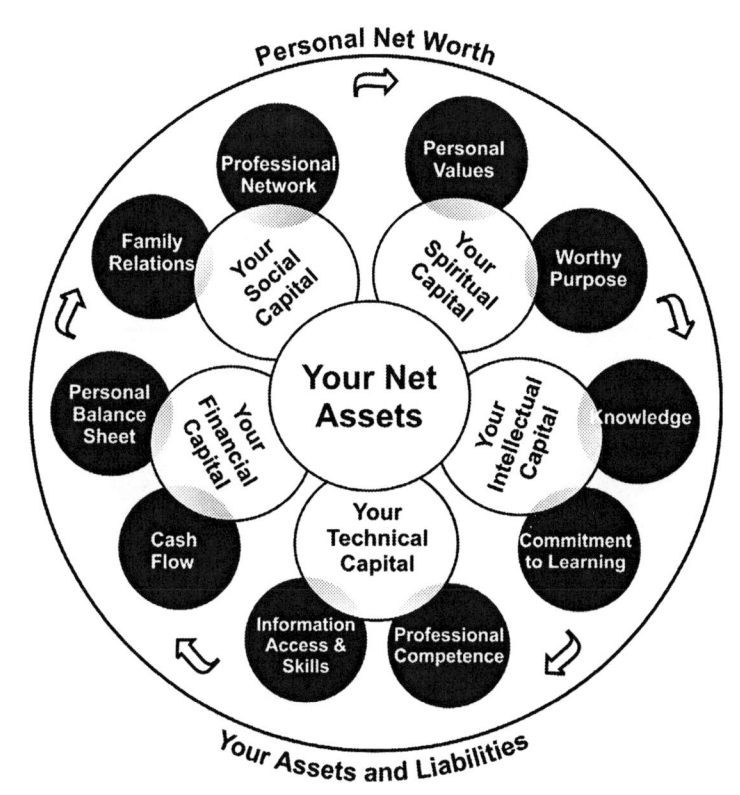

To my young friends I tell one personal story that may help understand the power of networks.

Many years ago, I worked for a consulting/training firm owned by the former football player Fran Tarkenton. I had become president of his company, yet with no prospect of gaining any significant ownership. I was feeling that this path was coming to an end.

Ken Blanchard of *One Minute Manager* fame had read a book and training manual I authored and we had mutual friends. We spoke on the phone and he told me that his co-author, Spencer Johnson was coming to Atlanta and I should get together with him. The truth is that I am not the most sociable person in the world and I had my doubt about this. But, for some reason I did go to the seminar he was putting on, promoting their book, of course, and I had dinner with him.

During our dinner, I told Spencer that I was working on another book and gave him what must have been a very loose description because, in fact, I had little more than an outline.

Six months later, I was on a consulting assignment in New York and was staying at the Grand Hyatt hotel. It was about ten o'clock in the evening when I went down to the lobby to find a newspaper. I was in my blue jeans and sneakers and I had no intention of meeting anyone. However, just as I was about to get on the elevator to return to my room, I was staring across the very large lobby and saw, all the way on the other side, Spencer Johnson standing and talking to some woman. For a few critical seconds I had an internal debate with myself – "should I go over and introduce myself? He probably doesn't even remember me. And, who is that woman ... who knows? It might be an embarrassment. Oh, what the heck!"

So, somewhat cautiously I walked over and reintroduced myself to Spencer Johnson. Spencer, always the salesman, told the woman he was with, that "this is Larry Miller and he is writing this great book, it is really going to be fantastic!" The woman was his literary agent, Margret McBride, who has had many best selling books to her credit. Margret immediately said, "Oh, well send it to me; I'd love to see it."

Now the reality of the situation was that Spencer Johnson could not have possibly known that my book was any good because as it was little more than an outline. But, he knew, perhaps intuitively, that he was giving me a break by saying nice things about my imaginary book.

Recognizing the potential opportunity of being represented by one of the most successful literary agents, I went back home and really got to work. In a few months, I produced the manuscript for *American Spirit*. Margret read it, liked it, and sold it to William Morrow for a hefty advance. That advance gave me the financial capital to allow me to leave Tarkenton's company and form my own. My company was reasonably successful and for many years allowed me to provide an excellent life style for my family. I eventually sold the company for a very nice gain.

But, that is not the end of the story. A few years later, my daughter, Layli, was in law school and became involved as an intern, representing Fauzi Kassinga, a seventeen-year-old girl from Togo who had fled to the United States seeking human rights asylum. She was fleeing a forced marriage and female genital mutilation. My daughter's fight to get Fauzi legal entry into this country and out of prison became the subject of three front-page New York Times stories, coverage on CNN and National Public Radio.

During this battle, I called Margret McBride. I said, "Margret I think I have another book for you." She replied, "Oh, what are you writing?" And, I said, "Well, it's not me. It is about my daughter." I am sure at this point, she had an uncomfortable expression on her face. Yeah, every dad thinks his daughter is a book!

I said, "Do you have the New York Times today?" She did. I asked her to read the front-page story on the case. A few hours later Margret called me back and said, "This is fantastic. This is a book – the story of two young women, one fleeing mutilation and imprisoned and the other young American college student trying to rescue her."

Well a few months later, Margret McBride had sold this story to a major publisher for a very large advance, one of the largest of the year in the publishing industry. The book, *Do They Hear You When You Cry*[64], was translated into several languages and became an inspiration to young woman around the world concerned about the status and treatment of women.

Layli and other supporters eventually won this case, setting precedent and establishing gender related issues as grounds for human rights asylum in the United States. From the proceeds Layli received from the book, she established a not-for-profit organization, The Tahirih Justice Center[65] in Washington to provide legal representation for woman fleeing human rights abuse. Many women from

---

[64] Kassindja, Fauziya and Miller-Bashir, Layli. Delacorte Press, New York, 1998.
[65] See www.Tahirih.org.

Afghanistan during the reign of the Taliban were represented as well as others. Over the past years, the Center has served over six thousand women, has three times established legal precedent and has authored and helped achieved passage of legislation in the area of human trafficking.

If I had not walked across the lobby of the Grand Hyatt hotel, at ten o'clock at night, and re-introduced myself to Spencer Johnson, and if he had not been so gracious in his introduction, it is likely that most of this history would be very different.

It is your network that makes you rich…financially, socially, and even spiritually. Remember it!

The following are some *critical success factors* for managing your professional network:

- I develop a high level of trust with co-workers and associates as demonstrated by their seeking my advice and counsel.
- I go out of my way to demonstrate interest in the lives and well-being of others at work.
- I have maintained lasting personal relationships with friends I have made through my work.
- Other associates trust that I will look out for their best interest and extend myself to be helpful to them.
- If I needed help finding another job, or if I had a job for someone else, there are many friends I could call who I expect, might be helpful.

Nurturing Your Spiritual Capital:

There are many books that discuss the benefits of following a religious path as a means to professional success. There are even books that ask, "What would Jesus do if he were CEO?" I think these are all thought provoking and may challenge us to follow a spiritual path. However, I also do not think that spirituality, nearness to God, or adherence to moral values is the property of any one religion. I have read the Holy Books of many religions and I believe that they are largely in agreement. For entirely human reasons, for material reasons, we tend to focus on the differences and this, in itself, is a sign of our spiritual failure.[66]

But spirituality is not religion. You have heard enough stories about leaders of some of the largest churches who were living a most sinful life. This is true not only in Christianity, but in Islam as well. No religion has a copyright on either sin or virtue. I do believe that religion, in general, serves as a spiritual discipline that is beneficial.

I have thought a good bit about what spiritual qualities are and what the word "spiritual" means to different people. Some time back I had a meeting with the staff and consultants of my firm to discuss and develop our mission statement. I had drafted a statement that included "…to contribute to the material, intellectual and spiritual wealth of our clients." Some of the consultants who were very analytic and intellectual wanted to know exactly what it meant to contribute to *spiritual wealth*. I wasn't sure myself. I asked the group what they thought it meant. No two people had exactly the same idea as to what the word "spiritual" meant. However, everyone agreed that it was a desirable set of qualities that gave the individual balance and grounding in values that had the authority of some higher voice outside oneself. Everyone agreed that it was a good thing, even though we couldn't precisely define it. We then agreed that coming up with a definition wasn't important. It was fine for people to have different ideas about what "spiritual wealth" might involve. As long as the methods we employed and the results we achieved contributed positively to the spiritual well-being of our clients, we were doing the right thing.

Some feel spiritual when they exercise and the endorphins kick in. Some experience a spiritual response to music or other art forms. Others feel spirituality on a mountain top or sailing alone on the ocean in a small boat. But, I think genuine spirituality requires something more than a temporary "high" from these activities. I believe that true spirituality requires some connection to a source, something

---

[66] The author is a member of the Bahá'í Faith which teaches that there is one God; all religions are chapters of the same book, revealed progressively as humankind matures; and humanity is one family, God's family. The author, however, does not intend to proselytize here, only to provide transparency.

unchanging; something that we believe is a source of eternal and infallible values and guidance for our personal life. Of course, for most, this is religious faith in a Supreme Being. Those with religious faith tend to suffer less anxiety and are generally happier than those who do not follow a religious faith.[67]

Spiritual development does not mean, in my opinion, the absence of material things or needs. Nor does it require a divorce from the intellectual self. And, I believe our spiritual development is necessarily related to our social relationships, trust in our family and friends, appreciation for others, and the ability to engage others in unifying dialogue.

Spirituality almost defies being divided up into any parts. It is transcendent. However, again, I have divided it into two larger segments: ***personal values*** and the pursuit of a ***worthy purpose***.

Many companies are providing ethics training to their managers, hoping to instill personal and professional values, boundaries that will guide them in their decision-making. It is very difficult to instill personal values in mature adults. The research on transforming values in adults is not very promising. It is far easier to teach ethical behavior or values to young children. This is when moral inhibitions, are best developed.

Almost everyone knows, in their mind, what is right conduct and good values. The test is whether, confronted with temptations, one is able to make the right choices. In business, these choices are often difficult and require personal, even professional sacrifice. It is a struggle.

The following are some *critical success indicators* for engaging in the struggle to apply personal values to our work lives:

- I can recall decisions I have made in the past few months that required me to consider and employ my personal values.

---

[67] Seligman, Martin E.P. Authentic Happiness, New York, 2002, The Free Press. P. 59.

- When choosing my current job I considered whether I could adhere to my values within this organization.
- When considering decisions at work I am comfortable raising the issue of morality or values as a factor in decision-making.
- My spouse, or family, and I discuss our values when we make important family decisions.
- If I was confronted with an opportunity to make a lot of money but required some compromise of my values, I know that I would have little difficulty making this choice.

Dedication to a *worthy purpose* is also a force that attracts others. We tend to like, and have confidence in people whom we know to be dedicated to a worthy life and worthy achievements. The third chapter of this book is devoted to the pursuit of worthy purpose as a critical factor in our own motivation. I will not repeat that discussion here.

The following are *critical success indicators* of the personal pursuit of a worthy purpose:

- If someone asked, I could describe my life's mission in one clear sentence.
- I can explain how my current work is a step along the path toward my mission.
- My spouse or family members know that my life has a purpose beyond merely achieving financial success.
- When I wake up in the morning, I feel energized by the challenges facing me because I know they are leading toward a worthy goal.
- I am willing to sacrifice short-term gain in order to continue on the path toward my higher purpose.

Building Your Intellectual Capital

The mind is not only too precious a thing to waste, as one advertisement said; but, it is our primary asset, our equipment, in the professional world. We all know that formal education and formal degrees are likely to contribute to our professional success. They are one, but only one, measure of our intellectual capital.

We should in no way confuse the development of the intellect, achieving knowledge, with success at academic institutions. Abraham Lincoln attended no academic institution, yet was of great intellect. Thomas Jefferson founded a great academic institution and was arguably the greatest thinker among our Founding Fathers, yet he attended college for two years and left without a degree. There is a long list of geniuses who made great discoveries, founded great companies, and served in public life, but who had little or no formal education. This is not to condemn formal education or academia, but rather to point out that formal education is only one path to the development of the mind.

Unfortunately, too many people make the assumption that intellect and academic training are one in the same. By making this assumption they give up the pursuit of the intellect. They stop reading and learning. They stop challenging their own mind to develop new capabilities.

Because the world has become very complex, the amount of knowledge needed to understand world events is overwhelming to many. Why were we attacked on 9/11? What do Muslims really believe and do they all hate Americans? What is the meaning of China's economic rise and are they still communists? Why has the United States become a debtor nation? What is the potential and threat of bio-engineering, genetic science and stem cell research? And, will we run out of oil anytime in the near future? Everyday we are confronted by hundreds of questions that can only be answered with a great deal of knowledge, knowledge of history, religion, culture, economics, ethics, technology and even psychology. Who can possibly have all the information to answer these questions? It is stressful to even think about it.

There are two possible responses to this stress. One response is to find comfort in simple answers, labeling and categorizing positions in a way that assures us that we are on the *right* side. You must be a lefty *liberal* to think that! Or, that's what all you wacko right wing *conservatives* believe! The entertainment news media has promoted the idea that everything can be divided into left and right and we can pick our team, and cheer for our players! It is the path of least intellectual resistance, which allows us to put aside the intellectual challenges that are implied by questions such as "do all Muslims hate us, or why do they hate us?"

Do dividing the world into left and right and quickly labeling people lead to the most accurate understanding and to the best decisions? I think not. In fact I think the entire mental model of *left* and *right* is largely nonsense. Is free trade with China a liberal or conservative position? Is reducing our deficit and balancing our budget liberal or conservative? The fact is that these simplistic labels and categories have become entirely dysfunctional and do little except provide an easy excuse for NOT thinking! Many people listen only to news media that supports their team, their simplistic explanation for almost everything in the world.

The alternative to simplistic labeling is to recognize that the world is, in fact, complex and answers are often difficult and require the consideration of different points of view. It may shock some, but occasionally I go on the Aljazeera website and read the news from their perspective. It is interesting. For example, some time back there was an article on a group of Saudi academicians who had been imprisoned without a trial and without a date of release because they were proposing the country develop a constitutional monarchy somewhat along British lines. The Aljazeera article was clearly on the side of the unjustly imprisoned academicians and not supportive of the Saudi government. I looked on the CNN website and the New York Times and could find no report of this same story.

Does this make Aljazeera liberal or conservative? Does this make Aljazeera pro or anti-United States or democracy? Perhaps these are the wrong questions.

Intellect is developed by questioning. How do things work? Why do they work this way? The process of inquiring is the process of exercising the mental muscle of the brain. I certainly do not have answers to all these questions and I do not feel a need to have answers. Simply understanding the different points of view, the cultural and historical context of events in the Middle East or China is mental exercise and fun!

Intellectual capital is built on questions, not answers. Answers are easy. My wife and I were taking our walk in Annapolis and passing a house with a sign in front that said: "War is Not The

Answer!" A young man was sitting on the steps in front of the house and I asked, as we walked by, "What is the question?" He was somewhat startled and didn't know what I was talking about. I said "Your sign says 'war is not the answer', I was wondering what the question is?" Somewhat taken aback, he said, "Actually, I have no idea." Those who have answers without knowing the question have certainly not thought very deeply.

Your intellectual capital can be assessed in terms of the degree to which you possess knowledge and your commitment to the process of lifelong learning.

No simple questions can demonstrate your depth of knowledge (knowledge of what, baseball, chemistry or world history?). However, one can divide the issues of intellectual capital into two categories. The first is the degree to which you *possess knowledge*. This is your database, the information in your head. I cannot write simple indicators of success for this, as I have with previous categories of capital. The range of potential knowledge is simply too great. The second is your *commitment to continual learning*. It is a certainty that if someone is committed to continual learning they will develop their intellectual capital.

The following are a few *critical success indicators* regarding your commitment to continual learning:

- I read at last one non-fiction book each month or a novel that provides insight into history or world affairs.
- I enjoy discussing world events with friends regardless of their political orientation. I always learn something from these discussions.
- I am interested in the advance of science and read articles on new discoveries in some field such as biology.
- I subscribe to news magazines and enjoy reading in depth articles on topics such as world events.
- When I watch television, I tend to look for programs that provide in-depth exploration of a topic or of historical events.

Building Your Technical Capital

In the previous chapter, I chose to label one of the forms of capital for a *team process performance*. It is hard to apply this same category to the individual, although if you work alone (like writing a book) there are processes that are followed that may be more or less productive. However for most, this is not particularly useful. What is more useful, I believe, is to consider **professional competence** and your use of **information systems and technology to access knowledge**. Together these comprise what I will call technology capital. It is technology in the broad sense of things you can do that are technical in nature.

In the previous section, we addressed general intellectual development, largely outside of work or profession. Here, let us consider your development of professional competence. Professional competence, whether you are a brain surgeon or an auto mechanic, a brick layer or a software engineer, is a critical asset that defines a measure of your wealth. If you have highly developed and in-demand professional skills, that is the equivalent to money in the bank.

The following are *critical success indicators* for professional competence:

- I am a member of professional organizations that share knowledge in my field.
- At least once a year I attend a conference or seminar to learn from other professionals in my field.
- I subscribe to at least one magazine or journal in my area of expertise.
- I mentor or provide training to others in my field.
- My colleagues come to me for advice and consultation regarding technical matters.

As with intellectual competence, it is not only important that you possess professional competence, but it is equally important that you are seeking improvement and employing the best methods for professional development and learning. The following are *critical success indicators* for the use of information technology and access:

- I read or participate in on-line discussion, information sharing, forums that are specific to my professional field.

- I have online access to the best research sources in my field to alert me to new technical developments.
- On my web browser, I have saved links to websites that provide professional insights into my field of expertise.
- At work, we have a database of shared files or research that I can access when researching areas related to my work.
- On my computer, I have organized files according to the major categories within my expertise so I can quickly access previous work, articles I have saved, or Powerpoints I have developed.

Building Your Financial Capital

Financial capital is the most well understood form of capital. Like a company, an individual or family has two types of statements or categories of financial well-being. The first is their bank account and checkbook balance that records income coming in (deposits) and expenses going out (expenses). If more is coming in than going out than you have positive *cash flow*. Although you may not maintain any record that you actually call a balance sheet, you have a balance in fact. Your *balance sheet* is the computation of all of your assets (money in the bank, real estate, stocks or mutual funds, furniture, jewelry, etc.) and all of your liabilities (your mortgage, credit card debt, car loans, etc.). Hopefully, you have a positive balance sheet, more assets than liabilities.

This may all be very obvious to anyone experienced in financial matters. However, many people do not understand the need for positive cash flow and do not understand their own balance sheet. More important they do not track and record these on a regular basis. Playing the business game, watching your income statement and balance sheet can be just as motivating and fun as it is in a business or on a team.

The following are *critical success factors* for you personal cash flow:

- I keep a checkbook or a spreadsheet that records my monthly income and expenses. I know how much my income exceeded my expenses (or the other way around) last month.
- I know how much my income increased or decreased year-after-year for each of the past five years.
- I know how much positive cash flow (income above expenses) during the past year.
- I have broken down categories of expenses (such as housing, utilities, entertainment, etc.) and I monitor the increase or decrease in these categories of expense.
- I have set goals for both income and for positive cash flow.

The following are *critical success factors* for maintaining your personal balance sheet:

- I have a spreadsheet or other record of my total assets and liabilities. I know my net worth.
- I have set goals for the growth in my net worth, either through increasing my financial assets or reducing my debts.
- I have a goal for the net worth required at the time of my retirement.
- I have a plan for employing my positive cash flow to increase specific assets or reduce specific liabilities.
- I know my credit worthiness from credit reports or other sources.

A Plan to Build Your True Net Worth

All good management, whether of a company or of yourself, begins with big long-term goals and then breaks those goals down into more immediate action and behavior. Building wealth begins with dreaming about where you want to be ten or twenty years from now, then asking yourself *what are reasonable goals for this year that will help get me toward that long term dream*; then asking yourself *what am I going to do this week and today to turn my goals and dreams into reality*.

Benjamin Franklin identified thirteen virtues. In the first part of this book, I identified nine disciplines that are central to achieving success in the new capitalism. These nine disciplines are the things you do, the actions and skills you need to exercise in order to create value for yourself and others. These are the wealth creating actions that result in capital or net worth. A corporation doesn't build its asset value, its share price and money in the bank, by focusing on those assets alone. Rather, it must design superior products, employ superior marketing and manufacturing. In order to increase your personal value you must do something in a different way. You must change in order to achieve different results.

Just as Franklin was systematic in working on one virtue each day, I think it is wise to focus on one of the nine competencies at a time. You will remember that at the end of each chapter you were presented a set of questions regarding your personal, as well as team and organizational, development of those competencies. Each of the needs you identified in those chapters can now become part of your personal development plan.

In the pages that follow, you will find five different planning forms. These start with defining your long-term dream and become more specific, down to planning your daily actions. Please do not just stare at the pages, pick up your pen or pencil and write. You may wish to go to the author's website (www.lmmiller.com) and download a set of these forms, which you may print out in any number you like.

Creating a Long Term Dream

When you were in school, your teacher may have reprimanded you for daydreaming in class. What your teacher may not have understood was that daydreaming could be one of your most productive activities. Most great achievements begin with a dream. A person without dreams is a person without hope, without motivation, without energy. Please…dream and dream BIG!

In the beginning was the Word. The Word is the inspired idea, the image or prophecy of something that can be in the future. The idea precedes action or achievement. A high performing individual is one constantly in the process of discovering new opportunities for growth, development and service. Those ideas or images become a motivating purpose for the work of developing oneself.

Close your eyes and visualize where you will be and what you will be doing in five and ten years. Where are you going, why are you going there, and how will it feel when you get there? Do you have an answer to these questions? It is important. It may be the most important question of all because the answer will determine the course of your life. Motivation springs from your personal desire to be somewhere, to be somebody, to be able to do things you can not now do. Achieving your vision is your purpose.

You have already considered the critical success indicators for each of the five forms of capital. Now make a decision. Imagine and decide where and who you want to be in twenty years. OK, how much money do you want to have? That's the easiest one. So, go ahead and get it over with. How much on your balance sheet and how much positive cash flow would you like to be generating twenty years from now?

Now that the easy one is out of the way, imagine your technical competence in twenty years. How do you want to be known professionally? What will be your professional legacy when you retire? Imagine that you have accomplished something very significant in your chosen profession.

For your intellectual capital, go back, and look at the critical success indicators, and imagine your ideal state of knowledge and intellectual achievement in twenty years.

Then consult your religious faith for a concise definition of the spiritual ideal you hope to achieve. It is found in every faith.

Finally, imagine your social relationships in twenty years. What will they be like and feel like?

My Long Term Dream
What is my dream for my future personal wealth?

Your Capital Assets		
Financial		
Technical		
Intellectual		
Spiritual		
Social		

Take account of yourself each day.

Create a One year Plan

Every business has a one year plan and for the same reasons, so should you. The long term dream is a strategic vision. Companies develop a strategic vision around which more specific plans can be developed. The strategy leads to a one year planning process.

Do a *gap analysis*. Do you remember the discussion about *creative dissatisfaction*, the gap between where you are or who you are, and where you could be or who you could be? Now think through the gap. Looking at your vision of what you want to achieve, there is not only a gap in the obvious things like how much money you will have or be making; but, there is a gap in your other assets. Again, if you refer back to the critical success indicators this will help you define the gap.

Now is the time to set realistic goals. Your long term dream is necessarily not realistic. Now consider your financial situation and set a goal for increasing your assets. How much can your reasonably, yet ambitiously, hope to generate in positive cash flow this year? By how much will you be able to increase your financial balance sheet?

Now look at the assets and decide how you can improve them during the next year. How will you improve your social relationships? What will those relationships look or feel a year from now? Do the same for the other categories.

In addition to setting goals for the growth of your capital it will also be helpful to ask yourself "How am I going to improve in each of the disciplines that create wealth?" The way you are going to increase your social capital will be by improving the currency of trust, improving your skills in dialogue, improving your demonstration of appreciation for others. Go back and look at the individual self-assessment questions in each of the chapters in the part one of this book. By studying those you will find specific things you can do to increase each of these nine disciplines.

My Yearly Plan
What Are My Goals This Year to Create Personal Wealth?
For each of the five forms of capital, what are my goals for improvement this year?

Your Capital Assets	
Financial	
Technical	
Intellectual	
Spiritual	
Social	

Take account of yourself each day.

My Yearly Plan

What will I _do_ this year to improve my performance in each of the nine disciplines?
Focus on specific behavior that you will do, behavior that can be observed and measured.

Unity	
Trust	
Purpose	
Dialogue	
Discipline	
Team-Work	
Appreciation	
Scorekeeping	
Flow	

Take account of yourself each day.

Develop Weekly and Daily Plans:

A few years back there was a movie starring Bill Murray and Richard Dreyfuss, *(What About Bob?)* about a somewhat lunatic patient (Bill Murray) and his psychiatrist. The psychiatrist (Richard Dreyfuss) had just published a book with the title *Baby Steps* and Bill Murray seeks his approval by demonstrating his ability to take baby steps on the path to improvement. It's a funny movie, but it actually contains an important truth about self-improvement. Have big dreams, but be willing to move down the path with baby steps.

We are an impatient society with expectations of instant gratification. Rarely does success or significant improvement come quickly or easily. You have no doubt heard stories about the musician or movie star who becomes an overnight success, *after* twenty years of diligent devotion to the art. Design your program of self improvement with diligent devotion to your dream and disciplined execution of small steps toward your goal. This is the purpose of daily or weekly planning.

It is probably not likely that many readers will want to complete both daily and weekly plans. But, I strongly recommend at least a weekly plan.

"What am I going to do?" may sound deceptively simple. But, plans often fail here. To develop greater *trust* and *teamwork* you might say, "I am going to communicate more with my team member." That is a good intention, but it is a poor definition of what you are going to do in an action plan. Your daily or weekly plan should define *pinpointed behavior*, not a general statement of intention. Pinpointed behavior is measurable or observable.

It is a good idea to print the weekly planner, fill it out on the weekend, and tape it to your mirror so you see it each morning as you prepare for work. This will remind you of your commitments to yourself. If you do this every week during the year, there is little doubt that you will either achieve your yearly goals or make great progress toward them.

Weekly Planner

What Will I Do This Week To Create Personal Wealth?

Which form of capital do I most need to develop this week?
Which discipline will most contribute to creating that capital?

The Value Creating Disciplines	Your Capital Assets				
	Social	Spiritual	Intellectual	Technical	Financial
Unity					
Trust					
Purpose					
Dialogue					
Discipline					
Team-Work					
Appreciation					
Scorekeeping					
Flow					

Take account of yourself each day.

Daily Planner

What Will I Do Today To Create Personal Wealth?

Which form of capital do I most need to develop this week?
Which discipline will most contribute to creating that capital?

The Value Creating Disciplines	Your Capital Assets				
	Social	Spiritual	Intellectual	Technical	Financial
Unity					
Trust					
Purpose					
Dialogue					
Discipline					
Team-Work					
Appreciation					
Scorekeeping					
Flow					

Take account of yourself each day.

Develop Your Capability through Action Learning

Learning any new skill is a repeated sequence of planning to do something (a behavior such as reading), then doing it, then reflecting on your experience. I find it very important that I take time to think about things I have read. If I read a chapter of a new book, I don't like to go on to the next chapter immediately. I have to process, reflect upon, the information in the chapter just completed. What is the important point, the "so-what?" in the chapter? If you can't answer the so-what question after reading a chapter, then why bother reading it? This is only one way to reflect on the meaning of an experience. Reflection often requires sharing and dialogue with others. This is why book clubs are popular and why it is advisable for a team to read a book at the same time and then discuss its importance to their own work or relationships.

In order to become a highly effective learner you must be willing to take action, even though you may not be entirely sure what you are doing. If you are going to learn to play a musical instrument, you must pick up the instrument and start plucking the strings. You cannot learn to play the guitar, for example, by reading a book. It only comes with practice. Now you must find opportunities to practice any skill you have the intention of learning.

Creativity almost always comes from studying some input, a book in your field for example, then experimenting, trying out possible applications of that knowledge, and finally reflecting on the lessons learned. Significant progress in organizations is usually a result of this kind of creative experimentation.

A creative genius of acoustic blues guitar, the blind Reverend Gary Davis, when asked about writing one of his great songs (Twelve Gates to the City) said "I never wrote that song, it was revealed to me in 1908." And, then commenting on another song he said, "That was from before noise came south!" Before noise came south was before radio or television. I imagine this blind boy in Greenville South Carolina with his guitar and no "noise" but the ability to listen and to reflect, to experiment and try out different "licks" on the guitar. This is the rich soil from which creative genius springs. If we can block out the noise for a period of time, if we learn the fundamentals and enjoy what we do, we will find that we will surprise our self with creative discoveries. Maybe you will even have a revelation!

Share your plan with others. Many years ago I worked with Stephen Covey in his Master's of Excellence series. These were a series of one day, once a month programs, in which the author of some current book would present, and the participants would then seek to apply, their knowledge. During the series, Covey repeatedly emphasized the necessity of going back to your work place and teaching the principles, or knowledge to someone else. We have all had the experience of preparing to teach others something, perhaps in a Sunday school program or perhaps teaching your children something and discovering that we learned more from preparing and doing the teaching then did our students. When you teach others you digest the information in a way you do not if you just consider it by yourself. You get feedback from those you teach and you see them understanding and appreciating the lessons and this deepens your own understanding.

One of the things that will inevitably happen when you share your learning is that your own sense of self, who you are and who you can become, will evolve and it will evolve toward a higher vision. The vision you start with is not the vision you will end with. Our vision will evolve upward as our capacity increases. The cycle of learning and development then begins again.

Chapter 13

A Modest Proposal For a National Strategy

In this age, the well-being and security of the country are not determined by the number of tanks or airplanes, but by the human capital, the spiritual wealth, the intellectual competence of our people, and by the degree to which people in other countries and cultures feel affection rather than alienation from us. I would argue that the five categories of capital discussed in the previous chapters are the essence of what should be considered in a national strategy.

When I started this book, I had no intention of entering into the shark infested waters of national policy or politics. However, as I wrote about the forms of capital and the currency, which drives the increase or decrease in that capital, I could not help but consider the possible implications for national policy.

Before I go further, let me caution the reader from falling into the trap of trying to place my comments into the usual dichotomy of left or right, liberal or conservative. My proposal regards the structure of a national strategy, not the specific policies that could be pursued within that structure. The content of strategy within this structure could be either liberal or conservative, although I am convinced that those labels have lost any coherent meaning and are less than useless.

You already know my bias regarding a strategic structure for understanding the wealth or capital of a company and there is no reason not to apply the same to the nation. And, one might well ask, does the country (choose your country) have a national strategy at all? Should the government of a country have a strategic purpose, intent and plan, like that of a well-managed corporation?

I believe that the leaders of a nation, led by the Chief Executive, and including the leaders of the various Cabinet departments, and the legislature, should develop a plan for the increase in total national wealth. Some may think I am speaking of old style Soviet planning. I don't mean anything of the kind. No federal democracy can impose a top-down national plan. However, it can provide leadership in a direction. It can present a budget and encourage legislation that would lead toward desired outcomes. And, the leader of a country, just as in a corporation, has great powers of persuasion. Persuasion, rather than control, is the key to leadership, whether in the public or private arena.

Strategy on a national level is essential because, just as in a company, there are budgetary or investment decisions that require priorities. No government can afford to invest in everything that may be worthwhile. It should invest around its strategic priorities. Of course, defense issues represent one priority. Debt payments and the social safety net items are also largely non-discretionary. But, after these, the strategy should be formed around a consideration of the future competitiveness of the nation.

I won't discuss the issue of national financial capital and a financial plan. It seems obvious that a country should have a coherent national financial strategy, a strategy to reduce debt, increase revenue, reduce unnecessary costs and make strategic investments in infrastructure related to future economic growth. Unfortunately, in my country there is nothing that can be accurately described as a national financial plan. Taxes (revenue) are treated as an entirely separate discussion from spending. It is very clear that there is no accountability for making income equal or exceed expenses as there is in every business.

Solving this problem is highly political and not where I wish to take this discussion. Rather, I would like to initiate the discussion about developing a plan to enhance other forms of capital, which will necessarily impact financial capital in the long term.

***

I want to be the moderator at the next Presidential candidate debates. There are a couple questions I would like to ask.

"Dear Candidate, given that the President is the Chief Executive of our government, and given that it is well accepted that CEOs should have a strategy for increasing the net value of that over which he or she is "Chief," what is your overarching strategy for increasing the total wealth of our nation? I have a few follow-up questions after you provide an over-arching framework."

We can then assume response that has little to do with our question, but will surely touch on the three talking points, which the candidate's polls have indicated are the hot buttons for their most important interest groups. It would be a shock if the question was answered with an actual strategic framework... but, we can hope.

"Thank you. I would now like to ask you about some of the specific aspects of your strategy. We know that democracy relies on internal sociability or what de Tocqueville called the "art of associating," a characteristic that has proven to be a leading indicator of economic well-being. What is your understanding of the trend regarding this quality, and what would you do to improve this foundation of democracy and free enterprise?"

"Well, that is an interesting approach. You have obviously given some thought to how you may influence the culture of our nation."

"This brings me to the issue of our external relations with the rest of the world. As you know, most corporate strategy includes a plan to improve the brand-equity, the market's perception of the firm's brand. As a nation, our ability to gain support on issues of security or trade, our ability to attract the best minds, or sell our products, is largely based on the degree to which we are trusted by the leaders and citizens of other countries. How would you go about improving the value of our nation's brand?"

Of course, our candidates would surely have given great consideration as to how they might improve both the internal and external social capital of the country and their answers would no doubt be illuminating. So we will now turn our attention to human capital.

"Madam Candidate, I would now like to ask about education and the competence of the American (insert your own country's name) workforce. As I am sure you know, China is now graduating three times the number of engineers, more MBA's, and the trend is similar in other countries. Given that our economy is built, as I am sure you agree, on the foundation of knowledge and technology, what is your strategy for ensuring that our country maintains its competitive advantage?"

Well, you get the idea. Is it unreasonable to judge candidates by the quality of their thought, for the logic of their plans, to improve the well-being of our country? I think not. Is it unreasonable that the legislative branch attempt to assess the wealth of the country in a comprehensive manner and develop a plan to increase all forms of wealth? Again, I think it is not unreasonable.

The skeptic is likely to resist the idea of a national strategy to address the five forms of capital due to the absence of a clear and universally accepted system of measurement and accounting. I will suggest that this is a lame excuse for failing to seek to improve the very qualities upon which our future economic well-being and security depend. Can we accurately measure our military might relative to other countries in any reliable way? I would argue that we cannot. The number of bombs, planes, or missiles was not predictor of success in Vietnam and it is likely not a predictor of success in Iraq or elsewhere. We don't know how to measure genuine military power. That has not stopped us from investing in military power. Why should it stop us from investing in social or human capital?

If I were President or King for a day, I would create an Institute of National Wealth Strategy (INWS, of course, it must have an acronym! Everything in Washington does.) I would charge the director of this new agency (it can be small in numbers and costs, by the way) with developing an index to measure each of the five forms of wealth, along with a strategic plan for the improvement of each. I would then charge each cabinet member with the task of defining his or her plans in light of the overall strategy to increase aggregate national wealth.

I would like to offer a few thoughts on each of the five categories of capital as they apply to a nation, particularly my own. It is not my intention to propose anything approaching a comprehensive discussion of this topic. Rather, my only intention is to stimulate thought in the direction of a comprehensive wealth strategy.

I served in the U.S. Army in the 1960's in both Europe and Vietnam. As a young man in Europe, my buddy and I traveled around Europe in my VW beatle. I remember one day very clearly. We were in Belgium and traveling through some very small country village. We stopped for lunch. An elderly couple came by to talk with us. They asked if we were Americans. When we said that we were, they both got a huge grin on their face and expressed their great appreciation for the U.S. Army and they recalled how their village had been liberated from the Nazis by the Americans. I have never forgotten the affection of this elderly couple.

Today it is very common, when discussing how the United States is viewed in Europe or the Middle East for Americans to respond by saying, "Well, they all hate us anyway, what does it matter?"

This is wrong. They, whoever they are, do not all hate us, and they have never all hated us. Unfortunately, it does feel that way to many Americans whose only points of reference are the evening news and commentators who are constantly denigrating other countries and cultures.

In fact, for most of the past century, the United States has had a great deal of "brand-equity," trust and affection by many people around the world. To a degree, most Americans do not realize, the ability of the United States to remain secure, to have allies in the so-called "war-on-terror", (and these allies are required for success) we have called upon our social capital. To the degree that we are losing that capital, and I don't think anyone would question that our social capital is diminishing rapidly, we are weaker and less able to remain secure.

Globalization, the global economy and increasing degrees of interdependence are indisputable and irreversible. This does not mean that we should not have secure borders, trade policies that give everyone a fair chance at competition, and economic policies that reduce our financial dependence on lending countries. But the days of isolationism and fanciful hopes for energy or economic independence, rather than interdependence, are long gone.

The ability of our country to succeed in the global world of security and economics will largely depend on the degree to which we are trusted by other countries and cultures. If the President is the CEO of this great enterprise, his job is to increase our social capital in the world and this will only be accomplished to the degree that we, ourselves, are sociable and trustworthy.

Arnold Toynbee's analysis of the emergence and decline of civilizations concluded that civilizations are never defeated by external barbarians; they are always defeated by internal decay and disintegration. He concluded that the fall of Rome and other great civilizations was an act of suicide, not an act of homicide. The fall is the result of a loss of common vision and values, the loss of the ability to exert will. This occurs because leaders have lost the ability to devise creative solutions in face of new challenges, but rely on yesterday's successful response to old challenges. These no longer succeed and the people lose faith in their leaders and increasingly turn against each other, eating at their own collective flesh. This is the process of national suicide.

To the degree that the members of a country or company are devoting their energies to internal combat, they lack the energy to succeed against external competitors. This is why the loss of internal trust or sociability results in defeat on the external battlefield.

Can the cycle of internal disintegration be halted? I believe it can. It can, if the people will elect leaders who do not devote their energies to the mindless left-versus-right, tired and useless characterizations, the genuinely evil skill of characterizing the opponent in exaggerated and frightening terms, and rather devote their energies to promoting genuine solutions to genuine problems.

Almost every corporate leader recognizes the degree to which they rely on attracting and developing human capital. The same should be true for the country.

Rarely do we step back and ask, "What are our national assets that will help us in our global competition?" "Can we devise a national strategy that will employ our assets?"

One of the great assets of the United States has been its system of universal and mandatory education up to grade twelve, and its excellent system of higher education. In my opinion, the single greatest asset of the United States is our intellectual and creative capacities. This human capital is the foundation of our economic life. It is, however, also a national asset in our international affairs.

For most of the last half of the last century, students from Africa, Asia or Latin America sought entry to the universities of the United States. If you were from Paraguay or Nigeria, there was little you prized more than an education at an American university. The experience of young foreign students in the United States taught them not only technical subjects, but it taught them our history, our value of democracy and human rights, the history of our Civil War and the value of our system of justice. It also exposed them to American brands and corporations and many of those students became distributors for John Deere or Caterpillar in Asia or Latin America.

These days are past. Of course, many students still come to the United States. However, I have worked closely with global youth organizations over the past six years and I can assure you that the preferred place of study is no longer this country. Perhaps it is only a transitory phase as a result of our seeking to adjust to international terrorism, but the United States is now viewed as unfriendly and a very difficult place to visit for education. Acquiring visas has become a nightmare for many students and, rightly or wrongly, they fear being looked upon and treated as though they were a threat, rather than as a welcomed guest.

To ensure long-term security, few more constructive things could be done than to attract the best and brightest young people to our shores to study and to seek employment. Just as corporations are competing for the best talent on a global basis, the country too, must compete for the best talent if we are to continue our leadership in the field of human capital.

It is a serious concern of many that in our desire to solve the problem of excessive illegal immigration, we may be throwing out the baby with the bathwater, cutting off the desirable immigration of talent that has built so many of this countries technology leaders.

There are many other aspects to developing our nation's human capital from head start programs through to our investment in basic research and development in the sciences. This subject is certainly worthy of an entire book. I will go no further than to say that I would instruct my new formed agency to develop a comprehensive plan to assure our global brand leadership in human capital.

What is our national technology or process capital? Dwight Eisenhower is responsible for one of the great investments in national infrastructure. It was he who initiated the construction of our national highway system. This infrastructure is a critical national asset.

Every president should have a plan to develop the technology and process infrastructure that will serve as the national highway system of the future. That infrastructure today is, most importantly, our information technology infrastructure. This is not to dismiss the importance of further investment in roads, railroads, ports and airports – all critical economic assets that serve as enabling processes.

Both education and commerce are now dependent on access to high speed Internet. In the future, every school will be using the Internet to broadcast classes, resources, tests and will provide access to their entire library for research. If our Chief Executive strives to maximize the human capital and competitiveness of our country, there must be a plan, whether through public or private funding, to have the world's best information technology infrastructure.

How does the United States rank now? In broadband Internet access per capita, the United States ranks 16th after South Korea, which is first, then Hong Kong, the Netherlands, Denmark, Switzerland, Canada, Norway, Finland, Sweden, Taiwan, Israel, Belgium, Japan, France, and the United Kingdom.

In the information age, when access to information is the key to education and commerce, there must be a national plan to develop the most modern, most effective, information system in the world. I am not proposing that the government take over the business of Internet access. However, if I were President (perhaps on my second day in office) I would call together the CEOs of the major service providers, telephone and cable companies, along with a few Congressmen and Senators, and I would do more than lecture or listen to them for an hour. I would ask them to show up at 8:00AM in the morning and I would advise them to make no plans for the rest of that day or the next. I would tell them in advance that I want no speeches or presentations, no platitudes, and no slogans would be allowed. I would have flips charts and markers at the ready and I would tell them that I don't want anyone to leave the room until we jointly develop the key elements of a plan that will make the United States the world leader in information access.

I don't know what the results of this session would be. But, I would insist that they display creativity and a shared sense of national purpose. If the mission were not accomplished in this session, I would set another date for them to gather within the month. If they refused, I would so publicly humiliate them they would live to regret it.

You get the idea. We need a leader who will dig in, drill down, and exert the pressure of the office to develop real plans that will make a difference to our competitiveness. No more slogans or excuses.

Is the concept of spiritual capital relevant at a national level? I will once more point out that I am committed to the pluralism and separation of church and state that were fundamental principles of this country's founding. I have previously defined spiritual capital as composed of the degree to which people are committed to an ennobling worthy purpose and the degree to which they adhere to moral values. This is entirely different from religion. Religion may, and often is, a source of these two qualities; however, I am not impressed with the correlation between those who loudly voice their religious commitment and the display of higher purpose and morality.

I believe that a nation does have spiritual capital and I believe the leaders of a country can promote this asset. In many ways the commitment to a higher purpose and moral values are a foundation upon which social and human capital are built.

What is our ennobling purpose as a nation? Do our leaders articulate a purpose that inspires our citizens? Is it possible for a country's leaders to develop a genuine sense of mission and a strategy around that mission, one that would be inspiring to the people of the country? Again, optimist that I am, I believe the answer is yes.

Of course, when we are attacked the leader must define and pursue the mission of security and defeating those who would attack us. However, this is an entirely defensive strategy, not a purpose to pursue something noble. That which is noble must be beyond self-interest, it cannot be merely to protect oneself.

The United States, with its immense power and influence, has the opportunity to create immense good. There are many possible ways to define our nation's purpose and no one has elected this author to do so. However, for the sake of discussion, I might propose something such as the following:

The mission of the United States is to promote democracy and the rule of law, human and civil rights, and education for all the earth's citizens.

It is not my intention to convince the reader that this, or any other mission, is the right statement of purpose for the United States. I am merely presented an example.

I would argue that to the degree this mission, or something like it, is pursued by peaceful means, we will have fewer enemies, more friends, less war and more social and economic progress.

I can imagine so many initiatives that could be pursued toward achieving that mission. Imagine an educational program for all the world's current and future leaders in democracy development, human and civil rights. Why not provide scholarships to the brightest students from every country, from China to Rwanda, from Cuba to Iran, to come here and study the best practices in developing the institutions of democracy; human and civil rights law; and the leadership skill necessary in a democratic world. Why not?

This mission could be the focus of all aid and foreign policy. This externally focused worthy purpose in no way detracts from our internal pursuit of economic well-being and security. Remember that all five forms of capital function as a whole-system, interdependent and mutually reinforcing. I believe that to the degree we pursued such a worthy purpose, we would develop greater social capital, and diminish threats.

I know that many readers will think the writer naïve at this point. I am not naïve. I have served in the military, worked in prisons, and run a business for more than twenty years and now spend a good bit of time managing investments. I live in the real world. But, if the spirit of the real world is dominated by the skepticism so prevalent in our society, if it is devoid of great dreams of a better society, it is a world not foreseen by the founders of our great religions or our great country. In fact, the acceptance of skepticism is the loss of faith, and I choose to keep my faith, for our children.

Index

Abilene Paradox, 87
Action Learning, 289
Adams, John, 36
Afghanistan, 270
African-American, 101
AIESEC, 267
Alexander the Great, 25
Aljazeera, 275
American democracy, 26
American Spirit, 268
American Truck Stop Owners Association, 45
Amoco, 242
Annapolis Mall, 19
Annapolis, Maryland, 19
AOL, 22
Apostle Paul, 25
Apple Computer, 178
Appreciative Inquiry, 145, 148, 151, 243
Apprentice, 10
Arab tribes, 25
Army, 103, 104
Arthur Andersen, 198, 263
association, 45
Atlanta Braves, 236
Authentic Happiness, 132
Authentic Voice, 94
Babe Ruth, 24
Bahá'í Faith, 25, 271
Baha'u'llah, 25
balanced scorecard, 166
Best Buys, 185
Bible, 25, 80
Blanchard, Ken, 268
blues, 101
Board of Directors, 83
boards of directors, 69
Bohm, David, 11, 75
Breen, Ed, 36

Broad-slicing, 17
Brodie, Marie and James, 93
Buddha, 25
Buddhism, 25
Business strategy, 193
Cameron, Kim, 138
Carnegie, Andrew, 194
Carson, Johnny, 100
Categorizing, 90
Change management, 105
Chick-fil-A, 19
China, 37, 275
Christianity, 26, 271
Chrysler, 174
church, 102
Circuit City, 185
civilization, 62
Clark-Schwebel, 112
CNN, 275
coaching, 106, 244
Coca-Cola, 242
Collins, Jim, 89
Command decisions, 123
Communication, 48
competence, 236
Competence, 237
competencies, 199
competition, 43
Conference Board, 113
Congress, 45
Consensus decisions, 124
conservatives, 274
construction industry, 106
Consultative decisions, 124
contracts, 107
Cooperation, 43, 44
Core Process, 177
core process., 179
core work process, 206
Corning, 213, 224

Covey, Stephen, 120
Covey, Stephen, 290
craft shop, 40
creative dissatisfaction, 263
creative response to challenge, 62
creativity, 62
Creativity, 289
Crossfire, 73
Csikszentmihali, Mihaly, 103
Csikszentmihalyi, Mihaly, 172
Dalai Lama, 132
Darwin, 114
Darwin Award, 175
Davis Reverend Gary, 289
Debate, 78
Dell, 19, 206
Delmarva Power and Light, 120
Deming, 160
Deming, Dr. Edwards,, 63
Deming, W. Edwards, 171
Design Charter, 222
design team, 173, 174
Design Team, 220, 222
Dialogue, 49, 73, 77
Dialogue and the Art of Thinking Together., 96
Discipline, 100, 107
Discussion, 78
Disney, 8
Divine Teachers, 67
Dixie Chicks, 80
Doc Watson, 10
Donald Trump, 10
Dr. Deming, 182
Dreyfuss, Richard, 286
Eastman Chemicals, 164
ecology, 91
economic development, 195
Emery, Fred, 213
Enron, 47
Enron board, 87
Enron Corporation, 82
Environmental Protection Agency, 93
executives, 69

fact finding, 77
Family relationships, 266
Federal Express, 149
financial capital, 231
financial system, 208
Financial targets, 208
First Union National Bank, 135
Florida Power & Light, 121
flow, 102, 172
Ford, 174
Fortune 500, 266
Founding Fathers, 26, 274
Franklin, Benjamin, 263
Frederick Taylor, 212
Frederickson, Barbara, 138
Ft. Dix, New Jersey, 103
Fukuyama Francis, 37, 39
Fukuyama, Francis, 156
Gains Topeka, 213
Geneen, Harold, 21
General Electric, 19, 21, 201
General Motors, 20, 174, 213, 263
Gladwell, Malcolm, 17
God, 67, 102
Goldblatt, Eliyahu, 175
Good To Great, 89
Google, 184
Great Britain, 37
Greek tragedy, 262
Group decision-making, 76
Grove, Andy, 33
Gulf of Mexico, 180
happiness, 59
Harvard, 93
Harvard Business Review, 83
Harvey, Jerry, 87, 115
healthcare provider, 173
Hemingway, Ernest, 85, 161
Hemingway, Ernest, 85
Henry Ford's factory, 41
hierarchy of purpose, 67
High performing organizations, 230
high performing teams, 230
Hinduism, 25

Home Depot, 206
Honda, 19, 174, 198
Honda America Manufacturing, 20, 148, 163, 213
Honda Way, 20
hubris, 263
Human capital, 198
human nature, 42
humility, 89
industrial engineering, 40
information systems, 207
Intel Corporation, 33
intellectual capital, 231
Intellectual capital, 275
Intellectual Capital, 273
intention, 64
International Standards Certification, 47
Isaacs, William., 96
Islam, 26, 271
ISO, 47
ITT, 21
Jack London, 65
Japan, 37
Jefferson, Thomas, 274
Jobs, Steven, 8
Johnson, Spencer, 268
Journal of Organizational Behavior Management, 161
Kampelman, Max M., 73
Kaplan, Robert S., 166
Kassinga, Fauzia, 269
Keller, Helen, 56
Kimberly-Clark, 213
King, Dr. Martin Luther, 80
Kingsport, Tennessee, 164
knowledge-based economy, 50
Kozlowski, Dennis, 35, 263
L. L. Bean, 206
Landmark Communications, 242
Lay, Ken, 87
Lay, Ken, 263
Leadership Solution., 49
lean manufacturing, 209, 213
Lean Production, 175

Learned Optimism, 132
learning theory, 142
liberal, 274
Liker, Jeffrey K, 175
Lincoln, Abraham, 274
Lindsley, Dr. Ogden, 142
Local Spiritual Assembly, 93
London, Jack, 58
Mager, Robert F, 140, 199
Maher, Bill, 80
manufacturing, 104
map of a process, 180
Market capital, 197
Martin Eden, 58, 65, 66
Marx, Karl, 194
Marysville, 20
mass production, 40
mass production factory model, 42
Master's of Excellence, 290
Mathew 12:25, 25
McBride, Margret, 268
McDaniel, Eugene, 42
McDonald's, 81, 184, 206
Met Life, 146
Microsoft, 201
Middle East, 37, 38
military, 103
Miller, Arthur, 203
Miller, Lawrence M, 62
Miller, Lawrence M., 27
Miller-Muro, Layli, 269
mission statement, 69
Mohammed, 25
Morgan, J.P., 194
motivation, 56, 199
Motivation, 199
Motorola, 121
Murray, Bill, 286
Musicians, 102, 107
Muslims, 274
NASCAR, 184
National Quality Award, 225
Native Americans, 25, 40
NBA, 45

Nelson, Jane, 103
Networking teams, 119
New York Times, 139, 269
Nonzero – The Logic of Human Destiny, 44
non-zero-sum, 45
North Carolina Correctional System., 133
Norton, David P, 166
Nummi, 213
NY Times, 139
Ohno, Taiichi, 23
One Minute Manager, 268
Open Book Management, 47
organizational strategy, 193
Parsons, H. M, 161
Peter Drucker, 60
Pipe, Peter, 140
Pixar, 8, 198
Plato, 26
Poland, 18
Polk Youth Center, 133
positive discipline, 103
positive motivation, 105
Positive Organizational Scholarship, 11
positive psychology, 11, 12
Positive Psychology, 132
POW, 42
prison, 101
Problem solving teams, 118
Process Owners, 179
Proctor & Gamble, 213
productivity, 40
productivity of the process, 238
Psychology Today, 264
punishment, 103
Purpose, 56
Purpose of Teams, 116
Putnam, R. D, 195
quality of the process, 238
Raleigh, North Carolina, 93
re-engineering, 175
Reliability, 50
religion, 101, 203

Responsiveness, 50
reward system, 51
reward systems, 52
Rewards, 51
Rolex Watch, 184
Root Learning, 164
Sabatini, Fabio, 196
sacrifice, 58
Schuster, John P, 47
scientific method, 40
Scorekeeping, 155, 161
Seinfeld, 65
self-managing teams, 125
Seligman, Martin E.P, 132, 265
Seligman, Martin E.P., 59
Seligman, Martin E.P., 59
Senge, Peter, 84
Seuss, Dr., 26
Shaffer, Jim, 49
shaping, 143
Shell, 242
Shoshone, 46
Simon, Neil, 100
Simon, Neil, 107
Six Sigma, 104, 161, 209
Six-Sigma, 175
slaves, 101
Sneetches, 26
sociability, 196
social capital, 38, 52, 111, 231, 233
Social capital, 39
Social Capital, 195, 265
social system, 83
Socio-technical systems, 212
Socrates, 26
Sonnenfeld, Jeffrey A, 83
Sonnenfeld, Jeffrey A., 83
Southerners, 80
Speed, 184
spiritual capital, 231
Spiritual capital, 233
Spiritual Capital, 203, 270
spiritual wealth, 271
spirituality, 203

Spontaneous sociability, 37
sports, 43
Stack, Jack, 47
statistical process control, 161
Steering Team, 220, 221
strategic planning process, 182
strategy, 21
Student Council, 95
Switzerland, 95
Systems thinking, 64, 84
Tahirih Justice Center, 269
Taliban, 270
Tarkenton, Fran, 267
Tarmac, 242
Team business performance, 240
Team Learning, 242
team management, 104, 118
Teams, 103, 238
Teamwork, 111
Team-work, 112
Technical Capital, 276
Texaco, 242
The Great Disruption – Human Nature and the Reconstitution of Social Order, 39
The Great Game of Business, 47
Theory of Constraints, 175
Tibet, 211
Time-Warner, 22
Total Quality Management, 161, 175
Toynbee, Arnold, 62
Toynbee, Arnold, 27
Toynbee, Arnold, 62
Toyota, 23, 174, 183, 213

Toyota Production System, 22, 186, 206, 213
Toyota Production Systems, 175
Transparency, 47
Trist, Eric, 213
Trust, 33
Trust: The Social Virtues & The Creation of Prosperity, 37
Tyco, 35
United States, 37, 40
United States National Quality Award, 121
United Technologies, 244
values, 204
Vince Lombardi, 24
virtues, 264
voodoo, 101
Wall Street Journal, 224
Wallace Company, 121
Wal-Mart, 40, 206
wealth, 37
Weisbord, Marvin R, 220
Whitlock, Scott, 20
Whole System, 91
whole-system design, 216
Whole-System Design, 212
whole-system thinking, 11
Whole-system thinking, 11
Win-Win Relationships, 51
Womack, James P, 175
work teams, 43
World Bank, 195
Wright, Robert, 44
YM/YWCA, 242
Yugoslavia, 18
zero-sum, 52